Praise for Linda McQuaig OCT - - 2019

On *The Trouble with Billionaires*

A devastating expose … An indispensable read.

— Naomi Klein

Magnificent — the book of the moment.
— George Monbiot, UK journalist and columnist for the *Guardian*

I don't know another book that illuminates the epic crime behind the current "economic crisis" as concisely, vividly and truthfully …
— John Pilger, UK-based journalist and documentary filmmaker

A narrative that moves along at the clip of a detective novel. I adore this book with its policy smarts and folksy style.

— Ellie Kirzner, *NOW* Magazine

This book is chock-full of hard economic facts — yet it's as readable as a crime novel. Come to think of it, this *is* a crime novel — except that it's true.

— Jim Stanford, economist and CBC–TV commentator

Cutting commentary on disproportionate wealth by one of Canada's most provocative journalists and a leading Canadian tax expert.

— Canadian Press

On *It's the Crude, Dude*

McQuaig's perceptive inquiry into the world's energy system … is an urgent wake-up call that should — and must — be read and acted upon without delay.

— Noam Chomsky

Canadian journalist Linda McQuaig's brilliant *It's the Crude, Dude* will give you an overview of "Iraqi" history and indeed of the frantic hunt for the last of the world's oil that will transform your view of everything current.

— Heather Mallick, *Globe and Mail*

D0290591

McQuaig gives the reader an entertaining crash course on the history of the oil industry ... It's a highly educational rant ... and a deliciously written one.

— *Gazette* (Montreal)

Extremely interesting ... McQuaig writes extremely well, and has clearly done her homework.

— *Winnipeg Free Press*

An analysis presented with passion and impressive detail.

— *Maclean's*

On *The Cult of Impotence*

Linda McQuaig's magnificent new book, *The Cult of Impotence*, is the slap upside the head we all sorely need.

— Heather Mallick, *London Free Press*

This fifth in her series of Establishment-debunking firecrackers is ... a significant and fascinating read.

— Peter C. Newman, *Globe and Mail*

On *Shooting the Hippo*

Part thriller, part financial expose ... McQuaig has written an accessible and essential introduction to Canada's economy for all Canadians ... I intend to send a copy to my federal MP, and hope that the book gives him the kind of nightmares it gave me.

— *Gazette* (Montreal)

McQuaig has laid out sufficient material to throw serious doubt on the economic policies that dominate our society.

— John Ralston Saul, *Globe and Mail*

McQuaig — one of the country's most effective journalists — has put together a devastating analysis of the debt/deficit fiasco.

— *Edmonton Journal*

Like Isaac Asimov, who popularized science for the masses, McQuaig has the gift of making the complicated world of economics understandable.

— *Financial Post*

If there is anyone who can make economics sexy, it's popular financial writer Linda McQuaig. Free of jargon and cant, down-to-earth enough to make media potentate Conrad Black white with rage ... this woman dares to unmask the arrogance and greed of the world's corporate money managers.

— *Times Colonist* (Victoria)

On *The Quick and the Dead*

Read this story about Brian Mulroney and get angry ... filled with solid reporting and excellent analysis and tells a story that is enough to make you weep.

— *Calgary Herald*

McQuaig has given us a masterly, intelligent analysis of what's happening to Canada ... provides a metaphor that absolutely and chillingly captures our prime minister's character and aspirations. Linda McQuaig gets my own private award — the Canadian Book of Greatest Cultural Significance.

— Brian Fawcett, *Books in Canada*

On *The Wealthy Banker's Wife*

The Wealthy Banker's Wife offers an opportunity to elevate the forthcoming ... debate to a more intelligent level than the boys in the back room are planning for us. Whether that opportunity is taken depends on whether readers and the media pick up ... the gauntlet McQuaig has thrown down.

— Stan Persky, *Globe and Mail*

Linda McQuaig is one of the most vibrant, effective and readable journalists in the country ... provocative and fascinating.

— Michael Coren, *Law Times*

On *Behind Closed Doors*

A tough and thorough analysis of how Canada's tax system rewards the rich ... a devastating profile of Mickey Cohen.

— Peter C. Newman

Courageous ... The brilliantly written chapter on Cohen is worth the price of the book by itself.

— *Books in Canada*

A page-turner.

— *The Hamilton Spectator*

McQuaig's book will undoubtedly enrage large segments of society. Equally, many will suggest that she is "right on" and will probably flood the Department of Finance with copies.

— *Globe and Mail*

A rave review for Linda McQuaig's *Behind Closed Doors*.... It's a classic piece of investigative reporting.

— *Toronto Star*

A stinging indictment of Canada's tax system and the people who shape it ... Whether you agree with her — and many business people will find her ideas repugnant — you cannot ignore her.

— *Financial Post*

The
SPORT
&
PREY
of Capitalists

The
SPORT
&
PREY

of Capitalists

*How the Rich Are Stealing
Canada's Public Wealth*

Linda McQuaig

DUNDURN
TORONTO

Copyright © Linda McQuaig, 2019

All rights reserved. No part of this publication may be reproduced, stored in a retrieval system, or transmitted in any form or by any means, electronic, mechanical, photocopying, recording, or otherwise (except for brief passages for purpose of review) without the prior permission of Dundurn Press. Permission to photocopy should be requested from Access Copyright.

Cover Image: istock.com/clu
Printer: Webcom, a division of Marquis Printing Inc.

Library and Archives Canada Cataloguing in Publication

Title: The sport & prey of capitalists : how the rich are stealing Canada's public wealth / Linda
    McQuaig.
Other titles: Sport and prey of capitalists
Names: McQuaig, Linda, author.
Description: Includes bibliographic references and index.
Identifiers: Canadiana (print) 2019012847X | Canadiana (ebook) 20190128534 | ISBN 9781459743663
    (softcover) | ISBN 9781459743670 (PDF) | ISBN 9781459743687 (EPUB)
Subjects: LCSH: Privatization—Canada. | LCSH: Wealth—Canada. | LCSH: Capitalism—Canada. | LCSH:
    Canada—Economic conditions. | LCSH: Canada—Social conditions.
Classification: LCC HD4008 .M37 2019 | DDC 338.971—dc2

1   2   3   4   5   23   22   21   20   19

We acknowledge the support of the **Canada Council for the Arts**, which last year invested $153 million to bring the arts to Canadians throughout the country, and the **Ontario Arts Council** for our publishing program. We also acknowledge the financial support of the **Government of Ontario**, through the **Ontario Book Publishing Tax Credit** and **Ontario Creates**, and the **Government of Canada**.

Nous remercions le **Conseil des arts du Canada** de son soutien. L'an dernier, le Conseil a investi 153 millions de dollars pour mettre de l'art dans la vie des Canadiennes et des Canadiens de tout le pays.

Care has been taken to trace the ownership of copyright material used in this book. The author and the publisher welcome any information enabling them to rectify any references or credits in subsequent editions.

The publisher is not responsible for websites or their content unless they are owned by the publisher.

Printed and bound in Canada.

VISIT US AT

@ dundurn.com | @dundurnpress | dundurnpress | dundurnpress

Dundurn
3 Church Street, Suite 500
Toronto, Ontario, Canada
M5E 1M2

To Don Smith, who is a chief in every way.
And to my adorable daughter, Amy.

I say on behalf of the Government, that the water power all over the country should not in the future be made the sport and prey of capitalists and shall not be treated as anything else but a valuable asset of the people of Ontario.

— James P. Whitney, Premier of Ontario, 1905

Contents

Introduction

By April 2018, Kinder Morgan, the Texas-based energy company, had had enough. After years of frustration fighting Indigenous and environmental groups in Canadian courts, it was ready to walk away. If Ottawa couldn't assure approval for a pipeline expansion, allowing the company to bring more heavy crude from Alberta's oil patch to the British Columbia coast, Kinder Morgan vowed to pull the plug on the mega-billion-dollar project by the end of the following month.

The deadline set off panic in Ottawa, where Prime Minister Justin Trudeau realized that all his efforts to win favour in Alberta suddenly hung in the balance. Then, with only days to go until the deadline, Trudeau announced that Canada would buy the pipeline, committing $4.5 billion of Canadian taxpayer money, and possibly many billions more if Ottawa ended up paying for the expansion of the pipeline as well. The surprise announcement produced a lot of high-fives in the oil patch — the majority of these were in the boardroom of Kinder Morgan, where the leaky, sixty-five-year-old pipeline had come to be regarded as something of an albatross.

Perhaps the oddest thing about the highly controversial purchase was Trudeau's insistence that it was in "the national interest." Quite apart from the risk of leaving taxpayers on the hook for a multi-billion-dollar project that might never be approved, there was another, far greater consequence that was barely mentioned in days of media coverage: the impact on climate change. The proposed expansion of the pipeline would triple its capacity to transport the province's heavy oil, which renowned U.S. climatologist James Hansen describes as "one of the dirtiest, most carbon-intensive fuels on the planet."[1] Hansen says it would be "game over" for any hope of solving the climate crisis if Alberta's oil sands are fully exploited.[2]

How can something be said to be in the national interest when it would compromise the ability to survive on this planet? Can something really serve our interest *as a nation* when it undermines our more basic interest *as humans*?

In purchasing the pipeline, the Liberal government was following a long Canadian tradition of establishing publicly owned enterprises. But Trudeau was using this important tool of national development in a new way: not in a way that would advance the interests of Canadians, but in a way that would — by any meaningful measure — set back those interests. He was turning the Canadian tradition of public enterprise on its head.

For the first century after Confederation, Canadians collectively created significant public enterprises and national programs that helped transform this vast stretch of land into a functioning and successful nation: power plants, a national railway, a public broadcaster, a nationwide postal service, coast-to-coast transportation infrastructure, strong public health care and education systems, a publicly owned pharmaceutical company that pioneered medical breakthroughs — the list goes on. Many of these key national projects came into being only after hard-fought battles that pitted the public against a narrow set of financial interests.

After fighting to put these public enterprises and programs in place, Canadians have spent the last few decades downsizing them or selling them off to private investors. After more than a century as nation builders, we've spent recent decades as dismantlers or vendors of our ambitious collective undertakings.

All this cutting and privatizing has far-reaching consequences. It diminishes our collective power to own and control key aspects of our economy, our country, and our lives, thereby shrinking our democratic capacity as a nation.

These sweeping changes have been made under the illusion that we're better off if we leave our economy and our lives in the hands of the private marketplace. Another influential but false notion has been that we can no longer afford things we managed to afford decades ago, even though we are a vastly richer country today.

In reality, we haven't made these changes because of the inherent superiority of the marketplace or due to financial necessity. Rather, we've made them because of the pressure exerted by powerful financial interests who have been keen to take over lucrative parts of our public domain so they can own them and milk them for profits.

Of course, all this is hardly unique to Canada. The push toward privatization started in Britain and the United States several decades ago, and it has had major impacts on both those nations. But its impact may be particularly profound in Canada — a country where public enterprise has played an especially important role, something that is now largely ignored as we've succumbed to the dogma that the market-place always does things better.

∽◎∾

Whether we ignore it or not, there is something distinctly Canadian about our reliance on public enterprise. It is deeply rooted in our history and our geography. As the Canadian historian H.V. Nelles notes, "the concept of the positive, interventionist state did not have to be invented.... [It] was the natural product of a colonial heritage and a unique economic history."[3]

Canada's historical distinctiveness can be appreciated most easily in contrast to the very different course pursued by our sprawling neighbour to the south. Rejecting Britain and its aristocratic traditions with their Declaration of Independence in 1776, the American colonies embraced an ideology of materialistic individualism as they embarked on an aggressive development of their frontier. Central to their ideology was the notion that each homesteader had a claim to the land and that by cultivating a piece of it through his own labour, he became its rightful owner, entitled to live as a free man in the American republic. (At the time, only men were considered able to claim that right.)

This highly individualistic creed left little room for a public domain. "Americans placed a premium upon the rapid transfer of the public domain, either by outright sale or preemption, into unrestricted private ownership …" observes Nelles. "[T]he retention of property rights by the state for the welfare of the community became an increasingly un-American notion with the passage of time. The public lands were public only insofar as they were waiting to become private."[4]

The British colonies that were to later become Canada (including the French colony of Quebec after 1763) followed a very different path. They stayed within the Empire, accepting a modified version of British governance, with ultimate control residing in the British monarchy. Immense tracts of the Canadian terrain were designated Crown lands, literally owned and controlled by the British Crown and at the disposal of the reigning monarch, who relied on the proceeds from them to pay for wars and for running the realm.

So, a settler could purchase a piece of Upper Canadian land, but the British Crown owned any minerals found on it. "Every deed to land issued in the colony carried the stipulation that both base and royal metals [gold, silver, and copper] were not conveyed with title," writes Nelles. Similarly, the British monarch retained the surface rights to the trees covering the land. "A timber licence," notes Nelles, "was not a deed to land; it was an authorization to cut trees, and to pay for that right according to a specified rate per board foot. Colonial officials were thus able to adjust the terms of timber licences in such a way that they became … productive sources of revenue." This also happened to suit the needs of the commercial lumber interests, who were focused on harvesting the wood, not owning the land. (By contrast, the American practice was to sell clear title to the land, which included full rights to the minerals and timber located on it.)[5]

As the British colonies developed in the nineteenth century, forming themselves into the Dominion of Canada in 1867, the notion lingered that there was a share belonging to the Crown — although this share was now seen as rightfully belonging to the Canadian public, rather than to the British monarch. By the 1890s, politicians in Ontario were campaigning on platforms clearly calling for the public to share in the benefits of the province's natural resources. As Nelles puts it, "The principle that a portion of the 'bounty of nature' properly belonged to the public had become one of the basic political values."[6]

In addition to these historical factors, there were significant geographic factors contributing to the different development paths of Canada and the United States. For instance, the vast Canadian Shield surrounding Hudson Bay and covering much of east-central Canada is made up of ancient Precambrian rock. Although rich in minerals and heavily forested, the shield is covered by only a thin layer of soil, making most of it unsuitable for farming. Thus Canada, at least in its early stages, lacked the endless frontier of potentially arable land that America had. Instead, much of Canada and its wealth existed in inhospitable places. So, whereas American geography suited agrarian development, based on individual ownership of the land and its resources, Canadians found themselves geographically located on a mostly cold, barren stretch of infertile land, which was nonetheless rich in mineral and timber resources — wealth that could be collectively shared.

As Canada expanded to the West Coast, a different geographic imperative encouraged the development of a strong public sphere. The sheer breadth of the country, with its small population strung out in settlements over great distances, meant that Canadian communities had difficulty communicating and doing business with each other. Canada, made up of isolated farms and villages, was unable to produce sufficient demand to entice private interests on their own to build railways and provide other key services. Since there was little private entrepreneurial interest in carrying out the development essential for a country, there was a pressing need for public enterprise if Canada was to successfully hang together and compete with the more aggressive, ever-expanding nation to the south.

Increasingly, as we've been led to believe that private enterprise is the appropriate engine for growth and development, we've failed to appreciate our heritage as a nation that has embraced public enterprise to great effect. Herschel Hardin, in his insightful 1974 book, *A Nation Unaware*, identifies the role that public enterprise played in Canadian history as "one of the most vibrant expressions of the Canadian character.... The great public enterprises in transportation and communication symbolize the independent, creative Canadian spirit."[7]

Prominent writers like Peter C. Newman and the late Pierre Berton made successful literary careers out of celebrating Canadian private enterprise heroes, often portraying them as more swashbuckling and trail-blazing than they really were. In fact, Canada has never had the dynamic, hyperindividualistic tycoons who strode boldly (for good and for bad) across the U.S. stage — Andrew Carnegie, John D. Rockefeller, Cornelius Vanderbilt, Jay Gould, John Jacob Astor, and Henry Ford. Our elite have displayed little of that free-enterprise entrepreneurial talent and grit. In French Canada, our elite came from repressive clerical and semi-feudal traditions; in Upper Canada (Ontario), they were a pale version of the British aristocracy, with a clique of powerful men known as the Family Compact ruling the colony and siphoning off profits for themselves along the way. As Hardin notes, "When the nation-building era began in Canada ... private enterprise boldness and tenacity was lacking, and when it was finished ... it was still lacking."[8]

Whenever entrepreneurial activity did break out in Canada, resulting in a successful company, its owners soon seemed happy to be bought out by a bigger American competitor. The result has been our uninspiring branch-plant economy, where much of industry reports to owners outside our borders. Mel Watkins, a University of Toronto economist appointed by the federal Liberals to study this phenomenon in the 1960s, put it bluntly in his 1968 report: "The extent of foreign control of Canadian industry is unique among the industrialized nations of the world."[9] Since the time Watkins authored his report, interest in the subject of foreign ownership in Canada has largely faded, although the problem has remained. "Foreign ownership is still the norm for large companies in Canada, giving a continuing branch-plant character to the Canadian economy typical of a less-developed country," Watkins said in a recent interview.

The rather unimpressive record of our free-enterprise entrepreneurs didn't prevent popular authors like Newman and Berton from embellishing their stories, especially since Canadian business people buy lots of books. Newman's 1959 treatise, *Flame of Power*, celebrated eleven Canadian business leaders who allegedly demonstrated a "phenomenal mastery of the entrepreneurial art" and "transformed Canada from a community of traders and land tillers into one of the world's economically most animated nations."[10] Stirring stuff. But in fact, the businessmen Newman eulogized were operating in a significantly modified free-enterprise system, one in which there was massive government support and subsidies. Without such government support, Canada's major "free-enterprise" projects — starting with the Canadian Pacific Railway — would likely never have launched.

Newman, in his keenness to applaud Canada's allegedly gifted entrepreneurs, carefully restricted his glance to those who operated in the private sector and oozed free-market values. This led him to pass over another set of entrepreneurs who arguably made a more significant contribution to the development of Canada: the entrepreneurs of public enterprise — Adam Beck, Henry Thornton, and Dr. John G. FitzGerald, for example.

Hardin turns the popular assumptions about private and public enterprise upside down, making the provocative argument that while Canada has a mediocre record of private enterprise, it has excelled in developing public enterprise. "Canada, in its essentials, is a public enterprise country, always has been," writes Hardin. "Americans have, or, at least had, a genius for private enterprise; Canadians have a genius for public enterprise."[11]

Yet, we've often avoided creating public enterprises out of some deference to the private sector — a deference that only really disappeared in times of war.

Indeed, the Canadian genius for public enterprise reached a zenith during the Second World War, when the usual ideological baggage favouring the private sector was trumped by the need to pull together to fight Nazi Germany. Canada's war effort was masterminded by C.D. Howe, the powerful Canadian wartime Cabinet minister who became known as the "Minister of Everything." Although a wealthy, self-made businessman, Howe felt comfortable departing from capitalist practices in order to mobilize a massive public industrial effort to win the war. Largely under his direction, Ottawa created twenty-eight wartime Crown corporations, which employed 229,000 workers and made significant technological advances in key areas like aviation, communications, and weaponry.

As soon as the war ended, so too did the government's interest in relying on public enterprise rather than private enterprise. It's extraordinary how men like Howe, who worked tirelessly in developing highly successful Crown corporations during the war, were keen to dismantle them once hostilities ceased.

This led to some missed opportunities for Canada. Sandford Borins, a professor of public management at the University of Toronto, notes, "The success of Canada's aircraft manufacturing industry during the war stimulated hopes for the post-war period."[12] A government committee concluded in 1943 that it would be in the national interest for Canada to design and develop both military and commercial aircraft after the war. Victory Aircraft was a Canadian Crown corporation that had proven highly effective in manufacturing complex, British-designed planes for the Allied war effort. With the expertise it had developed, it could have been involved in developing a postwar aviation industry in Canada. But Howe opposed its continuation as a Crown corporation. As he wrote to the committee, "I suggest that the airplane business in the post-war period must not expect to find itself a ward of the Government."[13] Suddenly, with the prospect of peace, the notion of public enterprise was once again something to be denigrated as a mere drain on the state.

Instead, Howe allowed British aircraft giant Hawker Siddeley to purchase Victory and set up a Canadian subsidiary known as Avro, which absorbed another successful Canadian wartime Crown corporation, Turbo Research. Ottawa continued to provide financial support for these now-privatized aviation operations, investing more than six million dollars in Avro from 1947 to 1952. This public financing enabled Avro to develop a promising fifty-seat commercial aircraft, the Jetliner, which caught the attention of American business magnate Howard Hughes, owner of airline TWA. Hughes offered to purchase thirty Jetliners for TWA, but the deal was opposed by C.D. Howe, who wanted Avro to limit itself to developing military fighter planes for use in the Korean War.

Although Avro missed out on the TWA deal, it went on to develop a military supersonic interceptor jet known as the Avro Arrow, which was considered one of the most advanced aircrafts of its time. But, apparently at the request of Washington, the Avro Arrow program was cancelled in 1959 by the Progressive Conservative government of John Diefenbaker. That cancellation abruptly ended Canada's ambitions as an innovative aircraft producer.

While the circumstances surrounding the cancellation of the Avro Arrow are beyond the scope of this book, what is clear is the role played by Crown corporations — Victory and Turbo — in laying the groundwork for Canada's emergence as a promising producer of modern aircraft.

Another example of a highly successful Canadian wartime Crown corporation was Research Enterprises, as Borins documents. Between 1941 and 1946, it teamed up with the National Research Council in Ottawa to design and produce more than $220 million worth of vital wartime components — radar equipment, binoculars, periscopes, rangefinders, radios, and wireless sets. Howe was reportedly particularly proud of Research Enterprises, sending Prime Minister William Lyon Mackenzie King the hundred thousandth optical instrument manufactured by the Crown corporation. Even so, by the end of the war, Howe had returned to his reverence for the private marketplace and had little interest in maintaining this highly capable entity as a public enterprise.

With the war winding down in May 1945, Howe announced the Liberal government's intention to sell Research Enterprises, provoking considerable controversy in the House of Commons. Unmoved, Howe defended the decision in Parliament with a glib "What are the peacetime uses of radar? There are a few limited uses and one will come into being on ships."

The Conservatives opposed the sale, pointing to potential job losses. But it was Alastair Stewart, a Winnipeg parliamentarian affiliated with the Co-operative Commonwealth Federation (CCF), who really seemed to grasp the peacetime potential for the Crown corporation. Stewart insisted that there was a future for radar, predicting that "eventually with the use of radar, we can expect that the day will come when aircraft will land with all the precision we associate with the movement of railway trains to-day." Stewart also understood that the expertise that Research Enterprises had developed during the war could be a springboard for diversifying into related fields such as "measuring instruments, cameras and photographic equipment, motion picture projectors ... television ... surveying instruments ... automobile and aero instruments ... medical and dental equipment, electronic equipment, control instruments, electrical and radio test equipment, commercial radio and FM sets."[14]

Sadly, however, Howe prevailed with his determination to shut down public enterprises, no matter how much potential they showed. Research Enterprises was sold, with thirteen of its manufacturing facilities purchased by Rogers Majestic, a Toronto radio equipment manufacturing concern that had been a major subcontractor for the Crown corporation during the war. Rogers Majestic was owned by Ted Rogers Sr., and the company went on to focus on broadcasting. (Ted Rogers Jr. would later become a billionaire in the Canadian telecommunications business.) By 1950 Rogers Majestic had sold the former Crown corporation's manufacturing facilities to multinational electronics giant Philips. For several years, Philips manufactured lighting products at two Canadian factories, but by 2003 both these factories had closed. Nothing was left of Research Enterprises, or of any of the ambitious diversification possibilities once described in the Parliament of Canada.

C.D. Howe was a towering figure during the war, and he has been credited with transforming Canada from a largely agriculture-based society into an industrial one. His legacy lives on today — somewhat ironically — through the C.D. Howe Institute, a business-funded think tank that has consistently promoted pro-market ideas. While Howe shared these ideas, it was actually his development of Canada's wartime Crown corporations, with their substantial manufacturing capabilities, that laid the foundation for Canada's evolution into a modern industrial nation. Once the war was over, Howe reverted to his conventional pro-market views, pushing for privatization rather than envisioning a future for the promising public enterprises he had built.

Many decades later, we are now faced with an urgent need to evolve beyond a modern industrial nation motored by fossil fuels. An enormous mobilization, on a scale similar to the one orchestrated by C.D. Howe, will be essential in order to fundamentally re-equip our economy and society for the global green energy revolution. Given the short time left, if we are to avert climate disaster, government planning, oversight, and ownership — along the lines of what was achieved through wartime planning and Crown corporations — will almost certainly be necessary for the massive undertaking ahead. (More on this later.) Of course, the political obstacles are enormous. Only once Canadians grasp that we face a threat today as great as during the Second World War will we demand the sort of public leadership and management the country got in that earlier crisis.

~ ⚙ ~

The voice of business is all around us, promoting the notion that the market is the appropriate vehicle for achieving economic growth and advancing our interests. Whether through the reports issued by business-funded think tanks, the public statements of advocacy groups, or the articles and programs made possible by virtue of its ownership of popular media, the corporate world has saturated us with ideas about the effectiveness of private enterprise while depicting government as inefficient and intrusive. And, on some levels, this narrative seems to make sense. After all, the free-market system, while inclined to produce inequalities, is based on acquisitive behaviour that seems rooted in our nature as humans. Indeed, looking around our world, it is tempting to regard the acquisitive instinct, with its insatiable desire for material gain, as the driving force in human behaviour.

However, if we broaden our focus to include other times and places in human history, we are able to identify an instinct that is even more basic to humans. As noted by Aristotle as well as by a host of social scientists in psychology, anthropology, and sociology, the most basic, dominant aspect of our nature is that we are social animals.

As humans, we naturally seek to relate to and be accepted by other humans. We want to belong, to feel part of a larger human community — family, clan, gang, club, network, village, country, or simply society at large. As part of that community, we generally participate and contribute willingly in order to achieve position and status in the social order. We desire approval, recognition, and respect from others as part of our yearning to be appreciated and considered worthy by our fellow humans.

The economic historian and anthropologist Karl Polanyi, in his classic 1944 book, *The Great Transformation*, observes that it is this social behaviour that has defined human societies throughout most of history and in just about every corner of the globe. All societies take care of their material needs, and the pursuit of private gain is always present. But the attainment of material possessions has been, for the most part throughout history, considered a less important mark of distinction and status than the demonstration of other traits, such as loyalty, honour, devotion, bravery, service, and dedication to duty.

According to Polanyi, this thinking fundamentally changed in the last five centuries and in parts of the Western world as, with the rise of capitalism, feudal society was reorganized around the principles of the marketplace. It is only in the resulting capitalist world that displays of greed and the pursuit of material gain have come to be considered worthy behaviour — behaviour that is actively encouraged and even regarded as the very essence of the human personality.

The point of raising all this is not to deliver a diatribe against greed, but rather simply to note that our capitalist society may be something of an aberration, that behaviour which we consider basic and natural may actually have been implanted and reinforced in us in recent centuries by forces driving the transformation to a market economy. This raises the question of whether our market-based society, built around the presumption that we are ultimately acquisitive animals, is accurately reflecting us and serving our true needs. If we are actually, above all, social animals, then surely we need to strengthen our social bonds and our communities and bolster our capacity to defend them against disrupting forces, including corporate greed and rapaciousness. Our focus should clearly be on building a stronger, more functional, and more inclusive social order, rather than on unleashing and stimulating individual acquisitiveness.

Public enterprises contribute to a strong social order, since they strengthen our collective capacity to organize our economy and to create a society with a place for everyone. The intrinsic appeal of public enterprises may explain why business interests, seeing them as competition, have been keen to disparage them. It's striking that business types, who cherish private property and remain on guard against any slight infringement of their right to private ownership, are quick to dismiss the benefits of *public* ownership. For millions of Canadians, the possibilities of private ownership are limited. Public ownership is the only kind of ownership that they will likely experience with anything of value.

For we social animals, public ownership has some real virtues, coming as it does with benefits and a stake in the community.

Given the longstanding resistance to public ownership on the part of our elite, it is all the more astonishing that the Trudeau government rushed in, pockets bulging with taxpayer cash, to buy the Trans Mountain pipeline from Kinder Morgan.

The case against purchasing the pipeline involves more than the need to address climate change — even though the prospect of further imperilling the planet should have been enough to decide the matter all on its own. There are significant other reasons that should have led to the rejection of this nationalization, including the opposition of the Indigenous Peoples whose ancestral lands the pipeline would intrude on and the environmental risks posed by additional tanker traffic in B.C. coastal waters.

Given the fact that there are so many negatives attached to the pipeline, you would think that there must be some major economic positive that might make the government prepared to overlook all the problems. Not true. The economic case for the pipeline expansion is actually remarkably flimsy.

The argument routinely advanced in the business media and by Alberta and federal politicians in favour of the pipeline is that Alberta's heavy oil (or bitumen) would fetch a higher price in Asian markets, if only it could get there. But it is effectively blocked because the existing pipeline to the B.C. coast lacks sufficient capacity. As a result, Alberta's oil is mostly sold to refineries in the United States, where it receives a lower, discounted price, thereby cheating Albertans (and the federal government) out of billions of dollars.

But as Jeff Rubin, an economist and senior fellow at the Centre for International Governance Innovation, notes, this oft-repeated narrative is just wrong: "Bitumen is not conventional oil, and nowhere in the world does it command the same price. It is an inferior crude with high sulphur content that must first be upgraded before most refineries can use it as a feedstock. It is the physical properties of bitumen, not the location where it is sold, that dictates a price discount."[15]

In fact, the evidence indicates that Alberta's heavy oil would receive a *lower* price in Asian markets than it does in North America, insists Rubin. That's because a number of North American refineries are configured to deal with heavy oil (from Mexico and Venezuela, as well as from Alberta) and are therefore willing to pay more for this inferior product than would be paid elsewhere in the world.

So why is the oil industry so keen for this pipeline expansion? Rubin says industry officials see pipelines as providing "optionality" — that is, the option to gain access to new markets in the future, when conditions and pricing may change.

But there may not be much of a future for Alberta's oil, regardless of how many pipelines get built. The recent boom in the U.S. production of shale oil, particularly in Texas, has provided a much cheaper alternative to costly oil sands production. Then, of course, there's climate change. The oil industry and its supporters are still putting up resistance to global efforts to wean us off carbon. But much of the world has started to move on, as reflected in the increasingly strict carbon reduction targets agreed to in international treaties and in the fact that some major European cities are moving to ban the internal combustion engine altogether. The electric car has emerged as a viable alternative, with Volvo announcing its intention that fully electric vehicles will make up 50 percent of its sales by 2025. As all the major car manufacturers move to develop electric models, Tesla now has a higher market valuation than General Motors.

Certainly, if the world gets serious about climate change, the global consumption of oil will fall significantly, possibly by as much as 50 percent within a few decades. In a world of declining oil demand, the first sources to be abandoned would be the expensive ones, such as the oil sands, where producers can't break even without a world oil price of at least sixty dollars a barrel. (Saudi-produced oil is profitable with a world price that is less than half that amount.) "If you can't compete at twenty-five dollars, you're out," predicts Stanford University economist Tony Seba. "Places like the Canadian oil sands are going to be stranded — essentially [they're] out of luck."[16]

These diminishing long-term prospects — combined with the gritty opposition of environmentalists and others determined to stop the development of the oil sands — have already caused an exodus of big multinational oil companies from Alberta. Shell, ConocoPhillips, BP, and Norway's Statoil all sold major oil sands assets in 2017, mostly to Canadian firms. The year 2017 was something of a watershed, with multinational companies selling off more than thirty billion dollars in oil sands assets. Investment in Canada's oil and gas sector fell by 19 percent in 2017, even as it rose in the United States by 38 percent.

By the spring of 2018, with prospects for the oil sands looking increasingly grim, it's likely that Richard Kinder, chairman of Kinder

Morgan, was losing some of his enthusiasm for the Trans Mountain pipeline expansion.

Kinder, a Houston-based multi-billionaire who made a fortune from his stake in Enron before the company descended into scandal, went on to create Kinder Morgan with college friend Bill Morgan. The company has grown into one of the largest energy infrastructure companies in North America, with annual revenues exceeding thirteen billion dollars. Kinder prides himself on being something of a tightwad; he told *Fortune* magazine that the corporate culture he has instilled at Kinder Morgan is "Cheap. Cheap. Cheap."[17] With his keenness for cost-cutting, he was undoubtedly displeased that by the spring of 2018 the projected cost of the Trans Mountain pipeline expansion had ballooned from $5.4 billion to $7.4 billion — even as multinational oil companies were signalling declining confidence in Alberta's energy future.

Kinder decided to demand that Ottawa provide the company with a guarantee the expansion would be approved, which wasn't really possible since the matter was being hotly contested in the courts. He may have been looking for a way out, hoping Ottawa wouldn't be able to deliver. An even better outcome for Kinder and his company was what actually happened: Ottawa stepped forward and paid good money for a pipeline whose value is likely to plunge, along with the other major assets in the oil sands, as the United States turns increasingly to shale oil and the rest of the world gets on with transitioning to cleaner energy. "Much of Canada's existing pipeline capacity will become redundant in the face of what can only be a massive contraction in oil sands production over the next three decades," maintains Jeff Rubin.[18]

Ultimately, the Trudeau government's rash $4.5 billion pipeline purchase — Canada's parliamentary budget officer estimates Ottawa may have overpaid for the pipeline by up to $1 billion — served no purpose beyond further enriching Richard Kinder and other Kinder Morgan shareholders.

Certainly, the notion that the Trans Mountain pipeline expansion is a viable project with a lucrative future has been undercut by the apparent lack of interest in it on the part of investors, who clearly see the project as risky. When the government announced its intention to purchase the pipeline, Finance Minister Bill Morneau stressed that public ownership was temporary and that Ottawa wanted to return the pipeline to the private sector as soon as possible. The government hoped to find a buyer before the deal closed in August 2018, according to news reports. But no buyer emerged. That should have been the end of things. The pipeline expansion — opposed by Indigenous and environmental activists and shunned by investors — should have been allowed to die a quiet death.

The larger point is that public ownership is a potentially powerful, transformative vehicle for national development, and Canada has a long history of using it wisely and effectively to advance the broad public interest. As we continue to sell off more and more of what we've collectively built as a nation, let's not desecrate the role of public ownership by falsely invoking the national interest when the only real beneficiaries are a set of immensely wealthy interests based in Houston.

A pipeline that facilitates the exploitation of the tar sands is something Canadians don't need. But something we do need is a strong national infrastructure: public transit, affordable housing, roads, and bridges, as well as hospitals and schools. During the 2015 election campaign, Justin Trudeau promised he would take advantage of historically low interest rates in order to rebuild our national infrastructure. Canadians liked what they heard and voted him into power. What they didn't know was that they would end up paying inflated prices for this new infrastructure and that they wouldn't end up owning it.

One

Justin Trudeau Meets the Smartest Guy on Wall Street

If the world's seven billion people were ranked on a ladder according to how much power they wield, Larry Fink would be on a rung way, way, *way* up near the top — just thirty-three rungs below the world's most powerful person, according to a ranking by *Forbes* magazine.[1]

So, although balding and rather mousy-looking, Fink turned heads at the annual gathering of the global elite in Davos in January 2016. Indeed, many at the gathering were keen to make contact with Fink. A legendary Wall Street figure, he manages BlackRock, the world's largest investment fund, worth no less than five trillion dollars. Fink, however, was focused on making contact with Canada's newly elected prime minister — a man who is neither balding nor mousy-looking, but is ranked many rungs below him on the power ladder.

Of course, Justin Trudeau, with his Cary Grant good looks and sudden superstardom, is no run-of-the-mill Canadian prime minister. Still, Fink wasn't one to be easily impressed by celebrity. Fink wasted very little time thinking about anything other than how best to invest his massive fund of global assets. He has developed BlackRock into a fabled firm, where the cream of Wall Street analysts and mathematicians discover trends in the millions of calculations churned out daily by the firm's five thousand computers, all in the interest of evaluating risk. Figuring out risk levels — and how to minimize them — is essential for successful investing, as Fink had learned early on in his Wall Street career. During a meteoric rise through the ranks at First Boston, a New York–based investment bank, he had recklessly compromised that success by failing to adequately assess risk and ended up losing one hundred million dollars of the bank's money in one quarter. It was a mistake he would not make again.

The quest to minimize risk now led him to Justin Trudeau, of all people. While most of the media coverage of the new prime minister dealt with his patrician lineage or his hipness in stocking his Cabinet with women, Fink was interested in something else: a Trudeau election promise that was receiving less attention, despite the big dollars involved. A centrepiece of Trudeau's platform had been a pledge to spend billions on Canadian infrastructure. Trudeau even campaigned on plans for a Liberal government headed by him to go into deficit to the tune of ten billion dollars a year, in large part to pay for this new wave of infrastructure.

This was a surprising move, given Canada's history of deficit hysteria — a hysteria methodically stoked by the business community for two decades. But Trudeau's bold gambit worked. Canadians had apparently gotten over their fear of deficits, had even come to realize that business had heartlessly played on those fears to justify cuts to well-loved social programs. The shift away from deficit hysteria should have benefited the New Democratic Party (NDP), traditionally the leading critic of austerity, but party leader Tom Mulcair veered rightward during the campaign and vowed to balance the budget come hell or high water. Sensing a huge opening on the centre-left of Canadian politics, Trudeau sashayed in with promises to spend billions on infrastructure to meet long-neglected social and environmental needs, like public transit and social housing. Voters liked what they heard, deficits and all, and gave him a healthy majority.

Larry Fink wasn't particularly interested in deficits or Canadian politics, but he did have a strong and growing interest in infrastructure. Big institutional investors — like BlackRock, as well as pension funds and insurance companies — are always looking for low-risk investments with a reliable revenue stream. There hadn't been sufficient opportunities of this nature since the 2008 global recession, a reality that had left trillions of dollars parked in bonds that were paying almost nothing. By comparison, investing in infrastructure offers major benefits. A 2015 analysis by J.P. Morgan Asset Management points out that, compared to other investment options, infrastructure offers very high returns at very low risk. The analysis, prepared for the company's clients, goes on to highlight other highly attractive features: infrastructure assets operate in monopoly situations, free from competition, and therefore produce reliable revenue streams, even during economic downturns. "Infrastructure assets have produced stable, predictable and growing returns," the J.P. Morgan report notes approvingly.[2]

So Fink and Trudeau shared an interest in building infrastructure. But their interests diverged in a significant way. Throughout his campaign, Trudeau had highlighted the fact that interest rates were extremely low and had insisted that this created a rare, not-to-be-missed opportunity for financing new infrastructure at very low cost. Trudeau had talked about creating an infrastructure bank that would enable Ottawa to use its strong credit rating to help municipalities reduce their borrowing costs.

This, however, was not at all what Fink had in mind. He had trillions of dollars to lend, and lending them at low interest rates didn't turn his crank. There seemed a fundamental mismatch. Trudeau had made no mention during his campaign of the possibility of Canada teaming up with big Wall Street players like Fink to finance new infrastructure. Indeed, if he had raised such a possibility, Canadians would likely have been much more wary of the whole infrastructure idea.

In the wake of the 2008 financial meltdown, most Canadians had developed a low opinion of — if not a downright aversion to — Wall Street. And Fink aptly represented what had gone so terribly wrong; indeed, he had personally played a role in the transformation of Wall

Street into a multi-trillion-dollar casino. As a young hotshot in the 1980s and '90s, Fink, along with Lew Ranieri of Salomon Brothers, had helped develop the market for mortgage-backed securities, a market that later got wildly out of control and eventually helped trigger the 2008 crash. Fink then played a significant role in managing — and profiting from — the chaos. In the heat of the crisis, he was advising top Wall Street CEOs as well as leading officials at the U.S. Treasury and the New York Federal Reserve Bank. Described by one insider as "the man behind the curtain," Fink effectively became the key person overseeing Washington's bailout of Wall Street — a bailout widely regarded as a gigantic government giveaway to some of the richest people on earth.[3]

Trudeau and Fink were introduced in Davos at a power breakfast hosted by Dominic Barton, global managing partner of the giant consulting firm McKinsey & Company, and it was obvious the two men shared an interest in building infrastructure. But was there a way to square Trudeau's promise of delivering infrastructure to Canadians at very low cost with Fink's interest in investing in Canada at very high rates of return? With their apparently diverging agendas, the two men met privately to see if something could be worked out. And so it was that Fink, considered one of the sharpest minds on Wall Street, sat down to negotiate with a man who had little experience as prime minister and who, before that, had distinguished himself not as a financial whiz but as a drama teacher.

By the time Trudeau headed home from Davos, his ideas about a Canadian infrastructure bank were changing dramatically — at least from what he had publicly talked about during the Canadian election campaign. Crucially, Trudeau now seemed open to a significant role for private capital.

Indeed, Trudeau gave Larry Fink an influential role in designing the proposed new Canadian infrastructure bank, inviting in a team of BlackRock advisers to work closely with senior Canadian government officials in drawing up plans for the bank. This BlackRock involvement was kept strictly confidential (and only became public a year later due to an application under the Access to Information Act from Ottawa researcher Ken Rubin).[4] Although Trudeau met publicly with Fink in New York in March 2016, two months after Davos, there was no public disclosure of the fact that a team of Fink's officials was working deep inside the Trudeau government — including with those inside the Privy Council Office — drawing up plans for shaping and promoting the new "Canadian" bank.

With BlackRock's guidance, the Trudeau government worked at a lightning pace to move the project forward and to shape it in a way that would please big institutional investors like Fink. Definitely onside with the new shape of things was Finance Minister Bill Morneau, who has a strong connection to the financial world. Indeed, although the new Trudeau Cabinet is famous for its diversity, with women and minorities well represented, Morneau — ensconced in the Cabinet's most powerful post — is a character straight out of the Canadian establishment. Morneau inherited a successful business from his father and married Nancy McCain, heiress to one of Canada's largest fortunes. After expanding his father's business into the giant human resources firm Morneau Shepell, Morneau consolidated his Bay Street ties by serving as board chairman of the C.D. Howe Institute. So, while some of the more flamboyant Cabinet ministers grabbed the headlines in the early days of the Trudeau government, Morneau was busy behind the scenes working with BlackRock, making multi-billion-dollar decisions that would have major impacts on Canada's future.

In March 2016, Morneau appointed the Advisory Council on Economic Growth, ostensibly to figure out how to raise the living standards of middle-class Canadians, a theme that Trudeau had trumpeted in the election campaign. But this council of economic advisers, made up mostly of business people and without a single labour representative, seemed less focused on how to raise middle-class incomes than on how to advance the goals of institutional investors like Fink. Prominent among its members were two other influential institutional investors — Mark Wiseman, CEO of the Canada Pension Plan

Investment Board (CPPIB), a Crown corporation managing more than three hundred billion dollars in pension assets, and Michael Sabia, CEO of the Caisse de dépôt et placement du Québec, which manages pension assets in Quebec. The advisory council was chaired by Dominic Barton, the managing partner from McKinsey who had brought Trudeau and Fink together at the breakfast in Davos. These three men — Wiseman, Sabia, and Barton — shared Fink's interest in devising a Canadian infrastructure bank that, above all, would deliver high rates of return for billions of dollars held in funds managed by institutional investors, rather than delivering on Trudeau's campaign promise of infrastructure at bargain-basement prices.

Although Fink operated behind the scenes, he clearly helped shape the new bank. Not only was his BlackRock team advising officials at the top levels of the Trudeau government, but Fink himself was close to Trudeau's key economic advisers Wiseman and Barton, having collaborated with them since 2013 on a business initiative promoting long-term capital investing. Fink's ties to Wiseman were further strengthened in 2015, when Fink appointed Wiseman's wife, banker Marcia Moffat, to head up BlackRock's Canadian operations.[5] Those ties were soon to get closer still; just two months after Wiseman was appointed to Morneau's advisory council, Wiseman left his very prestigious post running the CPPIB to accept a high-ranking job working for Fink in New York, as a senior managing director at BlackRock. Despite this move to New York and his clear allegiance to Fink, Wiseman remained on Morneau's advisory council — and declined to declare any conflict of interest, perhaps because his potential conflict was so glaring it hardly seemed necessary to flag.

The advisory council, although ostensibly focused on the Canadian public interest, seemed to function more like a lobby for institutional investors. Barton arranged for his firm, McKinsey, to provide the council with "research, analysis, and administration" — all for free. Given the heavy influence of Fink and other like-minded institutional investors, it's no surprise that the council quickly produced a report, *Unleashing Productivity through Infrastructure*, that gushes with enthusiasm about the "once-in-a-generation opportunity" Canada has to create an infrastructure bank — a bank that, oddly enough, would perfectly meet the needs of institutional investors like themselves.[6]

The report declares that Canada has an infrastructure gap that urgently needs to be bridged. However, it then concedes that there is "no nationwide source of reliable data on the current state of the country's infrastructure." Undeterred by the lack of evidence of a problem they are determined to solve, the report's authors toss out estimates of a Canadian infrastructure gap ranging from "as 'low' as $150 billion to as high as $1 trillion."[7] Not bad for a gap for which there is no reliable evidence! (If two people report seeing a UFO, with one describing it as large and the other describing it as small, is it reasonable to assume that the UFO was medium-sized?)[8]

In fact, there was an intriguing bit of evidence that the report's authors chose to ignore. In June 2016, the McKinsey Global Institute produced a report, *Bridging Global Infrastructure Gaps*, which includes a chart showing the estimated infrastructure gaps in eighteen major countries. While there are indeed countries with large gaps — including the United States, Brazil, Mexico, and South Africa — one country that bucks the trend is Canada. The report estimates Canada's infrastructure gap as precisely zero! That's because Canada is one of the few countries that has increased its infrastructure investment since the 2008 recession, the report explains. (This doesn't mean that all Canada's infrastructure needs have been met, but rather that, according to this report, money is already in the pipeline to address those needs.)[9]

Of course, this may not be an accurate estimate. Still, it's a striking finding, especially since it comes from the respected research arm of the company headed by council chair Dominic Barton himself. Furthermore, the council cites the McKinsey Global Institute as a source for other information. Of course, it's not hard to imagine why the council chose to ignore this particular finding by the institute. How could they go on to make the case that Canada's infrastructure gap urgently needed to be addressed, right after presenting research to suggest that the gap probably doesn't even exist?

But the obfuscation got worse. After the release of the advisory council's report, Dominic Barton strongly maintained in his public statements that Canada had a serious infrastructure gap. While the advisory council report at least acknowledges that there are no reliable sources of data, Barton apparently had no qualms asserting in media interviews that Canada's infrastructure gap was not only real but was in the range of five hundred billion dollars![10]

Having apparently established the seriousness of Canada's gap, the advisory council goes on in its report to insist that the way to bridge this gap is to attract big institutional investors. Now, surely the report should have disclosed the fact that Barton and Wiseman were closely connected to the world's biggest institutional investor, Fink, who actually employed Wiseman and his wife, and that Sabia himself was also a major institutional investor, whose fund managed some $250 billion in assets that he badly wanted invested in long-term infrastructure projects. Instead, the report simply makes the case that it is vital — indeed a "national priority" — to attract "institutional investors" (people like themselves)![11] By doing so, the report argues, the government would multiply the funds available for infrastructure projects and minimize the amount of Canadian taxpayer dollars that need to be spent.

This is, in fact, a bogus, deeply misleading claim, and we will deal with it in more detail later in the chapter. But for now, let's just note that the advisory council devotes much of its report to the question of how to attract these institutional investors. *If only we could catch their eye! Well, take heart*, we're told, *we can!* Yes, we can lure big, strong institutional capital to our modest Canadian shores, if only we "set the right conditions to attract it."[12] (Adjust our hairstyle, smile more, get them to talk about themselves ...)

In fact, according to the report, there was some twelve trillion dollars parked by investors around the world in negative-yield bonds, which investors would presumably much rather invest in high-yield, low-risk infrastructure. So, it wasn't really the case that Canada was the disadvantaged partner desperately hoping to seize this "once-in-a-generation opportunity" to solve a problem — a problem that may not even have existed. If anything, the shoe was on the other foot. It was institutional capital that was seeking a once-in-a-generation opportunity to earn high-yield, low-risk returns at a time when few such opportunities seemed to exist in the global marketplace.

So, it actually looks more like it was "advantage Canada" in this multi-billion-dollar infrastructure sweepstakes. But you'd sure never know it from the report put out by this council of advisers, who highlight all the things Canada must do to attract institutional capital. Essentially, they write, the country must create an infrastructure bank that would cater to the needs of institutional capital. This bank would deal exclusively with infrastructure projects big enough to interest these big private investors — projects worth a minimum of one hundred million dollars, they specify — and that have revenue streams attached, like toll roads or user fees. (Smaller projects, the advisers note, shouldn't be dealt with through the new bank, but rather just financed in the traditional way.)

But this is only the beginning of their requests. Crucially, the advisory council envisions allowing institutional investors to own pieces of Canada's infrastructure, like roads, bridges, hospitals, sewage systems, and electricity grids. Traditionally, most of Canada's infrastructure has been publicly owned. Recently, governments, particularly at the provincial and municipal levels, have entered into public-private partnerships (also known as P3s), with private interests building and operating infrastructure on long-term leases of twenty to thirty years. But in these P3 deals, the infrastructure remains publicly owned, and after the expiry of the lease, it is handed back to government to operate. (More on P3s later.)

However, Morneau's advisory council wanted private investors to be able to actually take ownership of our infrastructure. "The Bank's financial participation in projects will generally be in the form of subordinated equity and loan positions," the report states.[13] In other words, the federal government, through the bank, would own only a subordinated — that is, minority — equity position. In this rather flip, offhand manner, the advisers advocate that the bank facilitate the building of new infrastructure — the very physical structure and apparatus of our country — that would be owned by people other than ourselves. This departure from usual past practice cries out for some explanation justifying such a significant change. None is offered, however.

Instead, the matter is treated as if it were no big deal; the advisory council implies public ownership isn't necessary or important. Indeed, they devote little time to the subject in their report because ... well ... because they're in a rush! The authors indicate they are not ruling out public ownership. (Generous of them!) They maintain that it might be "worth considering" the possibility that provincial governments could have some ownership or a governance role at the bank, but "in the interest of expediency, we do not see these as imperatives to the launch of the Bank."[14] *In the interest of expediency!* Whoa! What's the rush? We're talking about hundreds of millions, even billions of dollars of Canadian infrastructure, paid for ultimately by Canadians, and yet these "advisers" are implying it doesn't matter who owns it! No, actually, they're implying it does matter — we must allow private investors to own it. After all, we must do everything possible to attract them!

The report also pays scant attention to the question of how much competition would be involved as the bank arranges infrastructure deals. "This may include a competitive bidding process,"[15] the report suggests, leaving open the possibility that there would be no competitive bidding. Who needs competition?

Oh, yes, and just one more thing. What hope will Canada have of attracting private investors if Canadians don't assume the lion's share of the risk? Even though infrastructure projects in a wealthy, advanced country like Canada are generally considered low risk, there is always some risk. To solve this problem, the advisory council suggests the nation should put in place measures to reduce that risk further still — in order to attract all those investors who apparently have nowhere else to put their money.

To do this, Morneau's advisers advocate that the risks be transferred to the bank (that is, to the government, and ultimately the public). "The Bank will play a critical role in addressing early stage risks associated with large infrastructure projects. This 'de-risking' will often entail investing equity upfront ..." the report says. "As a result, the Bank will likely earn below-market returns for some projects to 'clear the market' with institutional investors."[16] Indeed, with the bank (that is, the public) taking the risks upfront and earning only below-market returns, there should be lots of money left over so we can serve up generous above-market, risk-free returns to the private investors who would then own our roads, waterways, hospitals, and energy systems!

But hurry, before this once-in-a-generation opportunity disappears!

Reading the hastily assembled sixteen-page report issued by Morneau's team of economic advisers, one could be left with the impression that these advisers are rather shamelessly urging the government to create a bank that serves their interests, with little or no thought to the broader public interest. But then, let's face it; they are mostly just a bunch of business people, with private interests to promote. Fortunately, they were only advisers, with no decision-making powers. Morneau, on the other hand, is an elected minister of the Crown, with a clear obligation to serve the public. Presumably, he would spot the obviously self-serving nature of their advice and discount it appropriately.

But within a few weeks of the report's release, Morneau delivered his fall economic update, in which he outlined that the government would proceed to create an infrastructure bank, almost exactly along the lines called for by this self-serving crowd of "economic advisers." His fall update was followed, a mere two weeks later, by a glittering meeting — it had been in the planning stages for months, under the supervision of the BlackRock team in Ottawa — at Toronto's posh Shangri-La Hotel where Trudeau, Morneau, and Infrastructure Minister Amarjeet Sohi made a pitch about their new bank to international investors. Among that well-heeled crowd were Fink and his new employee Mark Wiseman. Then, just four months later, keeping up the breakneck pace of developments, Morneau used the 2017 federal budget to introduce legislation creating the bank. That legislation was tucked into an omnibus bill so that there would be little opportunity for the usual parliamentary scrutiny as the bill was rushed into law.

And so, within eighteen months of their encounter in Davos, Trudeau had used his parliamentary majority to pass a law creating an infrastructure bank that bore little resemblance to what he had promised during the election campaign but which, to a striking degree, lined up with the infrastructure plans of the thirty-fourth most powerful man on earth.

~⊘~

If you're a politician wanting to play fast and loose with the country's finances, Kevin Page is not someone you want on your trail. Page came to national prominence as the first parliamentary budget officer, appointed by Stephen Harper following Harper's election pledge to make government more accountable in the wake of the sponsorship scandal of the Chrétien government. As it turned out, Harper didn't actually want to be held accountable himself, and for five turbulent years the prime minister was deeply annoyed as his government was scrutinized by Page, a meticulous, principled economist who didn't shy away from speaking truth to power. So, for instance, when Harper announced there wasn't enough money to maintain Old Age Security benefits for sixty-five-year-olds, Page did his own calculations and then promptly informed Canadians that, on the contrary, there were definitely sufficient funds.

Now heading up his own creation, the Institute of Fiscal Studies and Democracy (IFSD) at the University of Ottawa, Page is still holding politicians' feet to the fire, trying to establish some accountability "at the dynamic intersection of money and politics." Accordingly, Page and his institute have been zeroing in, with critical ferocity, on Trudeau's new infrastructure bank. And they've been alarmed to find that, despite plans to invest a massive thirty-five billion dollars of Canadian taxpayer money, there's been a stunning lack of due diligence on the part of the government.

"There's no needs assessment, no plan, no white paper," says Page, who cautions that without a little more careful thinking on the part of government, the private sector players involved will easily get the better of us. "They'll rob us blind!"[17]

Certainly, the central concern about the new bank is the simple fact that bringing in private capital will substantially drive up the cost of building new infrastructure. Advocates for private sector involvement, such as Morneau's council of advisers, typically try to hide this reality. In fact, they suggest just the opposite: that partnering with private capital will save us money. They maintain that by borrowing funds from institutional investors we will be leveraging additional funds from the private sector, thereby sparing ourselves from having to come up with these amounts out of our tax dollars. But this implies institutional investors will be providing us with their money for free or at a discount. Nothing could be further from the truth.

In fact, it's easy to see why involving the private sector ends up being costly. Government can raise the money on its own — as it traditionally has — by selling government bonds or treasury bills to the public. Randall Bartlett, an economist at the IFSD, noted that thirty-year government bonds are paying interest rates in the range of just 2 percent, so "the federal government can almost literally get 'money for nothing.'" Yet, instead of going this sensible, low-cost route, the Trudeau government is planning to team up with big institutional investors, who are keen to invest about $140 billion of their funds. But they expect rates of return on that money of at least 7 to 9 percent, substantially higher than 2 percent.

With these higher rates, the cost of building our infrastructure will soar. And, Bartlett emphasized, it will be Canadians who make up the difference — through tolls or user fees or higher taxes. Toby Sanger, an economist with the Canadian Union of Public Employees, puts it this way: "No homeowner in their right mind would commit to a loan or mortgage at a rate of 7 per cent or more when they can borrow at 2.5 per cent — especially when it involves locking in over 10, 20 or 30 years."[18]

Certainly, over time, the difference between the higher and lower borrowing costs adds up to a staggering amount. Sanger notes that financing a $100 million infrastructure project at an interest rate of 2.5 percent would cost $42 million over thirty years. But the financing costs on the same project triple to $151 million when the interest rate is 7.5 percent. And the financing costs quadruple to $190 million at an interest rate of 9 percent — and that is enough to actually double the total cost of the project.

Sanger calculates that, with the involvement of private finance, Canadians could end up on the hook for an additional *$150 billion* in interest costs over the life of the infrastructure projects to be built. With numbers like this, Kevin Page's fear that "they'll rob us blind" starts to seem like a reasonable prediction.

The much higher financing costs expose the speciousness of the entire case for involving private capital. One of the key arguments made by Morneau and his advisers is that drawing in institutional capital will allow Canada to avoid spending tax dollars on major infrastructure projects so that the government can instead spend those tax dollars on socially needed projects, like clean water for Indigenous communities and affordable housing. However, once we admit that involving private finance will actually cost us more — *way more* — rather than less, these arguments can be seen for what they are: gibberish. Worse, they are gibberish dressed up in the garb of social justice. Indeed, Bartlett points out that, contrary to claims of advancing social justice, the higher private financing costs amount to a government subsidy to private investors.

Another argument used by Morneau is that involving private sector players allows Ottawa to shift over to them a big chunk of the risk involved in infrastructure projects. But an internal memo obtained by Canadian Press revealed that the government is actually planning to take on the bulk of the risk itself, in order to sweeten the deal for investors — just as Morneau's council of advisers urge in their report.[19]

Some commentators argue that we shouldn't be upset about the high rates of return for investors because some of the investment will come from Canadian pension funds and the earnings will therefore benefit retired Canadian workers. True, but if the goal is to strengthen pensions for Canadian workers, there are much simpler, cheaper, more equitable ways to do this than to dramatically overcharge ourselves for our own infrastructure. And, if the goal is to help Canadian workers, why is the government also interested in doing deals with Wall Street funds like BlackRock, whose five trillion dollars in assets probably doesn't include much in the way of assets owned by Canadian workers?

There's another big problem with Trudeau's plan beyond the fact that it will dramatically, wildly, needlessly inflate the price we'll have to pay for our own infrastructure. The other problem, perhaps the *real* problem, is that the bank will give private investors — even foreign-owned entities like BlackRock — the opportunity to actually own important pieces of Canadian infrastructure.

As we've seen, this was first recommended by Morneau's advisory council. And that is what is laid out in the government's actual plan for the bank — still without any explanation to justify it. Certainly, it won't save us any money. As Bartlett notes, whether our infrastructure is owned publicly or privately, it is taxpayers who will end up paying for it. "This does beg the question: Why would taxpayers sell their most valuable assets to the private sector?" he asks.

There's a tendency not to pay much attention to ownership, at least when it comes to *public* ownership. As we saw, Morneau's council of advisers quickly brush over the issue in their report, implying that the question of whether or not the public owned a piece of infrastructure isn't important. Indeed, the advisers recommend that government also put up for sale existing Canadian infrastructure, such as airports and seaports. "This does not necessarily mean an outright sale or 100 per-cent transfer ..." the report notes. "In many cases, the Federal government could retain control of these assets."[20] So, just like that, without any evidence that Canadians want to give up ownership of key infra-structure, the advisers are ready to toss our major airports into the sale bin for privatization.

It's worth noting that the idea of privatizing some or all of Canada's twenty-two major airports was taken up with some gusto by the Trudeau administration after it was given the thumbs-up by Morneau's advisory panel. The idea was not new. Canadian business interests had been quietly pushing for airport privatization through former Cabinet minister David Emerson, who headed a government transportation policy review that was started under Stephen Harper and completed under Justin Trudeau. Emerson, who relied on a large team of corporate and investment advis-ers similar to Morneau's advisory team, produced a two-volume report in 2016 keenly promoting the idea of selling our airports.

Clearly, the government intended to handle the question of whether to privatize our airports as an inside job. Accordingly, after both sets of advisers showed their enthusiasm for the idea, the Trudeau team hired the Bay Street arm of the Zurich-based investment bank Credit Suisse, which specializes in privatization, for advice on the matter. For the previous decade, Credit Suisse had been a major global player in the lucrative business of privatizing government infrastructure, including airports. In fact, in 2009 Credit Suisse went beyond merely providing advice; it jumped in itself, buying the United Kingdom's Gatwick Airport in a joint venture with General Electric. The fact that Trudeau had turned to an investment bank with fingers deep into the privatization business revealed that Ottawa was looking for advice on airport privatization that would run the full gamut from thumbs-up to thumbs-very-high-up.

Outside the immediate confines of the investment community, there was less excitement. Under the existing public system, Canada's airports are run by airport authority boards, which are non-profit entities that include local community representatives. A number of these airport authorities launched a campaign to oppose the privatization plans and to expose the claim that privately owned airports would manage to make profits simply by, for instance, selling more lattes. Instead, the airport authorities argued, passengers could expect higher parking costs, airport improvement fees, cuts to cleaning staff, and an end to services like free Wi-Fi. Although the Trudeau government apparently hadn't thought it necessary to consult with ordinary people who actually use our airports, it soon learned that Canadian air travellers agreed with the airport authorities. An Angus Reid survey in April 2017 found that 53 percent of Canadians considered the privatization idea to be either bad or very bad, with only 21 percent regarding it favourably.

By the spring of 2018, the Trudeau government knew it had a loser on its hands, and it shelved the airport privatization scheme — at least for the time being.

Privatizing airports regularly used by millions of Canadians turned out to be a controversial move that set off flashing red lights for a government starting to gear up for an election. Meanwhile, the broader, more nebulous idea of privatizing unspecified parts of our infrastructure through an investor-friendly infrastructure bank remained very much in play, and safely out of view.

⚬⚬⚬

When Trudeau or Morneau talk about their new infrastructure bank, the word *innovation* is never far from their lips.

But the innovation they're talking about isn't a better design for a road or an improved technology for building a bridge. Rather, they're talking about innovation in the *financing* of infrastructure — the kind of innovation Wall Street is famous for, the kind of innovation that is rarely good. Let's not forget that it was the incredibly innovative minds of Wall Street — Fink notable among them — who came up with mortgage-backed securities. These were assets, backed by a bundle of mortgages or a bundle of pieces of mortgages, that could be traded on the stock market. Wall Street devised increasingly tricky ways of slicing and dicing and repackaging mortgages so that low-cost, junk-quality mortgages could be thrown into the bundles without anyone really noticing. At first, this was regarded as a brilliant innovation, even as a way to attract more investment into the housing market. But as the demand for these new securities ballooned and the products became increasingly risky, this chaotic market helped trigger the 2008 financial collapse and worldwide recession.

So on the face of it, involving Wall Street in the financing of our infrastructure might not seem like the best plan. Yes, Wall Street players are talented innovators. But their innovation is aimed at contriving new ways to secure extremely large profits for themselves, with little regard for the consequences. It is not at all clear that their complex methods of extracting profits from our infrastructure are going to be in the interests of Canadians.

Certainly, there are plenty of clever minds working on innovative schemes to exploit profit opportunities in infrastructure. Recently, Sidewalk Labs, a U.S. firm involved in building infrastructure for an experimental new neighbourhood on Toronto's waterfront, devised a financing scheme that would allow it to get a share of property taxes and future increases in land values, diverting to itself revenues that would normally end up in city coffers. The company, a sister firm of high-tech giant Google, argued that its offer to provide light rail transit for the project was a great opportunity for the city to upgrade an undeveloped parcel of land. There was considerable resistance, however, when the financing scheme became public in February 2019. As city councillor Gord Perks put it, "Rather than wasting time chasing after a pot of gold at the end of that rainbow, we should get on and do what we know does work: build it with public dollars."[21]

But high-tech companies and Wall Street firms are likely to persist in their quest to score big profits through the privatization of infrastructure development. A 2015 BlackRock paper aimed at investors notes that "infrastructure has emerged as a distinct asset class" and that "institutional investors are increasingly keen to finance it." Titled *Infrastructure Rising*, the paper describes the explosive growth in worldwide infrastructure investment since the "watershed event" of the global financial crisis really kicked things off. And Wall Street has been there every step of the way, coming up with a range of innovative methods of packaging infrastructure assets. The BlackRock paper explains how investors can now choose from an "expanded toolkit of strategies — looking beyond core equity to consider infrastructure debt, core-plus equity, value-added equity and opportunistic equity," based on the level of risk they wish to take on. Infrastructure investments, notes the paper, are being organized into "distinct segments similar to those that make up the real estate spectrum."[22]

In other words, with Wall Street's help, the global market for infrastructure has grown like wildfire. In the decade between 2004 and 2014, infrastructure funds under management worldwide rose from just over $1 billion to an astounding $317 billion! In part, this reflects how private partners have managed to extract excess profits from infrastructure by scoring sweetheart deals in public-private partnerships. Typically, government negotiators fail to drive a hard bargain on behalf of the public, allowing private sector partners to overestimate the upfront "risk" they face. When those risks fail to materialize, the infrastructure asset turns out to be more valuable than originally assumed, and so the private partners are able to sell their equity shares and reap a speculative gain. Similarly, private partners can cut jobs or wages for workers (at hospitals or schools, for example) or raise tolls or user fees (on roads or energy grids), all actions that help to increase the revenue stream from what had been assumed in the original deal, thereby enabling the private partners to sell the infrastructure asset for an inflated price. Ultimately, such speculative activity leads to higher costs or reduced services to the public — or both.

This sort of profiteering lies behind the rise of the huge market for infrastructure assets. These assets can be sold to giant infrastructure funds for "super profits" — often with annual rates of return above 40 percent, according to Dexter Whitfield, a European-based analyst who has studied infrastructure funds. In addition to this private speculation driving up infrastructure costs, significant one-time costs are added due to the vast army of lawyers, accountants, consultants, and financial advisers involved in structuring these transactions. All these profits and fees typically end up in infrastructure funds located offshore, where disclosure requirements are minimal and annual dividends can be received tax-free. As a result, little of this multi-billion-dollar profiteering makes its way back to the coffers of the country whose infrastructure it is and whose citizens are ultimately paying for it.[23]

This high-finance profiteering is already going on with existing Canadian infrastructure that has been financed as public-private partnerships, according to Heather Whiteside, a political science professor at University of Waterloo. She believes that such profiteering will almost surely grow with the new infrastructure bank, which the Trudeau government has said will expand opportunities for private equity. This suggests that our infrastructure will increasingly be owned by unknown players reaping enormous speculative gains at our expense and accumulating those gains, beyond our reach, in offshore tax havens.

All this raises huge questions about the wisdom of allowing Wall Street to be involved in the financing of our infrastructure. We might be willing to take such a gamble if there was no other option. But, as noted, Canadian governments have a long history of financing

infrastructure largely by borrowing from the public — that is, raising money by selling government bonds or treasury bills to individual
Canadians as well as to Canadian pension funds. This financing method
is a made-in-Canada solution, using money borrowed from Canadians
to build infrastructure that we all end up owning and benefiting from.
As Whiteside observes, that's how most of the infrastructure in this
country was built and it was a system that worked very well.

This tried-and-true system was apparently what Trudeau had in
mind, based on his statements during the election campaign. But, once
in office, he did what Whiteside calls a "bait and switch": after campaigning on a progressive package of public investment, he ended up
delivering an infrastructure bank that offers ownership rights to private
capital. The result, she insists, will be much higher costs for Canadians
in the future as we find ourselves facing "a Canadian landscape dotted
with tolls and charges." Whiteside puts it bluntly: "Cutting through
the deception means seeing the Canada Infrastructure Bank for what it
is: the long-run theft of public dollars."[24]

Yet the media largely let Trudeau get away with this bait and switch,
even cheered it on from the sidelines. In a feature in the *Toronto Star* in
October 2016, the normally acerbic Paul Wells wrote excitedly about
this "rare opportunity for Canada" to link up with an asset manager
whose pockets are as deep as Fink's. "Writing about this stuff, for the
first time in a quarter-century in journalism, I'm getting used to typing
the word 'trillion,'" he enthused. At the end of the piece, Wells quoted
a Trudeau adviser warning that we shouldn't delay too long: "We just
don't know how long this [opportunity] will last."[25]

Well, we can assume that it will last about as long as there are
hucksters on Wall Street keen to make a buck at our expense.

Certainly, the media seemed to accept the central argument that
attracting institutional capital would amplify the funds available for
infrastructure, sparing us from spending our tax dollars. *Globe and
Mail* business reporter Barrie McKenna appears to buy into this logic
when he explains that the bank would allow Canada to multiply "limited federal dollars" by "persuading pension funds and other large private investors to pony up." *Pony up?* This is an expression typically used

when urging someone to stop resisting and pay what they owe. Used here, it reinforces the (mistaken) notion that institutional capital is reluctant to put its money in and that it's to our benefit that they do so. McKenna seems to completely miss the point: not only is institutional capital in fact extremely keen to get involved in financing our infrastructure, but their involvement will cost us dearly.[26]

From his office in BlackRock's posh headquarters on East 52nd Street in New York City or from his reserved table on "Chairman's Row" at Manhattan's swanky San Pietro Restaurant, Larry Fink is no doubt pleased as he contemplates the wildly lucrative new opportunities in the world of infrastructure finance.

And well he should be. It is not Larry Fink, but rather Canadian taxpayers, who will be ponying up.

∽ *Two* ∾

The Worst Deal of the Century

The privatization of Canada's public assets and services has become so pervasive that Canadians barely notice it these days, despite the serious consequences. But where did this impetus to privatize come from? An intriguing case can be made that the push for privatization in Canada has its roots in the pro-slavery Southern culture of colonial America.

In her insightful book *Democracy in Chains*, U.S. historian Nancy MacLean argues that the anti-government, anti-tax dogma that dominates U.S. politics today — with huge reverberations in Canada — is rooted in John C. Calhoun's defence of the interests of Southern planters. MacLean tracks the early nineteenth-century ideas of the prominent South Carolina senator to arguments expounded more than a century later by economist James M. Buchanan, who developed a school of thought known as public choice theory. Of course, by the 1960s, when Buchanan began articulating his theories from a perch at the University of Virginia, slavery was no longer an issue. But Calhoun's fiercely held notion that the wealthy were a particularly worthy minority, in need of special legal protection from a selfish majority eager to tax them, found great resonance in wealthy corporate sponsors, particularly Charles Koch.[1]

MacLean highlights the very different attitudes that existed historically in Northern and Southern states when it came to democratic government and taxation. In the more egalitarian Northern states, where slavery was less common and there was a broadly shared sense of civic purpose among the citizenry, early Americans chose to elect active governments that taxed them and used the revenues to provide roads, bridges, canals, and schools. This more egalitarian situation in the North favoured the development of democracy, where people willingly pool their resources in order to pay for things they need but can't afford on their own.

It was a different story in the Southern states, where slavery was the dominant institution, creating a small but wealthy and powerful elite of white plantation owners. Below them was a yeoman class of struggling white farmers, and beneath those farmers were black slaves and their families, who vastly outnumbered whites in many parts of the South. It was a very hierarchical, repressive society, where planters lived in luxury, but in constant fear of slave uprisings. There was little trust or sense of common purpose among the factions: none between black people and white people, but also little between rich white planters and poor white farmers. The top priority of planters was preserving slavery — the source of their tremendous wealth — and this made them conscious of their political isolation at a time when the Western world was increasingly abolishing slavery, including Britain in 1833. This sense of being on their own, lacking allies at home and abroad in their most important political cause, left them deeply suspicious of democratic government.

It also left them deeply suspicious of taxation. Yeomen white farmers in the South pushed for what Northerners had: roads and schools and canals. The planters resisted, fearing that the tax burden to pay for these facilities would fall unduly on them. In particular, planters resisted any scheme that taxed slaves as property, since this would be a simple way to transfer the tax burden onto them. So fearful were they of the taxing power of the majority that the planters pushed hard for constitutional protections against such "confiscatory" taxes. For them, the term *minority rights* referred to their right to be protected from the taxing power wielded by the majority of citizens in a democracy, or what one contemporary judge dubbed "rapacious public power."

The planters had a highly articulate advocate in John C. Calhoun, who, in addition to being a U.S. senator, served as vice-president of the republic. Calhoun was a wealthy slave owner himself and an unabashed champion of slavery; he defended it as "sanctioned by the Gospel, and especially favourable to personal and national liberty."[2] The liberty that he had in mind, of course, was that of the plantation owner. Calhoun fought hard against anything that threatened the interests of the slave-owning elite. When a federal tariff was slapped on imported manufactured goods in 1828, helping the industrial North at the expense of the cotton-exporting South, Calhoun and other planters dubbed it the "Tariff of Abominations." Calhoun called for a tax revolt in protest, making him "America's first tactician of tax revolt," according to MacLean.[3] A serious showdown over the tariff — including possible armed intervention by the federal government against defiant South Carolina — was avoided when a compromise tariff was worked out in 1833. Calhoun's brinksmanship not only foreshadowed the South's secession from the Union a few decades later, it also demonstrated the intense determination of Southern planters to shield their wealth from the taxing power of the majority.

Calhoun's ardent defence of the planter class went considerably beyond that of James Madison, the key drafter of the U.S. Constitution, who was himself a slave owner, as were a number of the other Founding Fathers. Madison had been careful to ensure the Constitution protected private property rights, including the property rights of slave owners, and that it included features that made it difficult for the majority to impose collective action. (The Electoral College and the Senate, for instance, were designed to favour less populous states, making it more difficult for the nation's majority to get its way.) Ultimately, however, Madison supported the right of the majority — excluding black people and women — to impose its collective will, seeing that as essential to the republic living up to claims of democratic governance and popular sovereignty. Calhoun, a generation later, was less interested in democratic niceties; he advocated a form of minority veto power that would effectively restrict what the majority could achieve to what was acceptable to the wealthy minority.

This notion that the wealthy should be able to block policies that threaten their interests lies at the heart of James Buchanan's public choice theory.

Buchanan was one of a number of conservative economists who were enormously frustrated in the early years following the Second World War, when the impressive performance of government in lifting America out of the Great Depression and winning the war against Hitler had generated great public confidence in government's ability to act to improve the lives of Americans. With the public applauding the extension of government, particularly into areas like social security, a small international cadre of distinguished conservative economists famously met at Mont Pèlerin, Switzerland, in 1947 to strategize about undermining the considerable public and academic support for government's expanded role. These economists, including Friedrich Hayek, Ludwig von Mises, and Milton Friedman, were to play a significant role in overturning the consensus supporting John Maynard Keynes and his advocacy of government intervention in the economy. The Swiss gathering was the launch of a robust revival of laissez-faire economics.

Buchanan was still in graduate school at the time of the Mont Pèlerin meeting, but he went on to play an important, if less well known, role in the major counter-revolution in economic thinking that would soon be underway. Indeed, he pushed that movement even further to the right.

Much of economics has traditionally focused on identifying "market failure" to determine how government intervention could correct such problems. (Even advocates of laissez-faire economics were concerned with market failure but sought to keep government intervention to a minimum.) Buchanan, however, turned the very idea upside down, zeroing in instead on how *governments* fail. So, although conservative economists typically regard government as inefficient and consider its interventions in the market to be intrusions on economic liberties, Buchanan's critique went further, hitting at the very legitimacy of government.

In particular, Buchanan tried to destroy the notion that government acted in the public interest, suggesting that this was based on a distorted understanding of human nature. According to Buchanan, humans are simply self-interested, and nothing more. Public officials, like everyone else, are focused on feathering their own nests and incapable of a broader, societal perspective. Therefore, Buchanan maintained, there is no basis for the notion that government is able to advance the public good.

What Buchanan did was provide an intellectual foundation for what became, over the next few decades, a massive attack on virtually all aspects of government and its capacity for beneficial collective action. The notion that government — even democratically elected government — could in any way represent the public interest was presented as fraudulent; there was no overarching public interest, he argued, just a collection of individual desires and preferences. The concept of public servants operating in the interests of the broader community was rejected and replaced with the concept of bureaucrats, who are interested only in increasing the size of their bureaucracies to maximize their own power and income. Politicians were dismissed as self-serving, controlled by the largest donors, and government in general was portrayed as little more than a trough that everyone tried to feed out of.

Of course, some of this is certainly credible: many politicians can be easily swayed by campaign contributions, and governments do often bend to the wishes of powerful donors. Less convincing is the assertion of Buchanan — and other academics who adopted his oddly named public choice theory — that human beings are incapable of caring about anything other than their own narrow self-interest and that they utterly lack public-spirited motives. Public choice theorists would, for instance, conclude there must be self-serving motives in the behaviour of all those who devote time, energy, and resources championing social justice causes, including ones in faraway places where they have no apparent interests.

Much of public choice theory simply doesn't jibe with our observation of human nature, as Nobel Prize–winning economist Amartya Sen captured with the following scenario: "'Can you direct me to the railway station?' asks the stranger. 'Certainly,' says the local, pointing in the opposite direction, towards the post office, 'and would you post this letter for me on your way?' 'Certainly,' says the stranger, resolving to open it to see if it contains anything worth stealing."[4]

But although public choice theory seems intellectually weak in parts, its political usefulness became clear. "Public choice theory is, more than anything else, a theory of government failure," notes Lars Udehn, a sociologist at Stockholm University. "The argument is that government is too big, and public expenditures in Western democracies a gigantic waste of resources."[5]

Given their conclusions about the deeply flawed nature of government, public choice theorists developed strong arguments about taxation. Like other conservatives, they staunchly opposed progressive taxation. But they went further and favoured strict limits on government taxing power, on the grounds that there is no broad public interest, only individual preferences. Echoing John C. Calhoun and his planter class from the previous century, public choice theorists pushed for constitutional protections against majority rule in taxation. And those constitutional protections, they argued, should not be subject to change without unanimous or near-unanimous public agreement, thereby effectively handing the rich a veto over popular attempts to increase their tax burden.

They also developed a deeply radical critique of education. When student radicalism erupted on campuses in the late 1960s and early '70s, conservatives consistently called for tough measures against activists. But Buchanan went further, insisting it was time to rethink the very nature of universities and their incentive structures. Rather than considering universities important public institutions, Buchanan argued that higher education should be regarded as an industry in which individuals seek to maximize their personal advantage and minimize their costs. The problem with universities was public ownership, he maintained, and the solution was to apply the corporate model: "Students should pay full-cost prices, and universities should compete for them as customers. Taxpayers and donors should organize 'as other stockholders do' to monitor their investments."[6] In *Academia in Anarchy: An Economic Diagnosis*, Buchanan and co-author Nicos Devletoglou offer a public choice critique that sets out a blueprint for the corporatization of the university, along the lines of what has taken place in the last few decades.

While much of the writing of Buchanan and other public choice theorists remains little known outside the academic world, its impact has been broad and significant. Buchanan created a radical new way to look at government, portraying it as not merely inefficient and intrusive but as inherently untrustworthy, with no higher purpose or beneficial capacity. And, particularly after he was awarded the Nobel Prize for Economics in 1986, his approach has been seen as having intellectual heft. Even so, his deep assault on government might have had limited reach had it not been for the keen interest it aroused in the multi-billionaire brothers Charles and David Koch, whose combined net worth is an estimated eighty-six billion dollars.

Many wealthy American families and corporate interests have contributed to the funding of the conservative assault on Keynesianism and New Deal thinking over the past four decades. But none of these donors stands out like the Koch brothers, who built a family-owned, oil-related business into one of the richest corporate empires in history. Along with business acumen, the Kochs undoubtedly learned extremist political views from their father, Fred, one of the co-founders of the far-right, anti-Communist John Birch Society. Charles and David readily embraced their father's passionate hatred of collective action and came to see entrepreneurs like themselves as the unsung heroes of the modern world, deserving much more deference as well as freedom from government regulation and taxation.

Like their father, the Koch brothers have always been considerably to the right of mainstream right wingers. In 1980, David Koch tossed his hat into national electoral politics, running for vice-president on the

Libertarian Party ticket, which called for an end to public schools, Social Security, and taxation. He and his running mate won only 1 percent of the vote, losing to Ronald Reagan in the Reagan landslide.

Undeterred, the Koch brothers set about to push America, particularly the Republican Party, much further right. Operating mostly behind the scenes, and driven by an abiding hatred of government and anything that smacked of distributing wealth more broadly, the Kochs invested massively over the next few decades in creating a vast network of think tanks, academic programs, front groups, political action bodies, campaigns, and lobbyists to influence the public, the media, and politicians, as *New Yorker* writer Jane Mayer documents in her powerful book *Dark Money.*[7]

Although the Kochs have funded many right-wing academics over the years, they were especially drawn to the work of Buchanan. Nancy MacLean notes that Charles Koch "bypassed" conservative economic superstars like Milton Friedman to concentrate on promoting the more uncompromising James Buchanan. MacLean writes, "Koch referred to Friedman and the rest of the post-Hayek Chicago school of economics he led ... as 'sellouts to the system.' Why? Because they sought 'to make government work more efficiently when the true libertarian should be tearing it out at the root.'"[8]

Buchanan's relentless attack on government combined with Koch's massive resources and steely determination have made for a lethal combination. Together Buchanan and Charles Koch, who co-chaired the governing board of the Koch-sponsored James M. Buchanan Center for Political Economy at George Mason University in Virginia, have been shockingly successful in bringing their extremism into the mainstream. They've been instrumental, over the past forty years, in slowly changing the shape of American politics, by nudging the Republican Party from one that espoused traditional conservatism toward one that embraces radical libertarianism, and then by orchestrating Republican domination of state governments as well as the federal government and the courts.

The success of this anti-government crusade has transformed the American political landscape, replicating some of the extreme anti-democratic aspects of the colonial Southern states, in a way that is deeply out of sync with more democratic historical traditions in the United States, not to mention with the political aspirations of millions of Americans today.

The ideas behind the anti-government movement are even less of a fit for Canadians, as our history and geography have inclined us to be supportive of strong government enterprises and programs. However, like so much else that becomes big in the United States, these ideas have penetrated north of the border, where they've been absorbed into our political culture, shaping our retreat from public ownership and our embrace of privatization. Strangely, the subject of privatization hasn't really been central to our public debates. Rather, without much debate at all, we've largely adopted significant aspects of an anti-government agenda financed by two ultra-right-wing U.S. billionaires, designed by an extremist libertarian economist, and rooted in the pro-slavery culture of the colonial planter class.

One Canadian politician who ran — and got elected — on a platform that at least included privatization proposals was former Ontario premier Mike Harris. Once in office, the Harris government carried out the biggest privatization in Canadian history when it sold Highway 407 in 1999 for $3.1 billion. The sale was highly controversial, but even its critics probably wouldn't have been able to imagine at the time just how much it has ended up costing Ontarians — and how much more it will continue to cost them until the deal expires in 2098, just two years before the next millennium, when anyone now reading these words will almost certainly be dead, or at least too old to celebrate.

Certainly, if we want to see what can go terribly wrong with privatization — and why we should be very wary of moves by Justin Trudeau and other Canadian political leaders to lead us further down this road — we need look only at the sad tale of the 407.

Harris, a folksy-talking, small-town politician from North Bay, Ontario, won the 1995 provincial election with a pledge to bring in a

"Common Sense Revolution" that would cut taxes, balance the budget, and reduce the size of government. During the campaign, he and his Progressive Conservatives talked about privatizing major Crown corporations like the Liquor Control Board of Ontario, Ontario Hydro, and TV Ontario. As premier, Harris followed up with a show of privatization zeal, appointing the Privatization Secretariat and the Cabinet Committee on Privatization, which was headed by his good friend and newly appointed finance minister, Ernie Eves.

Still, the Harris government proceeded cautiously when it came to privatization; the politically savvy Eves sensed that there wasn't a groundswell of support for selling off any of the province's major Crown corporations. By 1998, three years into its mandate, the government had only privatized a few small entities. But it decided to make a big move. Based on a task-force recommendation, it proposed privatizing the 407, a highway north of Toronto designed to relieve traffic congestion in Canada's fastest-growing urban area.

The 407 already had an unusual history. Unlike other Ontario highways, which had been financed out of general revenue and were fully owned and operated by the province, the 407 had been built, in the early 1990s, mostly in partnership with the private sector — an approach that was still relatively new in Canada. This involvement of the private sector had been particularly notable since it had been carried out by the left-leaning NDP government of Bob Rae.

The Rae government had been attacked every day in the legislature and the business press over Ontario's large deficits. Although those deficits were mostly caused by the Bank of Canada's overly tight monetary policy (which manifested itself in extremely high interest rates, something that had extreme negative effects on businesses and, in turn, produced significant unemployment), the Rae government was being blamed and was desperate to dispel the suggestion that its spending was out of control. Accordingly, it teamed up with a private consortium to build the 407. Although the government financed the project by borrowing through the Ontario Financing Authority, it was able to shift some of the considerable costs of highway construction off its own books in the short term, so that its debt load at least looked lighter. The Rae team was also clearly hoping to establish some credibility with the corporate world by showing its openness to working with the private sector. The co-operation worked fairly well. Even so, the Rae government failed to receive any credit from an unreceptive business community.

In another deficit-inspired departure from normal practice, the 407 had been developed as a toll road, allowing the Rae government to avoid increasing its deficits by transferring part of the construction costs to 407 drivers. Although Ontario drivers hadn't faced road tolls since the last tolls were removed from the Burlington Skyway Bridge in 1973, the decision to reintroduce tolling was relatively well received by the public — perhaps because it was accompanied by a promise that the 407 tolls would be used exclusively to cover the highway's construction costs and would be lifted once those costs were fully covered, likely in about thirty years.

By comparison, the Harris government's announcement in 1998 that it was considering selling the 407 was greeted with considerable resistance; critics immediately charged that a private owner would raise the tolls. Without vowing to take steps to ensure this didn't happen, the government simply downplayed the possibility. Tony Clement, minister of transportation, and Rob Sampson, minister for privatization, insisted that, on the contrary, tolls would likely decrease because the private owner would be keen to attract more users.

Although there was substantial skepticism among the public about that, the Harris team was getting lots of encouragement from inside and outside its own ranks. It relied heavily on advice from its Privatization Secretariat, which was stuffed with recruits from the business world who were full of ideas about the superiority of the private sector. There was also an enthusiastic banging of drums from Bay Street brokerage houses, along with law and accounting firms, which knew how much their services would be needed in a privatization deal of this scale. Goldman Sachs made a fancy presentation to the Ontario Transportation Capital Corporation. The financial services giant Merrill Lynch and the Royal Bank, the country's largest bank, were retained by the Privatization Secretariat to provide advice throughout the process (at a cost that ended up totalling twenty million dollars). Perhaps not surprisingly, their advice favoured privatization — a route that would incidentally bring them more business as well.

These outside financial advisers therefore consistently backed the positions urged by the government's own Privatization Secretariat, which had been set up, after all, to promote privatization and was extremely keen to do so. With this cacophony of voices in its ear, the Cabinet weighed the options: Should the 407 be fully privatized or should the government remain involved through a Crown corporation and just sell the public some shares? The Cabinet concluded a full privatization was best.

Another contentious question was this: Should there be a time limit on the deal? Typical privatization deals involved thirty-year leases. But the secretariat instead suggested lease periods of 55, 99, or even 199 years, and asked the prospective buyers to make non-binding bids on these various options. When the longer leases produced higher bids (all non-binding, rendering these bids fairly meaningless), the secretariat used this to push the Cabinet toward a longer lease. Staff inside the secretariat understood that a key Cabinet aim was to amass revenue to help make good on their promise to balance the budget just before the next election.

The difference between the bids for a thirty-year lease and those for a ninety-nine-year lease amounted to just one hundred million dollars — not a large amount to cover a period of almost seventy years. But making a commitment for an extra seventy years seemed to be unduly tying the hands of future governments and future generations. However, from the viewpoint of members of the Harris Cabinet, that extra one hundred million dollars looked mighty appealing as they struggled to balance the budget. The longer lease also fit well with their ideological distaste for public ownership. So, grabbing the extra one hundred million dollars, the Cabinet opted for a ninety-nine-year lease, thereby "handing over a lucrative franchise to toll the Highway 407 corridor for almost a century," note Chandran Mylvaganam and Sandford Borins in their detailed study of the deal in a book titled *"If You Build It ... ": Business, Government and Ontario's Electronic Toll Highway.*[9]

Although Ontario had never privatized a highway before, the Harris government proceeded at full speed. After only one day of public hearings, it passed legislation facilitating the privatization in December 1998. A few months later, having considered offers from three major consortia, it selected the highest bidder — $3.107 billion from 407 International Inc., which was owned by Cintra Concesiones de Infraestructuras de Transporte, a subsidiary of the giant Spanish construction firm Grupo Ferrovial, with a passive interest held by the Quebec-based engineering firm SNC-Lavalin. Since taxpayers had already spent $1.5 billion building the 407, the government declared it had scored a "profit" of $1.6 billion in offloading it to the Spanish company. The deal closed May 5, the same day an election was called, with the proceeds from the highway sale enabling Harris to head into the campaign boasting a considerably smaller deficit than expected — as well as delivering a two-hundred-dollar cash rebate to every Ontario taxpayer.

Just how bad a deal the government had struck first became evident almost three years later, in 2002, when SNC-Lavalin sold part of its 407 holding in a transaction that showed that the value of the highway had already more than doubled to $6.3 billion. Then, a year later, in 2003, the U.S. financial services giant Standard & Poor's valued the highway at between $8 billion and $13 billion, indicating that it may have quadrupled in price in just four years. More recent estimates by the National Bank put the value of the 407 at a staggering $27 billion to $28 billion. Ferrovial predicts that, by 2026, the highway could be worth $45 billion. These mega-billion-dollar price tags reflect how much revenue is expected to be collected — in other words, how much Ontarians are going to pay for the privilege of driving on this road over the coming decades.

Given all this, it is absurd to merely call the Harris government's sale for $3.1 billion nothing stronger than a bad deal; it is an unconscionably bad deal. And it's more than just a question of hindsight. At least part of the reason for the highway's dramatic jump in value was that, when it was put up for sale in 1999, it had been operational for less than two years and the number of users was still growing.

Mylvaganam and Borins argue that if the government had waited at least another couple of years, the true profit potential of the highway in the explosively growing Toronto market would have been easier to establish, and it would have commanded a considerably higher price. Of course, that didn't fit the Harris government's election needs.

Another example of a serious lack of due diligence on the part of the Harris Cabinet was its failure to insist on adequate protection against unreasonable toll hikes in the future. The Spanish-led consortium was buying a revenue stream: the right to charge drivers for using the 407 to escape traffic gridlock on Highway 401, the main east–west roadway that cuts through the north part of Toronto. If the government insisted on selling what amounted to a vital piece of the southern Ontario traffic system, surely it had a duty to ensure that the public was properly shielded against the enormous tolling power it was surrendering to private interests.

But, astonishingly, the Harris team utterly failed to provide even minimal safeguards. As Mylvaganam and Borins point out, the only protection built into the deal involved traffic volume; as long as the highway attracted a certain number of drivers (thereby fulfilling its function as a relief route), the new owners had total freedom to raise the tolls to whatever level they chose! Sampson, minister for privatization, reflecting the Harris government's blind faith in the marketplace, assured the public at the time of the sale that "tolls would not skyrocket because new owners need drivers if they are to pay off debts. The limit is what the market is prepared to pay and that's a realistic limit."

Sampson had evidently reached this comforting conclusion based on his understanding of how free markets work. It apparently hadn't occurred to him, or the others inside the Harris government, that the 407 doesn't operate as a service in a free market; it is a monopoly. If there were other, similar roads for drivers to choose from — in other words, if it weren't a monopoly — the new 407 owners would indeed have had to keep tolls down in order to compete. But there are no other such roads. That is why the 407 was built in the first place, and why it is so valuable. David Turnbull, who had replaced Clement as minister of transportation in 1999, even had the audacity to suggest that motorists had market power and if they didn't like the higher tolls, they should stop using the 407 — even though they had paid to build it through their taxes!

The reality is that the new 407 owners can keep raising the toll rates without losing customers because there is a great hunger for a relief route in the Greater Toronto Area, which had already reached five million people by the time of the sale. The government had just handed over to a private foreign company the power to effectively extort significant amounts of money from Canadians who use that highway to escape gridlock; many of them would otherwise face daily commutes of three or even four hours. While the Harris government had predicted that the 407 tolls wouldn't rise by more than 30 percent over fifteen years, in reality, the tolls rose by more than 300 percent over that period, pushing the approximate rush-hour cost of driving from Burlington to Pickering to more than forty dollars.[10]

Also absent from the privatization deal was the original promise that the tolls would go exclusively toward the costs of building the highway and would be removed when those costs were covered. Of course, that pledge had been made by the Rae government, so it was easily discarded by the Harris Common-Sensers — even though it was, when you think about it, the epitome of common sense. It must have been obvious to the Harris Cabinet that, even if this sale would help them get re-elected, it was a very bad deal for Ontario taxpayers, who had already paid $1.5 billion to construct the highway and now would be obliged to pay to drive on it for the rest of their lives. In 2014, 407 International reported annual revenue of almost nine hundred million dollars — money straight out of the pockets of Ontarians.

The sale of the 407 also created needless court battles and enormous hassles for thousands of drivers. That's because, in order to sweeten the pot when it put the highway up for sale, the government had agreed to deny licence-plate renewals on cars owned by drivers who failed to pay fines for unpaid tolls. Thus, the government's sweeping power to deny citizens the right to drive their vehicles — not just on the 407, but on any road — was effectively transferred to a private company. Amazingly, by February 2000, only nine months after the completion of the highway sale, fully 80,000 Ontario drivers had already been denied plate renewals as a result of unpaid fines related to 407 tolls, and a further 110,000 were listed as having delinquent accounts, a situation that would lead to the same punishment. This massive inconvenience — not to mention employment jeopardy for those needing a car to get to work — was a direct result of the privatization. The freshly re-elected Harris felt obliged to admit there had been a "screw-up."

This was just the beginning of years of conflict between the private owners of the 407 and the people of Ontario. One of the reasons there were so many plate denials was that the new owners frequently made billing errors and yet had few staff handling the phones to deal with complaints. It also practised something called bill suppression — if initial bills weren't paid, the company stopped sending follow-ups but continued to keep track of penalties and interest charges. Then, years later, it demanded payment of stunningly large overdue accounts. In 2014, forty-five-year-old engineer Andrew Bird received a bill for forty-three thousand dollars from 407 International when he returned to Ontario after living in Alberta for six years.[11]

The extent of the financial problems created by the 407 can be glimpsed in the fact that the company, in 2016, agreed to pay eight million dollars in a class action suit brought by Ontario drivers, after the Supreme Court of Canada ruled the company couldn't pursue collection from people who had declared bankruptcy.

All this helped turn 407 tolls into a contentious issue in the October 2003 election, with Dalton McGuinty's Liberals vowing to "stop the 407 rip-off" by rolling back what were reported to be the world's highest road tolls. But after he was elected premier, if not before, McGuinty discovered this was more difficult than his campaign slogan suggested; the Harris government had signed a deal with ironclad terms — favouring the company. When the company thumbed its nose at the new government by announcing a hike in tolls, not a rollback, McGuinty decided to take them to court. That was the beginning of two years of failed litigation. Finally, in 2006, an embarrassed McGuinty government announced it was abandoning its multi-pronged legal battle and acknowledged that the company had the power to set the tolls it wanted and to insist that the government deny plate renewals to delinquent accounts. It was a complete victory for the private owner.

~⊙~

Although Mike Harris managed to leave office without the 407 being considered a scandal, it is difficult to see it any other way in retrospect. Clearly, the premier sold the highway for a fraction of what it was worth, which is a fraction of what it will be worth in a generation (or two or three), when it will still be in private hands. While it is never possible to know the future, the trend toward rapid growth was already well underway in southern Ontario in 1999, at the time of the sale. It is outrageous that Harris set the lease for ninety-nine years — in order to score an extra one hundred million dollars for cosmetic pre-election deficit reduction — when a thirty-year lease would have been a vastly better financial deal for Ontario taxpayers and drivers.

The sheer amount of money the Harris government gave up is astonishing. In a 2017 note to investors, the Canadian Imperial Bank of Commerce (CIBC) described the 407 as a "cash cow," just on the basis of the returns it produces for minority shareholder SNC-Lavalin. (By February 2019, when SNC-Lavalin was enmeshed in a major Ottawa controversy involving political pressure related to a foreign bribery charge against the company, SNC-Lavalin's relatively small 16.7 percent stake in the 407 was estimated to be worth five billion dollars. This would put the value of the entire highway in the thirty-billion-dollar range.) The CIBC pointed to the population projection for the Greater Toronto Area, which is expected to expand to 9.6 million people by 2041 — not even halfway through the 407 lease! As a CIBC analyst commented in the letter to investors, "We note that 407 International still has flexibility to increase tolls for 81 years."[12] Flexibility, indeed! Mike Harris may have fashioned himself "the tax cutter" before he got out of town, but he left Ontarians saddled with paying ever-rising tolls to a foreign company far into the future for the privilege of driving on a publicly financed road.

Even with a ninety-nine-year deal, Harris could have reduced the financial losses for Ontarians if he'd insisted that the province have a minority stake in the winning consortium. This would have allowed the province to share in the massive profits reaped by 407 International, in the way SNC-Lavalin has from the beginning. With its 16.7 percent stake, SNC-Lavalin has reaped enormous profits, as the following language from a National Bank analyst in 2017 reveals: "407 continues to be a *value-generating monster* for SNC" (italics added).[13] The Canadian Pension Plan Investment Board (CPPIB) also bought a 10 percent interest in 407 International in 2010 and has since increased that stake to 40 percent. So, both SNC-Lavalin, a Montreal-based company, and, more recently, the CPPIB, the investment arm of Canada's public pension system, earn profits from their 407 holdings that benefit Canadians. There would have been a much bigger benefit for many more Canadians, however, if Mike Harris had been properly watching out for the interests of the people he had been charged with representing.

There's a problem more fundamental than the fact that the people of Ontario didn't get a shorter lease or a cut of the action. The real travesty is that the Harris government rejected the better option of retaining public ownership — for reasons that seem largely ideological and illogical. Had the 407 remained publicly owned under the original terms, the highway would, by the year 2028, become part of the toll-free system of Ontario roads, saving Ontarians a great deal of money in the years to come. Or the electorate could have decided to keep the tolls in place and use them as a large and reliable source of revenue for the province — a "revenue-generating monster," if you will — with that revenue dedicated to a specific purpose such as funding public transit.

Instead, by selling the 407, the Harris government has denied Ontarians decision-making power over some key questions about how we will live together, such as how highways fit into our plans to fight climate change and whether it's fair that low-income individuals may be unable to afford to drive on faster roads even though those roads have been constructed on public land and largely paid for with public funds. It might be possible for us to make changes involving the 407 for environmental or social reasons, but it won't be easy to do so. The contract signed by the Harris government imposes severe restraints, as the McGuinty government discovered when it attempted to alter the tolling arrangement. Having a privately owned highway smack in the middle of the most populous section of our country is a problem that limits our democratic options. That limitation will only become more problematic as the Toronto-area population swells over the next eighty years and we're faced with environmental and transportation problems we can't even imagine at this point.

～◯～

Mylvaganam and Borins also argue that the sale of the 407 amounted to an important missed opportunity, since the technology used for electronic toll collection on the 407 was the most advanced of its kind in the world at the time the highway began operation. Therefore, they note, public ownership of the 407 could have been used as the basis for developing Canadian expertise in tolling technology, which may well become an enormous industry.

Tolling is a potential item in the tool kit of green energy solutions. In addition to collecting revenues, it can be used to discourage drivers from using their own vehicles rather than public transit. And electronic tolling — rather than manual collection at booths — is more efficient, making it easier to collect tolls in high-volume areas with many access points. London, England, for instance, has used electronic tolling since 2003 on all vehicles entering the city between certain times, in the interests of reducing congestion and pollution as well as generating revenue. The London system involves hundreds of cameras that produce video images of all vehicles entering the city. "While this technology is impressive, it is still less advanced than that of Highway 407," Borins noted in an interview.[14]

And it was the Ontario government, under Bob Rae, that took the initiative in developing that more advanced technology in 1994 as part of the building of the 407. At that time, there were already electronic tolling systems that could effectively track regular highway users by attaching transponders to their vehicles. But Ontario also wanted to be able to apply tolls to occasional users who lacked transponders. In order to meet those requirements, three companies, Bell Canada, Bell Sygma, and Hughes Aircraft, worked together, winning the contract for the 407 tolling and developing a new technology involving video imaging of licence plates on vehicles.

If an Ontario Crown corporation had owned and operated the 407, with the advanced electronic tolling system developed specifically for it, it would have been well positioned to market that technology and Canadian expertise to other countries developing highway projects. "Highway 407 could have therefore been used as a springboard to create a Canadian presence of global significance in state-of-the-art highway and transportation development," insists Borins. Instead, that opportunity seems to have been seized by Cintra Concesiones de Infraestructuras de Transporte. Certainly, the 407 was critical to Cintra's corporate development strategy, and the company has built on the expertise it has acquired operating the 407. As Cintra's website points out, the 407 was the company's first venture into North American highways. Since then, it's been awarded seven more major highway contracts in North America and now claims a global investment in roadway improvements worth more than twenty-four billion dollars.

It's sad to imagine what prospects there might have been for Ontario — and the province's workers — if the Harris government hadn't been so hell-bent on privatizing one of Ontario's major arteries. This missed opportunity only adds an additional sting to the weighty financial burden Ontarians face in the coming decades as a result of the 407 sale, amounting to literally billions of dollars in tolls to be paid before the century is done.

What makes this tale sadder still is that no lessons appeared to have been learned from it. One might have expected, for instance, that the Liberal McGuinty government, having seen the pitfalls of the 407 privatization, would have given serious consideration to the alternative that had been so blithely rejected by Harris: public owner-ship. But there would be no such reset when the Liberals sought to build infrastructure. While McGuinty lacked Harris's gung-ho ideo-logical commitment to privatization, he nevertheless accepted the busi-ness groupthink that assumes the superiority of the private sector and defers to the business community in all key matters. And so the new government readily signed dozens of infrastructure deals partnering with the private sector for hospitals, courthouses, and power plants. Those power plant deals led it into a major scandal that eventually forced McGuinty to resign in disgrace.

That scandal continues to resonate in Ontario politics — although, oddly, little mention is made of what lay at the root of it: privatization.

The story of the power plants had a promising start. In response to growing scientific evidence of the dangers of climate change, a group called Ontario Clean Air Alliance successfully pressured the McGuinty government to phase out the province's coal-fired power plants, which were producing high levels of greenhouse gas emissions. This sensible move was unfortunately coupled with the decision to turn to private developers to build the new, less-polluting, gas-fired power plants the province required to replace the coal-fired plants it was closing.

It wasn't necessary to bring in private developers. In the past, Ontario governments had developed new power plants by allowing the projects to be handled by Crown corporations — Ontario Power Generation and, before that, Ontario Hydro — which would manage the projects while signing limited contracts with private builders to do the actual construction. The Crown corporations had experience in developing new plants and engaging with local communities about them. More importantly, as agents of the government, Crown corpor-ations had the advantage of being able to borrow money in financial markets at very favourable interest rates.

But instead of making use of this considerable expertise and bor-rowing advantage, the McGuinty government sought out private developers. In 2005, it awarded a contract for two power plants in the Toronto suburb of Mississauga to Eastern Power Ltd., a small firm run by two Canadian brothers, Gregory and Hubert Vogt. The brothers, who had trained as engineers at the University of Toronto, already had a small contract with Ontario Hydro to turn trash into energy at a local landfill site. And, oddly, they had already sued Hydro over that contract, demanding $121 million in damages — a case that was still tied up in the courts. Nevertheless, the government considered the Vogt brothers suitable to be in charge of building plants that would be required to produce about twenty times as much energy as their little landfill project.

Problems began almost immediately. While the government inexplicably had confidence in the brothers' ability to handle such a major project, the financial markets were more skeptical. As a result, the brothers had trouble getting financing, forcing them to scrap one of the two plants just three months after winning the contract. Their financing problems persisted, leaving the Vogts to eventually turn to eight hedge funds, based in the United States and the Cayman Islands. Taking full advantage of the brothers' desperation, the hedge funds struck an unusual financial deal under which the Vogts were obliged to pay an extremely high interest rate of 14 percent, compounded quarterly, and face crippling penalties in the case of default.

That unfortunate predicament soon happened, when the McGuinty government, faced with mounting local opposition to the plant, cancelled the project during the provincial election campaign in October 2011. The following month, government officials asked the brothers for a copy of their eight-year financial contract with the hedge funds. The brothers refused to provide it. Even so, anxious to get the controversial matter settled and unaware of the onerous terms spelled out in the deal with the hedge funds, the government signed an agreement accepting responsibility for the Vogt's financial obligations to their creditors.

The hedge funds quickly pounced. Although the Vogts had borrowed just $59 million in the six months before the project was cancelled, the hedge funds insisted the brothers pay them the equivalent of 14 percent interest for the full eight years of the contract — and not just on the $59 million actually borrowed but on the full $263 million line of credit. In total, the hedge funds were demanding a flabbergasting $228 million, and they launched a lawsuit in New York to retrieve that amount the following spring. Ontario's auditor general described their demands as possibly amounting to a "criminal" rate of interest, exceeding what is permitted under the Canadian criminal code. At the same time, the aggressive hedge funds also sued Ontario for $310 million in damages.

After legal battles in New York and Ontario courts, the McGuinty government settled in July 2012, paying the hedge funds a total of $149 million — more than double the amount the hedge funds had actually loaned to the Vogts. The government also paid the Vogts $31 million to cover their costs, and threw in $10 million to settle the old lawsuit the brothers were still fighting against Ontario Hydro, even though a judge had suggested the Vogts should receive just $5 million.

The cancellation of another plant in nearby Oakville was even more needlessly costly. There was already strong local opposition to the proposed plant in September 2009 when the government signed a contract with energy giant TransCanada Corporation to build it anyway. The Town of Oakville was committed to blocking the project and refused to grant the necessary building permits. With appeals pending, high-level officials in the premier's office met with TransCanada representatives in October 2010 and pledged that, if the plant was cancelled and relocated, the company would be "kept whole" — meaning that it would be guaranteed the profits it was anticipating receiving from the Oakville plant.

This was an odd promise to make, since the government's contract with TransCanada had stipulated that if the plant were cancelled due to forces beyond the control of the parties — as Oakville's legal opposition presumably was — the government would not be obliged to pay the company for lost profits. Two days after the meeting between the Office of the Premier and the company, the government announced the cancellation of the plant and entered into negotiations with TransCanada to relocate it. But, by waiving its rights to not be held responsible for lost profits, the government ceded the upper hand to the company, which drove a hard bargain. The company refused to accept the government's preferred relocation site of Kitchener-Waterloo. Instead, TransCanada insisted the plant be located in Napanee, in the eastern part of the province. This was advantageous to the company's parent firm, TransCanada Pipelines, which would have to make significant capital expenditures to expand its pipeline capacity to transport gas to the Napanee location — capital expenditures that could be billed to the province's ratepayers.

All this amounted to a sweetheart deal for the company. Ontario auditor general Bonnie Lysyk suggested that the relocation to Napanee would make the company "better than whole." And the eventual cost to Ontarians, she concluded, would be more than $675 million, mostly in the form of higher electricity charges in the future. Combined with the Mississauga plant, she estimated that the gas plant fiasco would cost Ontarians somewhere between $950 million and $1.1 billion.[15]

The condemnation directed at the McGuinty Liberals was fully deserved. They had cancelled and relocated power plants for highly political reasons, in order to hold on to two key ridings in what was shaping up to be a close provincial election. Furthermore, they had been inept in handling the cancellations and then had attempted to eliminate embarrassing evidence by wiping clean the hard drives of computers in the premier's office. Understandably, the criticism — from the other political parties and the media — focused heavily on the government's responsibility. With the political scandal sucking up all the oxygen in the media, there was little interest in a subplot about how the involvement of private developers in these deals had dramatically driven up the cost of cancelling and moving the plants.

Even with the government's political meddling, it is highly unlikely that the costs would have been anywhere near as high if the McGuinty team had originally opted for the tried-and-true method under which the government builds and owns the power plants itself. A Crown corporation could have borrowed funds at attractive interest rates, avoiding the absurd situation of the Mississauga plant being financed with money borrowed from shark-like hedge funds charging near-criminal rates of interest.

In the case of the Oakville plant, if the government had handled the development itself, it could have relocated the plant to its preferred location of Kitchener-Waterloo, avoiding potentially hundreds of millions of dollars in higher electricity rates. Of course, the government should have been more aggressive in pushing for the Kitchener-Waterloo location anyway, given the clause in the contract that apparently protected it from being responsible for the private developer's lost profits. This could have led to a lawsuit from TransCanada, with an uncertain outcome, and the McGuinty government wanted to avoid getting into a court battle with the company. Its willingness to bend over backwards to keep the company "whole" seems puzzling, but also reflects the tendency of today's political leaders to defer to powerful business interests.

Globe and Mail reporters Karen Howlett and Paul Waldie astutely observe that the gas plant fiasco serves as "a cautionary tale for governments as they increasingly shift services from bureaucrats to the private sector. The risks associated with these projects are supposed to be borne by the private sector. But when deals unravel, it is taxpayers who are left on the hook."[16]

In the case of the gas plants, the deals unravelled. Whether out of fear or deference, the government went out of its way to accommodate the needs of its private sector partners. It accepted all the risks that theoretically had been transferred to the private players. Both TransCanada and the Vogt brothers emerged better off as a result of their gas plant contracts, while the residents of Ontario will go on paying huge extra costs for decades to come.

According to *Toronto Star* columnist Martin Regg Cohn, the gas plant scandal should have served "as a teachable moment" in illustrating "how the ideology of privatization trumps practicality."[17]

Indeed, the push to privatize seems disconnected from any practical advantage achieved. More often than not, privatization seems to lead to disadvantage, to considerable extra costs imposed on society.

Those higher costs were highlighted in a 2015 report by the Canadian Centre for Policy Alternatives, which compared the telephone systems of Manitoba and Saskatchewan. Both provinces were served by publicly owned telephone companies for many decades until Manitoba privatized its system in 1997. The report, written almost twenty years later, found that publicly owned SaskTel was providing much better value for its customers than the privatized Manitoba Telephone System. SaskTel's basic telephone service was 27 percent cheaper, its CEO compensation one-tenth as high, and it had delivered $497 million in dividends to Saskatchewan over the previous five years, as opposed to the measly $1.2 million in provincial corporate taxes paid by Manitoba Telephone System over the same time period.

But the most compelling evidence of the higher costs of privatization came from a 2014 investigation by Ontario auditor general Bonnie Lysyk. In an audit of seventy-four infrastructure projects, Lysyk found that the province's decision to partner with the private sector, rather than building the projects itself, cost Ontario taxpayers an extra $8 billion.[18] This exorbitant additional cost was mostly because private financing is so much more expensive than government financing, according to Lysyk. Such a striking finding by such a respected authority should have led sensible politicians to begin to seriously examine their increasing reliance on privatization. But nothing of the sort happened, even as the auditor general continued to document the excessive costs of P3s in her subsequent reports. The privatization juggernaut remains in place, rarely even questioned.

Among other things, one wonders if those who promote privatization even believe what they say about the superiority of the private sector — or if their motivation boils down to simple self-interest. There is a great deal of money to be made in privatization for those who end up owning or operating crucial public infrastructure, as well as for those involved in drawing up the complex public-private partnership deals or providing related financial, legal, and accounting advice. So, does the privatization mania really just come down to pressure from a lot of people who are excited about making a lot of money? Is it really immersed so deeply in hypocrisy?

It's striking to note that the U.S. billionaire Charles Koch and the Austrian economist Friedrich Hayek — two individuals who have been hugely influential in discrediting government and promoting privatization — don't even seem to be true believers themselves. Or at least one could conclude that from an intriguing exchange of letters between these free-market apostles. Their 1973 correspondence, discovered by investigative reporter Yasha Levine in the Hayek archive at Stanford University in California, captures the two men calmly considering the merits of the U.S. Social Security system, America's largest social program, which they both fought long and hard to dismantle.[19]

The exchange springs from Koch's attempt to entice Hayek to accept a special teaching post at Koch's Institute for Humane Studies, a libertarian think tank in Menlo Park, California. Hayek, by then in his early seventies, responded that, having undergone gall bladder surgery earlier that year, he feared "the problems (and costs) of falling ill away from home." He wouldn't have to worry about such things in Austria, where there were strong public health care and social insurance systems.

As it turned out, Hayek had paid into the U.S. Social Security system when he taught at the University of Chicago in the 1950s. When Koch found out about this, he wrote to Hayek: "Since you have paid into the United States Social Security Program for a full forty quarters, you are entitled to Social Security payments while living anywhere in the Free World. Also, at any time you are in the United States, you are automatically entitled to hospital coverage." For added benefit, Koch helpfully enclosed a government pamphlet on how to apply for U.S. Social Security benefits and then alerted Hayek to the approaching application deadline.

Koch seemed downright enthusiastic as he explained how the massive U.S. government program works, and neither man expressed any embarrassment about the prospect of benefiting from a public program they had gone to great lengths to disparage. Shredding Social Security had long been one of Koch's central political goals; his brother David had vowed to scrap the system completely, along with taxation and public schools, when he ran for vice-president on the Libertarian ticket in 1980. Hayek was equally hostile to this centrepiece of the modern welfare state, even though he had made the choice of paying into the program while teaching at the University of Chicago in the 1950s. That didn't stop him from devoting an entire chapter to attacking U.S. Social Security in his 1960 book, *The Constitution of Liberty*, insisting that such coddling by government led to moral decay and, ultimately, tyranny.

Of course, even if Koch and Hayek were full-fledged hypocrites, other free-market advocates may actually be sincere when they argue that the public sector is inherently inefficient and the private sector can be trusted to do things better. Still, it is startling to consider that two men who have done so much to undermine the public's confidence in government were willing to write letters acknowledging how effective government-run social insurance is — and to personally make use of it — as long as they thought no one was paying attention.

The campaign to disparage government, to turn people against it, has been phenomenal in size, scope, and fury over the past few decades. And, although it originated south of the border, the campaign has been largely effective in Canada.

As a result, a resistance has developed here to government involvement in many sectors of our economy and our lives. Or, it might be more accurate to say, such a resistance has developed among our political and business leaders, the people who make the decisions. As they've embarked on their sweeping privatization plans, they've tried to convince us that our needs and interests will be better served by private sector players — despite no evidence that this is true, and plenty of evidence that it's not true.

In this chapter, we've looked at a few examples of how the public was very negatively impacted when important facilities — a key highway and two gas plants — were sold or contracted to the private sector. The rest of this book could easily be filled with many more tales of woe resulting from privatizations across the country.

But there's another serious consequence of this massive anti-government campaign: it blocks us from seeing the enormous benefits that can be achieved through government ownership and stewardship, and therefore prevents us from taking advantage of significant opportunities. We'll return to these missed opportunities later in the book. For now, it's worth noting that the anti-government dogma that infects our politics prevents us from appreciating — or even being aware of — what has been accomplished in Canada over our history through what can best be described as public enterprise.

Unlike the profit motive that has stirred the loins of capitalist entrepreneurs, those who built our public enterprises responded to a different set of motivations. It seems fair to say that they were driven, at least in part, by the goal of advancing the collective interests of Canadians, and that this served as a potent incentive. This meant that our public enterprise entrepreneurs often ended up aligned with popular movements of ordinary citizens, facing off against private interests who were keen to block these public enterprises from moving in on their lucrative turf. The resulting conflicts were often bitter and intense, with long-lasting impacts on the country.

It is to these largely forgotten stories of public enterprise entrepreneurs and popular movements battling powerful private interests that we now turn.

~ *Three* ~

The Thrill of Hearing Organ Music on a Train Crossing the Prairies

The building of the transcontinental Canadian Pacific Railway (CPR) in the 1880s has long been regarded as one of the great accomplishments in Canadian history — and with some reason. It's not surprising that Canadians have applauded the construction of thousands of miles of tracks across Canada's huge, physically challenging terrain and that we've hailed as heroes the entrepreneurs who made this feat happen. The famous 1885 photograph of the last spike being driven into the ground in British Columbia to complete the railway is one of the most iconic images in the history of Canada.

So, the celebration of the CPR and its story is understandable — although perhaps not entirely deserved.

Of course, the true heroes of the building of the railway were the ordinary workers, including the roughly fifteen thousand Chinese labourers, who suffered back-breaking toil for little pay, not to mention the estimated six hundred who died in the course of completing the physically treacherous project. Some of the railway's ordinary workers do appear, nameless and unidentified, in the background of the last-spike photo. But it is the financial wheelers and dealers who are prominent in the photo. Front and centre is Donald A. Smith, a major CPR stockholder and later president of the Bank of Montreal, who wields the hammer driving in the last spike — probably the only spike he ever actually drove in.

The building of the CPR has another dark aspect. The railway was a key vehicle for the incursion of colonial settlers into the vast western plains, which were the traditional lands of Indigenous nations and the Métis people. As railway tracks, farm fences, and towns continued to invade deeper into what is now Saskatchewan and Alberta, resistance to the intruders grew. In 1885 an armed Métis force, led by Louis Riel, declared a provisional government in what became known as the Northwest Rebellion. The Canadian government — with the help of the CPR — quickly moved three thousand soldiers and militiamen westward by rail to reclaim control. The suppression of the insurgency after five months of resistance, and the hanging of Riel, was a devastating defeat for the Métis and their allies, and it left a bitter legacy.

There is also reason to question the celebration of the CPR as a feat of Canadian entrepreneurialism. While the CPR financiers were certainly gung-ho capitalists, eager to make a buck, they were heavily subsidized by the Canadian government every step of the way. Ottawa gave them a cash subsidy of twenty-five million dollars, plus twenty-five million acres of prairie land (of their choosing), plus long stretches of already-constructed railway track.

Of course, given the considerable risks they were taking in building a railway across some extremely difficult terrain, government support was necessary. No private company would have considered taking on the job without a substantial subsidy. Still, in retrospect, economists and historians have generally concluded that the subsidy was too generous; economist P.J. George described it as "grossly excessive," with no provision for any repayment once the scope of the profitability became apparent.[1] In any event, the point here is not to judge the appropriateness of the CPR's subsidy. Rather, the point is to stress that, even this widely saluted example of capitalism in action was a very coddled, government-supported kind of capitalism. At least some of the financial heroics that contributed to the building of the CPR were performed by the Canadian taxpayer, who provided a good chunk of the risky upfront money — and ended up paying for the construction of the railway many times over.

Still, it's not surprising that Canadians have been taught the CPR story in school and encouraged to celebrate its legacy. It is surprising, however, that we seem to know very little about another railway that also shaped our history. This other railway was publicly owned, and it also ran coast to coast. And although its story may lack the track-building escapades of the CPR tale, this publicly owned railway pioneered some stunning innovations that led directly to the development of Canada's nationwide public broadcasting system, at a time when much of our population was isolated and disconnected and highly vulnerable to being swept up into the maw of the eagerly expanding American empire.

It was a blustery evening in December 1922 when Sir Henry Thornton arrived for a private dinner in the glittering Rose Room of Montreal's grand and elegant Windsor Hotel. Thornton, an American engineer who had started his railway career in Pennsylvania, was the guest of honour at this exclusive gathering, which included some of Canada's most powerful financial men. Thornton was himself a man of considerable accomplishments; he had gained a knighthood for running Britain's military rail operations in France during the First World War and had then gone on to great success as general manager of an important railway in Britain.

And now he had just accepted the job of president of the new Canadian National Railways (CNR), the publicly owned railway Ottawa had created out of five bankrupt rail companies in an attempt to stave off a financial panic and to keep key transportation routes functioning. With that amalgamation, the CNR became the biggest employer in the country, with more than one hundred thousand employees. But the task of creating a coherent company out of this massive army of workers and thirty-five thousand kilometres of decaying railway track was daunting, and it was made a lot more daunting by the fact that most of the men honouring Sir Henry in the Rose Room that evening wanted nothing more than to see him fail.

These distinguished business titans, including William Birks (founder of the jewellery store) and Sir Joseph Flavelle (president of the Canadian Bank of Commerce), were fierce adherents of the economic orthodoxy that ruled Montreal's St. James Street, then the financial centre of the country. That orthodoxy called for tight control over government spending, and for letting private capital — not government — run things and make the key economic decisions. It was up to the individual to fend for himself, so the theory went, without relying on a supporting hand from government.

So the decision of Liberal prime minister William Lyon Mackenzie King to create the CNR as a publicly owned railway had been highly unpopular with this crowd, who saw it as a dangerous opening up of the public purse for an enterprise that would rely on government largesse. In addition to their outrage over the government's defiance of free-market dogma, the men in the Rose Room had another reason for their unhappiness over the CNR's creation. Many of them had close ties or stockholdings in the CPR, the privately owned railway that had been operating since the 1880s.

The CPR had developed into Canada's leading private enterprise, an efficient and profitable company whose standing in world money markets was considered a gauge of Canada's own creditworthiness. Even so, the CPR had continued to push Ottawa to give it a railway monopoly, which CPR stakeholders considered their just reward for the initial risks they had taken in building the railway across the vast, perilous Canadian terrain. In their calculations of what was due to them, these men rarely took into consideration what they had already received from the Canadian taxpayer. Nor did they apparently see the irony in their stern opposition to government handouts to public enterprise, even though their private enterprise had pocketed government handouts that would certainly be categorized as generous, even, in P.J. George's assessment, "grossly excessive."

What was so frustrating to the CPR men at the dinner, including CPR president Edward W. Beatty, was that circumstances had finally seemed to bring their company's dream of a railway monopoly within reach. The five different railway lines being amalgamated to create the CNR had been struggling for years in different parts of the country, trying to achieve profitability under difficult circumstances, including the task of competing with the CPR. Some of these rail lines predated the CPR, such as the Grand Trunk (built in the 1850s linking southern Ontario and Quebec) and the Intercolonial Railway (built in the 1870s to link the Maritimes to central Canada as part of the promise of Confederation). After the CPR became the dominant railway in the 1880s, the other lines began a reckless spree of track building in an effort to consolidate and increase their share of the nation's railway business; it was, after all, the most advanced form of transportation available and often highly lucrative.

Following the First World War and the difficult economic conditions of the 1921 recession, the CPR had emerged clearly triumphant, with the other lines finally pushed into bankruptcy. This had left many communities across the country suddenly lacking a way to get their produce to market. Something had to be done. The CPR believed it had the answer: allow it to absorb these bankrupt railway lines and create the monopoly it had longed visualized. But the overbearing attitude of the CPR had already created considerable public resentment, particularly in the West, pushing the Liberal government to instead establish the publicly owned CNR.

Much as all this displeased the men in the Rose Room that evening, they were confident at least that Sir Henry was almost certainly going to fail at the hopelessly difficult task he had foolishly agreed to take on. And when that happened, their prize would once again be within reach. Certainly, as the evening wore on, with its forced sociability and bonhomie, they had little sense that Sir Henry was about to plunge them into a decade-long competitive battle for dominance, that he would transform the five failed and dysfunctional railways into a gem of a company whose innovations the CPR would struggle to match. The men in the Rose Room also had little inkling that Sir

Henry would set a new standard for labour relations, thereby winning unprecedented loyalty from his workers and putting pressure on other employers to follow suit. Certainly, Edward Beatty and the rest of the CPR-connected crowd that evening had little idea that the "national white elephant," as the new public railway had been dubbed, was about to turn into a svelte and agile tiger.

Sir Henry was not particularly intimidated by the wealthy financial players he encountered that evening in Montreal. As general manager of a major railway in Britain, he had had plenty of experience handling those types. Endowed with enormous personal charm and a talent for engaging with people, Sir Henry had dealt extensively, and effectively, with London's corporate barons as well as with Britain's leading political figures, and even royalty.

His ability to connect with people appeared to be deeply rooted and genuine; he treated ordinary people with the same respect and interest he showed members of the elite. He had barely settled into his new Montreal accommodations before he embarked on an extensive tour of the railway lines he had just taken charge of, first through the Maritimes and then all the way out to Prince Rupert, B.C., via the former Grand Trunk Pacific. The tour was about far more than surveying the extent of the track and equipment repairs needed. More importantly, it was about engaging with people — meeting as many as he could of the thousands of CNR employees and residents of towns along the route, all of whom were deeply dependent on the railway for their livelihood and their connection to the outside world. Everywhere he went, Sir Henry got out and talked to people, speaking to every local group that would have him and to the small crowds that gathered at the train station to meet him.

He was originally met with considerable skepticism and even heckling. The country was still recovering from the 1921 recession, and there was plenty of fear about the future and little reason to trust this unfamiliar giant of a man, who stood a striking six feet four inches tall. But Sir

Henry persisted, showing endless patience in answering questions and dealing with every concern raised. Above all, his message was one of confidence about the future. And gradually the heckling subsided, as the people he encountered began to appreciate and absorb some of his optimism. "He became something of a symbol — a symbol of unconquerable enthusiasm, both for the railway and the Dominion of Canada," noted D'Arcy Marsh, a journalist and author writing in Sir Henry's time.[2]

From the beginning, Sir Henry had ambitious plans to develop the CNR into a successful railway. He realized that this would involve attracting more settlers to the country, particularly the West. In fact, Sir Henry understood that his job required him to achieve nothing less than "*the economic development* of the Dominion," observes John Walker Barriger, a prominent U.S. railway executive who wrote a monograph about Thornton. "He could not wait for the country to grow up to its railroads; it had to be built up to them."[3] To this end, Sir Henry established the Department of Colonization and Development within the CNR. Working with provincial and federal authorities, the CNR set out to attract immigrants, promote land settlement in rural areas, and encourage improvement in agricultural methods.

With CNR offices in London, Paris, Boston, and Seattle, the colonization efforts turned out to be highly effective. Sir Henry asserted in 1929 that the CNR had been directly responsible for attracting more than forty thousand immigrants. "Colonists are our new blood," he declared. "We solicit them in Europe, we escort them across the seas, we advise them as to plans of settlement; often we help them select the cows and pigs and horses and equipment that will go with these farms. They are the backbone of tomorrow."[4]

Indeed, the scope of the activities carried out by the CNR (and the CPR) is surprising to the modern observer. In addition to operating transcontinental passenger and freight trains, the railways ran steamship services along both coasts and national telegraph services. They also built impressive hotels across the country, many of which are still operating today. Under Sir Henry, for instance, CNR developed Jasper Park Lodge as a way to attract vacationers and to compete with the stunning hotels the CPR operated in Banff and Lake Louise.

But, as mentioned above, the characteristic of Sir Henry that most set him apart from other corporate leaders of his time (or any other time, for that matter) was his unabashed support for workers' rights and even unionization. At that first dinner with the financial elite of Montreal, Sir Henry openly declared his support for the working person: "I believe that every employee of every industry ... should receive the minimum wage which will enable him to live in decency, in comfort and under proper sanitary conditions, and to educate and bring up his children as self-respecting members of society." Sir Henry appeared unconcerned that such a sentiment likely wasn't well received by the gentlemen in the room. He simply continued: "Any other policy makes for social unrest, and if carried on long enough is likely to create political upheavals."[5]

And it wasn't just talk. As the CNR became successful, its employees shared in the prosperity. While the CNR workforce remained about 108,000 in size, the company's payroll rose from $154 million in 1923 to $170 million five years later.[6]

Sir Henry exhibited an extraordinary rapport with his employees, as he had with the railway workers in Britain, partly by expressing appreciation when they did particularly good work. A CNR porter was delighted, for instance, to receive a congratulatory letter directly from Sir Henry after an elderly passenger had been so impressed by the porter's helpful behaviour that she'd written a note of thanks to the CNR head office. It was this sort of personal touch — along with pay raises — that made the CNR workforce fiercely loyal to the man running the company.

And although Sir Henry exuded personal confidence, he lacked the haughtiness and self-importance so often found in those occupying high positions. On one occasion, Sir Henry attempted, early in the morning, to check into the Royal York Hotel, part of the CPR chain, before delivering a speech later that day to the Empire Club in Toronto. The front desk clerk at the Royal York recognized him and apparently decided to demonstrate loyalty to his own railway company by being impolite to the president of the rival railway. "You'll have to wait your turn," the clerk said coolly. "There are a good many people ahead of you." Sir Henry thanked the young man and said he would return after having some breakfast. But his breakfast was interrupted when a more senior CPR official rushed in to apologize for the clerk's rudeness, which had been overheard and reported by another employee. The senior official told Sir Henry that he would immediately be accommodated in the suite that Mr. Beatty, the CPR president, used when he was in Toronto. Furthermore, the official assured Sir Henry that the rude clerk would be dismissed.

"Perhaps," Sir Henry responded, "if the man were fired for ten minutes it would be long enough. Most men are taught as good a lesson by getting a fright as by losing their jobs." Sir Henry went on to urge that the young man be allowed to retain his employment, which he was.[7]

In fact, Sir Henry's unusually sympathetic attitude toward working people was part of a larger commitment to equality and the breakdown of privilege, a worldview that was downright radical for a corporate leader. In an address to the St. James Literary Society in Montreal in 1924, Sir Henry described his belief that the highly unequal distribution of wealth in the world was fostering a growing resentment among working people everywhere. He went on to indicate his strong support for public ownership. He was not against private ownership of railways — his previous work experience had been with privately owned railways — but he felt that private railways needed to be carefully scrutinized and regulated to ensure they operated in the public interest. He suggested that, eventually, railways and most other industrial activities that have important impacts on the community would likely end up under public ownership.

Certainly, he believed that a publicly owned railway should and would advance the interests of the community in a way that a privately owned railway would not. D'Arcy Marsh describes Sir Henry's view that the CNR had a sense of "service to the community the railway had built and was pledged to serve," which was distinctly different from a private railway's "service to the unknown investors and the financial high command to whom it was, and would remain, a medium for the accumulation of private profits."[8] Indeed, Sir Henry's belief in the

CNR's obligations to the community led him to support branch lines in remote regions where rail cars were used to help children get to school and to enable Red Cross units to reach the sick.

Although his political views placed him at odds with many in the country's business elite, Sir Henry turned out to be a remarkably good businessman. For that matter, his egalitarian ideas may have actually contributed to his business success. He inspired loyalty and dedication in his workforce, as well as in many people living in the communities his railway served. He also knew the rail business thoroughly and worked tirelessly to upgrade the CNR's equipment, to improve service levels, and to introduce innovations that would appeal to customers.

While few observers had considered it possible, Sir Henry managed to transform the five bankrupt railways into one big thriving railway, in just one year. Even with significant investment in repairs, new equipment, and overseas outreach programs, the CNR's net earnings rose from $2.8 million in 1922 to a staggering $20 million the following year. Throughout the country, there was delight — and no more talk of white elephants. Meanwhile, inside the posh offices on St. James Street, there was astonishment and more than a little panic.

But the success of the CNR was only beginning.

Starting in 1924, the CNR launched a dramatic innovation: radio on trains. At the time, radio was a relatively new technology. There were only a few stations, mostly located in the United States, whose signals could be heard in Canada, and only in the evening hours. Still, radio was an enormously exciting new form of entertainment that brought music — often live performances in studio — into homes hundreds of miles away.

Sir Henry was determined to make this exciting new technology part of the pleasure of train travel. There had been some earlier dabbling with radio technology by several U.S. rail lines, but no follow-up on these limited experiments. The CNR therefore became the first to overcome the considerable technological challenges and actually outfit railway cars so they could receive radio signals while in motion. On January 5, 1924, the first radio-equipped transcontinental train, operated by CNR, left Montreal bound for Vancouver.

The concept proved popular. Passengers were delighted to be able to stroll to the train's lounge car, put on a headset, and suddenly, almost magically, hear live music broadcast by a radio station somewhere out there in the dark. The addition of radio service quickly became known as an attractive aspect of travelling on CNR, and there was a noticeable shift of passengers from CPR to CNR on the well-travelled Montreal–Toronto run, which had long been dominated by CPR.[9]

The enormous appeal of radio to the ear of a railway passenger in the 1920s is captured in an anonymous account from the CNR archives. The writer describes a scene in the observation car of a CNR train passing through the Prairies. The passengers are bored and waiting for lunch. Suddenly, the sound of organ music fills the car, grabbing their attention. The organ strains are followed by a sermon, Bible readings, and hymns broadcast live from a service in a Saskatoon church many miles away. When there is a pause in the church service to take up a collection, a passenger on the train rises, puts a five-dollar bill into a hat, and then passes the hat to the other passengers, who all contribute something. When the train pulls into Saskatoon later that day, thirty dollars are delivered to the church from the enthralled passengers.[10]

In addition to putting radio on trains, Sir Henry also moved quickly to develop CNR's own broadcasting stations. In the long run, this turned out to be a more important innovation. In February 1924, CNR opened a radio station in Ottawa, followed later that year by one in Moncton, New Brunswick, and about a dozen others across the country in the next few years, forming an early all-Canadian network of radio stations.

The CNR stations were committed to providing high-quality music for Canadians listening in their homes, as well as on trains. The stations broadcast a wide range of popular and classical music, performed by local singers, choirs, musicians, and bands, all of whom were paid honorariums plus travel expenses for coming to the station to play. In

Ottawa, the CNR station carried live broadcasts of the Château Laurier Orchestra. (In the 1920s, large hotels often had their own paid orchestras, and the CNR's flagship hotel in Ottawa had a particularly good one, which attracted large crowds to the hotel's splendid rotunda.) In 1925, the CNR station in Toronto was broadcasting opera singers, and it signed the Hart House String Quartet, then considered the leading performer of chamber music, to an exclusive broadcasting contract.

Sir Henry also regarded the CNR stations as important vehicles for transmitting public-interest messages, promoting the railway and its settlement programs, and linking the country together. A group of five Scottish editors, sent to Canada in 1924 to report on the conditions faced by immigrants, praised the newly created CNR broadcasts for enabling newcomers to cope with the twin challenges of loneliness and isolation. Sir Henry himself provided fifteen-minute talks that a 1925 article in *Maclean's* magazine described as "really fireside chats [that] were friendly, intimate, timely, and dealt with a great variety of topics." In Sir Henry's view, the radio broadcasts were an extension of the CNR's role in encouraging national development and cohesion. In a 1929 address, he described the vital role the broadcasts played in promoting "a feeling of kinship between all parts of the country, to bring home to all sections more vividly our common aspirations and achievements."

The CNR also broadcast programs for children, book reviews, scientific discussions, comic operas, and information about grain prices. It aired a hockey game for the first time in 1924 and in 1927 carried a widely praised nationwide broadcast commemorating the sixtieth anniversary of Confederation. There was even an early attempt by CNR's Radio Department to develop an educational political program called *The Nation's Business*. The program featured Cabinet ministers and opposition politicians describing the various functions of government. However, the show was cancelled after six months due to political bickering and fears on the part of the opposition Conservatives that it was providing a propaganda opportunity for the ruling Liberals.

Meanwhile, the development of carrier current technology led to significant improvements in radio, enabling the linkage of stations and simultaneous broadcasting across a national network. By the late 1920s, the CNR was able to link its thirteen stations from the Atlantic to the Pacific, making it the first coast-to-coast radio network in North America. Among other things, this brought in considerable revenue from sponsors. (Despite restrictions on advertising imposed by the CNR and the federal government, businesses were permitted to sponsor programs.) The success of carrier current technology and the promising future it suggested for radio prompted the CPR to finally jump into the radio game, too. In 1930, six years after the CNR had paved the way, the CPR completed its own installations and was broadcasting national programs on the airwaves — although still not on its trains.

Public excitement about radio continued to grow, and the CNR continued to lead the way. In 1930, the CNR launched a weekly program of concerts by the Toronto Symphony Orchestra, and there were soon groups around the country assembling on Sunday afternoons specifically to hear these broadcasts. About a year later, the Columbia Broadcasting System (CBS) created a similar series of radio broadcasts featuring the New York Philharmonic, followed by the National Broadcasting Company (NBC), which launched its own series highlighting international symphony superstars such as Walter Damrosch and Arturo Toscanini. The CNR was once again out in front of the major U.S. broadcasters when it created a popular radio drama series based on Canadian history called *The Romance of Canada*. The Toronto playwright who wrote those scripts, Merrill Denison, then took the idea to New York, where he ended up producing a very similar series for NBC called *Great Moments in History*.[11]

~❦~

The dramatic rise of radio — and the rapidly growing reach of the U.S. broadcasting networks — led to a realization in Ottawa that Canada would have to take action if Canadians wanted to have any broadcasting of their own.

The NBC network had been established in 1926, followed by CBS in 1927. By the end of the 1920s, corporate consolidation in the United States involving all radio activities, from manufacturing to broadcasting, had led to a small number of players taking control of the business and becoming immensely powerful. While the Canadian government had pushed for allocation of channels to Canadian broadcasting interests, Washington largely ignored these demands, and the American broadcasters simply appropriated the available channels.

The signals of the high-powered American broadcasters increasingly came to dominate the airwaves in Canada. The less-extensive reach of Canadian radio stations, which were all centred in urban areas, particularly Montreal and Toronto, left people in vast stretches of the country able to hear only the sounds coming at them clearly and loudly from the U.S. networks. Adding to the problem, four private Canadian stations in Montreal and Toronto signed up to become part-time outlets for the American networks.

Amid growing public concern over the implications of such American dominance, the Mackenzie King government appointed a three-man royal commission in 1928 to consider what should be done. Headed by Sir John Aird, president of the Canadian Bank of Commerce, the commission crossed the country by rail, holding public hearings in twenty-five Canadian cities, and concluded in their 1929 report that Canadians definitely wanted broadcasting that was Canadian. Furthermore, the commission recommended that the way to achieve this was to nationalize the broadcasting industry in Canada. One of the commissioners, Dr. Augustin Frigon, a prominent Quebecker, underlined the importance of public ownership: "That is the fundamental of the whole case — whether broadcasting is a business for profit-making or an instrument to be used for the benefit of the public at large.... [I]f you want to accept the point of view of broadcasting in the interests of the nation, it cannot be left to private enterprise."

The commission's report won wide support, and even sparked a popular movement to push for a national public broadcaster. It was a highly organized movement, led by two energetic young men, thirty-year-old Graham Spry and twenty-six-year-old Alan Plaunt, who were deeply committed to the goal of achieving a publicly owned national broadcaster in Canada. They turned out to be brilliant organizers and effective advocates, and their Radio League soon attracted an astonishing array of support: from women's organizations, labour and farm groups, university presidents, religious leaders, former prime ministers Sir Robert Borden and Arthur Meighen, future prime minister Louis St. Laurent, and future Ottawa mayor Charlotte Whitton, as well as some leading figures from the banking and business worlds.

There were, however, some influential forces lined up against the nationalization of radio — the Canadian Manufacturers' Association, as well as private radio station owners who had formed the Canadian Association of Broadcasters. Importantly, the CPR, the country's largest private enterprise, also came out actively against nationalization. Instead, it proposed two national radio networks: a private network, to be run by the CPR, which would handle commercial programming and cater to advertisers, and a public network, run by the CNR, which would carry public-service information and be funded by government. Graham Spry denounced the CPR scheme, noting that it was aimed at shutting down competing private stations, grabbing advertising dollars for the CPR, and creating a weak public network.

Once again, the different visions represented by the privately owned CPR and the publicly owned CNR seemed to be central to a key Canadian debate about the future of the country. But this time there was an additional factor that was to shape the debate: the 1929 stock market crash had plunged the country into depression, producing tremendous hardship and dramatically reducing profits for much of the corporate world. Among other things, train travel was greatly reduced. And, while both railways suffered financially, the CNR was in a more vulnerable position. As a public railway, it was obliged to keep serving the communities that relied on it, and it was under the control of Parliament.

As its revenues plunged, the charmed position the CNR had enjoyed in Canadian public life quickly disappeared, and it was accused of having undertaken years of costly expansion and extravagance that were now making the railway a burden on the taxpayer. Complaints that Sir Henry had created unnecessarily luxurious passenger services resonated with many for whom train travel itself now seemed like an out-of-reach luxury. Such accusations became increasingly vehement after Mackenzie King was swept from office in the 1930 election and replaced by Prime Minister R.B. Bennett, whose Conservative Party had deep ties to the CPR and who had personally spent much of his career as a CPR solicitor.

The Conservatives launched parliamentary hearings that became a showcase for the alleged misdeeds of Sir Henry — including his divorce and remarriage — with the Liberal-leaning press supporting the beleaguered railway executive and the Conservative-leaning press calling for his ouster. The CPR was only too pleased to have its long-time rival railway in the public crosshairs, forced by Parliament to cut back its services in a way that made it less competitive with the CPR. All this brought the CPR closer to its goal of achieving a railway monopoly in Canada.

Although no evidence ever emerged that Sir Henry had received any improper personal benefits, the Conservative attacks continued relentlessly at the public hearings held by the Parliamentary Committee on Railways and Shipping — dubbed the "hanging committee." In July 1932, a distraught and overwhelmed Sir Henry handed in his resignation.

Trying to recover from his very public fall from grace, Sir Henry and his wife embarked on several months of travels through the Maritimes and the southern United States before settling in New York. At sixty-two, after having achieved what D'Arcy Marsh calls "the most spectacular success in Canada's commercial history,"[12] Sir Henry was wasting away, increasingly weak, depressed, and in failing health. The following March, the CNR unions organized a dinner in his honour in New York, to be attended by prominent U.S. labour leaders. But Sir Henry didn't make it to the dinner; he died that evening in a New York hospital.

Although his name is not widely known in Canada today, his legacy has lived on in the highly successful railway he created and the foundation it laid for a national public broadcaster. With the Radio League enjoying robust public support in its crusade for such an entity, the Bennett government endorsed radio nationalization.

Even as the Conservative government was delivering cruel blows to Sir Henry, it gave its full backing to the national radio network that he had pioneered.

In a noteworthy speech to Parliament in May 1932, Prime Minister R.B. Bennett declared his unequivocal support for legislation creating a national broadcaster, insisting that "this country must be assured of complete Canadian control of broadcasting from Canadian sources, free from foreign interference or influence." The prime minister went on to strongly endorse public ownership of the airwaves: "The use of the air ... that lies over the soil or land of Canada is a natural resource.... I cannot think that any government would be warranted in leaving the air to private exploitation and not reserving it for development for the use of the people." The legislation, which led to the purchase of the CNR radio network and eventually to the establishment of the Canadian Broadcasting Corporation (CBC), passed with near-unanimous parliamentary support.

As for the CNR, it had experienced its heyday in the roaring 1920s under the leadership of Sir Henry. After he was driven from office, the railway continued to operate as a Crown corporation for many years. In the late 1970s, its passenger train operations were spun off to a separate Crown corporation called Via Rail, leaving the CNR primarily in the rail freight business. In 1995, as part of a wave of privatizations by the federal government, CNR (by now renamed CN) was sold to private investors.

The privatization of CN was part of a wave of changes in the operation and oversight of Canadian railways — changes that have had huge impacts on Canadians. Many communities, especially in the West and North, lost access to rail service altogether as CN cut back operations to become more competitive in the lead-up to privatization. Thousands of kilometres of track, which had once linked remote communities to each other and to the rest of the country, were simply ripped out of the ground and replaced with gravel beds.

The diminished travel options got a lot worse in October 2018 when Greyhound Canada, citing a significant drop in ridership, stopped operating all bus service in northern Ontario, Manitoba, Saskatchewan, and British Columbia (except for one line between Vancouver and Seattle). The move left three hundred western communities without bus or rail service, and considerable uncertainty about whether one of the small regional bus carriers might expand operations to fill the void. The virtual disappearance of bus service certainly compounds the isolation and lack of mobility experienced by those living in remote communities, and it highlights how much of a setback the CN privatization has been for tens of thousands of Canadians — and for the cohesion of a vast country with a spread-out population.

In a number of communities, portions of the old CNR lines have been bought by private rail lines, allowing some transportation links to be maintained. But these private lines operate differently than the publicly owned CNR did. One major difference is that their commitment to providing train service continues only as long as they're turning a profit — as the eight hundred residents of Churchill, Manitoba, recently discovered.

Located on Hudson Bay, 1,000 kilometres north of Winnipeg and only 110 kilometres south of the Nunavut border, Churchill is best known as a place to observe the northern lights and polar bears. Its school is surrounded by a high metal fence to keep out the five hundred polar bears known to roam within range of the town; one local sign reads, "Stop. Don't Walk In This Area. Report Bear Sightings."

Yet, despite its location far from population centres, Churchill had been connected to the rest of the country by rail since 1929, when the CNR completed a line to the outpost community. As Canada's only deepwater Arctic port, the town served as an important part of the country's transportation network, helping to ship prairie grain and other exports to countries in both Asia and Europe. In 1997, following the CNR privatization, a Denver-based railway holding company called Omnitrax purchased the seven-hundred-kilometre rail line that connected Churchill to The Pas, a town in central Manitoba near the Saskatchewan border. The line, known as Hudson Bay Railway, allowed

Churchill and a number of isolated communities along the route to enjoy rail service in recent decades.

But that changed abruptly in the spring of 2017, when an enormous flood following an unusually large blizzard left Churchill and the surrounding area under water. By the time the water receded, much of the track on the Hudson Bay Railway line was severely damaged. The track bed was completely washed away in twenty locations, and more than thirty bridges along the line were no longer considered structurally sound. The federal government's Canadian Transportation Agency ordered the railway to carry out the needed repairs. But Omnitrax claimed it had been on the brink of financial insolvency even before the flood and insisted that it had no way of coming up with forty-three million dollars for repairs. The company also noted that, under the Canada Transportation Act, its own financial health came before its duty to deliver train service.

For more than a year, the railway remained shut down. Since there is no road to Churchill, the loss of the railway was devastating, turning the town into a much more isolated, fly-in-only community. That dramatically drove up the price of food and supplies and left residents cut off from the world unless they could afford the twelve-hundred-dollar return fare to Winnipeg. The future of Churchill seemed bleak.

But the crisis was eventually solved in an innovative way, one that could be a solution for other remote towns as well. A group of thirty Indigenous communities and eleven non-Indigenous communities teamed up with each other and two private sector partners, with the aim of buying the railway. The resulting Arctic Gateway Group — an equal partnership between the northern communities and the private interests — engaged in extensive and difficult negotiations that finally resulted in a sale. The federal government contributed seventy-four million dollars to help with the purchase and repair costs.

On Hallowe'en night in 2017, with the prime minister on hand, a street party broke out in downtown Churchill, with several hundred residents signing "O Canada" to celebrate the arrival of a train — the first one in four hundred days, and now part of a railway line partially owned by the local people themselves.

～ℚ〜

Not only have the changes in the management of our railways led to service cuts, but there has also been a dramatic decline in railway safety standards. Indeed, it is not overreaching to blame this steep decline in safety standards for the horrendous Lac-Mégantic rail disaster, which killed forty-seven Quebeckers in 2013. That tragedy was entirely preventable. As Bruce Campbell documents in his insightful book *The Lac-Mégantic Rail Disaster*, the devastating crash of a train loaded with oil was rooted in dozens of decisions by Canadian political leaders who severely slashed Ottawa's ability to enforce rail safety, all in the cause of pleasing the powerful, profit-crazy private railway industry.[13]

Ottawa's infatuation with privatization and deregulation, which began under the Progressive Conservative government of Brian Mulroney in the 1980s, resulted in a dramatic departure from the way in which railways had operated and been supervised in Canada. "CN and CP's historic covenant to bind the country together was … rewritten," notes Campbell. "No longer were the railways to balance profit with an obligation to the citizens of Canada — who had, after all, collectively subsidized these companies for their entire history. Now the two railways were free to sell off or simply abandon unprofitable branch lines like the one running through Lac-Mégantic."[14]

Located in southeastern Quebec near the U.S. border, the picturesque town of Lac-Mégantic had been built in 1884 as part of the CPR's transcontinental rail line. But by 2013 the section of the old CPR line still running through Lac-Mégantic was owned by Montreal, Maine and Atlantic Railway (MMA), a regional carrier that was part of the railway empire of Chicago-based U.S. rail tycoon Edward Burkhardt. Burkhardt had a reputation for relentlessly maximizing profits by pushing down wages, firing railway workers, and allowing equipment and tracks to deteriorate. Among his cost-cutting measures, he had pioneered the practice of operating large freight trains with just one crew member, a practice that would end up being a crucial factor in the Lac-Mégantic disaster.

Still, this immense tragedy would never have happened if Ottawa hadn't abdicated its responsibility to enforce safety regulations for railways operating in Canada. Instead, Canadian politicians embraced neoliberal economic policies, championed by Margaret Thatcher in the United Kingdom and Ronald Reagan in the United States, that argued for getting government "out of the way" so that the market could work its magic. This involved radically reducing regulations, which were increasingly depicted as nothing more than a costly regulatory burden on business, one that hampered the ability of corporations to get on with the task of creating jobs and wealth.

Right from their election in 1984, Mulroney's Conservatives made deregulation a top priority. Mulroney appointed Deputy Prime Minister Erik Nielsen to head a task force to identify the scope of the regulatory burden. When the task force quickly concluded that Canada was overregulated, Mulroney set up the Ministry of State for Privatization and Regulatory Affairs to start eliminating regulations. On the railway front specifically, the Railway Safety Act of 1988 began the process of transferring responsibility for safety enforcement from government to the railways themselves. This dubious notion of self-regulation was pushed further by the Liberal governments of Jean Chrétien and Paul Martin, as the oversight authority of Transport Canada was dramatically reduced, its budgets slashed, and its on-site inspections cut back.

But it was the hard-right Conservative government of Stephen Harper that brought the deregulation agenda to a fever pitch, particularly after Harper attained a parliamentary majority in the 2011 election. Not even bothering to conceal its deregulatory aims, the Harper government launched the Red Tape Reduction Committee, and then used the committee's findings to draw up the Cabinet Directive on Regulatory Management in the spring of 2012. A key aspect of the directive was the abandonment of the "precautionary principle," the principle that, if there is any scientific doubt about the safety of a product or practice, regulators should be cautious and restrict its use. This basic, common-sense principle — err on the side of safety! — was turned on its head. Under the Harper directive, the burden of proof was placed on the regulator to show solid evidence of harm; otherwise the company had the green light.[15]

Another shocking aspect of Harper's deregulatory policy was an initiative known as the one-for-one rule, which required the elimination of at least one regulation for every new one introduced or old one amended. Campbell reports that this was part of the government's little-known regulatory budget, under which a private sector committee was set up to monitor progress in eliminating government regulations and to ensure that civil servants weren't able to thwart the government's deregulation intentions.

Meanwhile, even as Harper was gutting safety regulations, there was a dramatic boom in transporting oil by rail. With delays in pipeline approvals, oil companies were increasingly turning to railways to move their highly flammable product; the number of tank cars full of oil skyrocketed from 500 carloads in 2009 to an incredible 160,000 carloads in 2013. Trains with more than a hundred tank cars full of oil were now routinely barrelling through Canadian cities. (The train that crashed in Lac-Mégantic had passed through densely populated sections of Toronto.)

There was, however, little public alarm over this frightening combination of reduced safety surveillance and increased movement of dangerous goods. After all, there were government agencies — with reassuring names like the Rail Safety Directorate and the Transportation of Dangerous Goods Directorate — that presumably enforced strict safety measures. The public had little sense that these agencies had been largely stripped of their regulatory muscle and were now operating under political masters who had drunk the Kool-Aid of the new dogma that government's role was to get out of way of the corporate locomotive.

CP (formerly CPR) was a big player in the oil-by-rail business. By 2013, CP was headed by Hunter Harrison, an even more aggressive — and relentless — U.S. railway executive than Burkhardt. After heading the Illinois Central Railroad, Harrison had served from 2003 to 2009 as CEO of the privatized CN, where he introduced an unrelenting downsizing that eliminated staff and unprofitable lines and resulted in fewer and longer trains. When CN workers went on strike in 2007, Harrison quickly brought in strikebreakers from south of the border. His bare-knuckle profiteering won Harrison kudos from the business community — the *Globe and Mail*'s Report on Business named him CEO of the year in 2007 — but deep mistrust and hostility from CN workers.[16]

Harrison brought this same brash, outta-my-way approach to CP when he took the top job there after a 2011 takeover by a U.S. hedge fund. As Harrison told the *Financial Post*, "I kind of went through Canada maybe like Sherman went through Atlanta."[17] Certainly, Harrison had little interest in slowing down operations for safety reasons; he reduced the number of CP trains while adding to their size and speed. His severe cost-cutting paid off handsomely for company shareholders — CP stock rose from $75 to $242 a share in just two years.

Cost-cutting was once again top of mind in the spring of 2012, as CP signed a contract to transport oil from North Dakota to an Irving Oil refinery in Saint John, New Brunswick. Since CP no longer had track all the way to Saint John, it had to subcontract to another rail line for the last part of the trip. Both CN and MMA operated rail lines to Saint John, but MMA's route was shorter. Under Ottawa's weakened safety rules, CP was required to choose the safer route — but it was up to CP to make that determination. CP decided to go for the MMA route, even though MMA had a safety record that was worse than CN's. Concerns were raised by several staff members within the Rail Safety Directorate, but their warnings were ultimately ignored. After all, this was the Harper era, and regulations were nothing more than a burden to be eliminated.

And so the stage was set. As Bruce Campbell puts it, "With Transport Canada's blessing, [MMA] would be running these giant oil trains along a poorly maintained track, using shoddy locomotives. And with a single operator."[18]

In the early morning hours of July 6, 2013, an MMA train carrying almost ten thousand tons of highly combustible oil got loose from its moorings at the top of a hill eleven kilometres from Lac-Mégantic. The runaway train raced forward, reaching a speed of 105 kilometres. It finally derailed at a curve in the track in the centre of Lac-Mégantic, engulfing the town and dozens of its people in a gigantic inferno. The fire soared to 1,650 degrees Celsius. Water streaming from firehoses simply evaporated in the scorching heat. There were no survivors. Everyone caught up in the flames in the little town died.

There was a huge public outcry, but the Harper government managed to ride out the storm without calling a public inquiry. Instead, three railway workers were tried for criminal negligence and acquitted. Outside the courtroom, someone yelled, "It's not them we want!"

Harper and his officials were never held accountable for their reckless deregulation. Nor were the greedy rail barons who pushed — and continue to push, mostly successfully — for relaxed safety laws.

All these people got off scot-free. CP CEO Hunter Harrison, whose company chose the more dangerous rail route through Lac-Mégantic, took home eighteen million dollars in pay in 2016. Meanwhile, twenty-seven children in Lac-Mégantic are without parents due to the rail disaster.

It's hard to imagine such a horrendous tragedy happening if Ottawa had not surrendered so much control over our railways to the private marketplace in recent decades. Certainly, the days of a publicly owned CNR, managed by the likes of Sir Henry Thornton, with his concern for the railway's employees, for the communities it served, and for the broader public interest, seem lost in the mists of time — and sadly, strangely forgotten.

∽ *Four* ⌒

Niagara Falls, Berlin Rises

S tanding on a commanding ridge, Henry Pellatt realized he had found just the spot where he could build a sprawling mansion enabling him to look down over the budding city of Toronto and live, almost literally, like a king.

It was 1903, and Pellatt had already made a considerable fortune for himself. Born into a well-to-do family, Pellatt had attended prestigious Upper Canada College before joining his father's prominent Toronto stock brokerage firm. The ambitious young man had taken to the financial scene, making full use of his father's extensive contacts in the interconnected world of Canadian business and finance. His father had taught him a great deal about investment strategies. But, quite on his own, Henry had developed a way of operating that, even by Bay Street standards, was notable for its greed, ruthlessness, and cavalier disregard for any rules preventing him getting exactly what he wanted.

Henry Pellatt had thus become a kingpin in the Toronto business world, heading more than twenty companies and sitting on the board of more than a hundred. He was among two dozen men who were known to control the entire Canadian economy. Partnering with prominent railway financier William Mackenzie and entrepreneur Frederic Nicholls, Pellatt had gained control of the Toronto Electric Light Company, which had the exclusive franchise to provide street lighting in the city, and the Toronto Street Railway, which had a thirty-year contract to run the city's streetcars. Toronto's population exceeded two hundred thousand by the turn of the twentieth century, so with monopolies over lighting and transportation that allowed Pellatt and his partners to control the supply and price of these badly needed services, the three men had been able to become extremely rich and powerful.

Now, at the age of forty-four, Pellatt was poised to become vastly richer; hence his need for this magnificent stretch of property overlooking the city, where he was already making plans to build the grandest residence in the country. He and his partners were closing in on winning a fabulous new prize: a franchise for the exclusive right to develop and transmit power from Niagara Falls to Toronto. The franchise would allow them to control access to newly available hydroelectric power, setting whatever rates they wanted and making it possible for them to earn riches beyond their wildest dreams. Their chances of scoring this prize were extremely good. Not only had they demonstrated their dominance in the business world, but they had very highly placed friends — politicians at the top of the Ontario government, which had ultimate authority over the water rights to the Canadian side of the falls.

The only obstacle the financiers faced was a loosely organized group of citizens and civic politicians with a seemingly far-fetched goal: to establish a publicly owned system that would break up the power monopolies and make the miraculous new form of energy cheap and available to all.[1]

One of the world's most powerful waterfalls, with more than six million cubic feet of water plunging over its crest every minute, Niagara Falls had long been appreciated for its stunning beauty. By the end of the nineteenth century, it was also being appreciated in another way: as a source of energy with the potential to dramatically transform the economy and society.

Since ancient times, waterfalls and other rapidly moving water had been harnessed to turn water wheels, creating energy that could be transmitted through the wheel's shaft to attached devices. These water wheels — the first real substitute for human and animal labour — provided sufficient energy to grind grain and even operate textile mills. But their use had been limited to small, local projects near water sources. That was changing by the 1880s. The invention of more sophisticated water turbines, along with advances in electricity generation, made possible the development and transmission of significant water power over distances, suddenly making the large-scale harnessing of energy from Niagara Falls a serious and intriguing possibility.

By 1896, an American firm, the Niagara Falls Power Company, had generated hydroelectric power from the falls and managed to send it surging through thirty-two kilometres of transmission lines all the way to Buffalo, New York, where it immediately illuminated lights specially set up for the occasion. The accomplishment — considered nothing short of magical — soon transformed Buffalo into a booming industrial town, with its population jumping from 3,300 to 19,500 within a few years.

On the northern side of the border, Canadians were keen to get in on this significant development. Indeed, it was clear that they would have to if they wanted to be able to compete economically with Americans, who had the advantage of significantly larger markets.

Certainly, hydroelectric power offered a dramatic improvement over the existing energy sources in Ontario in the 1890s. Gas was primarily used for lighting. But hydroelectric power was capable of providing much brighter, safer, and more reliable lighting, for use both on streets and in homes. Similarly, hydro power was a much better, more efficient energy source for the province's industrial establishments — hundreds of sawmills, flour mills, furniture factories, tanneries, textile mills, and machine shops — which mostly operated with steam power.

In fact, steam power was becoming problematic. It required burning wood or coal, and after decades of cutting down forests, wood was no longer in easy, nearby supply. Coal had to be imported from the United States and its supply was precarious. A massive strike by coal miners in Ohio, Pennsylvania, and West Virginia in the summer of 1897 led to exorbitant prices as well as a temporary American embargo on coal exports to Canada. The vulnerability of Canadians was again demonstrated during a 1902 strike in Pennsylvania, when coal prices in Toronto tripled and, even at these extortionate rates, the black fuel was again scarce. By contrast, water was abundant and unlimited, and the immense potential power of Niagara Falls was nearby, with Canada owning the rights to the Canadian side of the falls. Hydro power promised to be truly transformative, if only Canadians could gain access to this natural treasure, and at a reasonable price.

But the power scene was already dominated by wealthy corporate interests that held monopolies for distributing gas and locally generated electricity in cities and towns across Ontario and Quebec. These companies had enormous leeway in setting their rates. While favoured businesses (including, of course, the ones these wealthy interests owned or had invested in) paid reasonable rates, less preferred enterprises and households often faced greatly inflated rates. Typically, it was small and medium manufacturers and more modest households that were unable to get power at an affordable price, creating great resentment in these quarters toward those who held the monopolies.

Among the most resented were Pellatt and his partners. As they plotted to also grab control of the promising new hydroelectric power from Niagara Falls, they seemed on the verge of consolidating their monopolistic position well into the future. This prompted the rise of an unusual alliance of individuals convinced that the only way to achieve the goal of accessible and affordable hydro power was through a publicly owned system.

Among the earliest advocates of such a system, in the late 1890s, were small manufacturers and businessmen who were worried about being at the mercy of unscrupulous private power interests. Two Toronto jewellery manufacturers, P.W. Ellis and W.K. McNaught, had travelled to Switzerland on business and observed the enormous industrial benefits of cheap hydroelectricity there. When they returned, they were eager to spread the word about the extraordinary benefits of cheap power, and they urged Toronto City Council to consider building its own generating station at Niagara Falls, along with its own transmission lines and distribution system. The idea attracted considerable support at city council, where Alderman Frank Spence emerged as a popular and eloquent champion of a public system.

Another strong supporter was William Hubbard, the first black person ever elected to Toronto City Council. Hubbard, whose parents had escaped slavery in Virginia and come to Canada via the Underground Railroad, was born in a cabin on the outskirts of Toronto in a rural area then called "the bush" (now called the intersection of Bloor and Bathurst Streets). As a young man, Hubbard was working as a driver of a horse-drawn livery when he came upon an accident where a man was in danger of falling into the icy waters of the Don River. Hubbard saved the man, who turned out to be George Brown, one of the Fathers of Confederation and editor of the prestigious *Globe* newspaper. A grateful Brown hired Hubbard as his personal driver and later encouraged him to enter city politics, which Hubbard did, winning his first election in 1894 at the age of fifty-two. Hubbard became an early advocate of what he dubbed "public power," chairing an important city committee that orchestrated plans to replace Pellatt and his private interests with a public system dedicated to serving popular needs. Hubbard, a powerful speaker and committed social reformer, went on to be elected fourteen more times in annual civic elections.

Along with voices from the business community and civic politics, the push for public power got important support in the first decade of the 1900s from some Toronto newspapers and periodicals, particularly the *Toronto Telegram* and the *Globe* (although George Brown had died in 1880). At the same time, however, there was strong opposition from the *Mail*, a conservative newspaper that vehemently denounced public power as a form of socialism, infringing on the rights of private property.

But while momentum was building for public power among the broader electorate, the Ontario Liberal premier George William Ross showed little interest in the idea, which he insisted would require costly investments and only increase public debt. Instead, the Ross government favoured involving private interests in the development of hydroelectricity from Niagara Falls, and his government initially turned to an American subsidiary of the Niagara Falls Power Company, which had brought power to Buffalo.

The province granted the American subsidiary a generous twenty-year exclusive contract to develop hydro power on the Canadian side of the falls for an annual rent of just twenty-five thousand dollars, with the possibility of renewing the contract for four additional twenty-year terms. Astonishingly, this meant that the province was willing to hand over to an American company monopoly rights to our side of Niagara Falls for a period of one hundred years — virtually the entire twentieth century! (This was an even worse deal for Canadians than Mike Harris's decision to lease Highway 407 to a Spanish consortium for ninety-nine years.) And the American subsidiary would be free to sell its hydro power south of the border, provided that at least half of what it produced went to Canadians. Yet, despite these wildly generous terms, the subsidiary was slow to get transmission lines operating, even though its parent company had already demonstrated the technological know-how. Strangely, provincial authorities bent over backwards to accommodate the subsidiary, extending the firm's deadline.

When the project was still not operational in 1899, the province extended the deadline again, although it cancelled the monopoly rights in the contract. This left open the possibility of another developer gaining access to the Canadian falls. Toronto City Council quickly applied to be that developer, hoping to establish its own generating station so that it could provide Torontonians with affordable power. City councillors were also motivated by a desire to block the new franchise opportunity from falling into the hands of Pellatt and his partners, known as the Syndicate, whose high prices in its streetcar and lighting monopolies had left many in the city unable to afford these services.

Certainly, the city appeared to have a strong case, backed by considerable public support. But the Syndicate had better political connections. In addition to the Ross government's general inclination toward business, the premier had special ties to Pellatt and his partner William Mackenzie. That's because, at the same time as being premier, George

William Ross was also serving as president of the Manufacturers Life Insurance Company, and the company's board included Pellatt and Mackenzie. It wasn't unusual at the time for political leaders to hold high-level positions in the business world. But the premier's personal links to Pellatt and Mackenzie through the company's board certainly helps explain why their application seemed to receive more favourable treatment than the bid put forward by the City of Toronto.

Indeed, several years later it came to light (due to the 1907 federal royal commission into questionable practices in the insurance industry) that Manufacturers Life had actually invested in the Syndicate. This raises the possibility that the premier may have stood to benefit personally from the Syndicate getting the Niagara contract, even while he was also in the position of controlling who got the contract.

In any event, the Ross government quickly rejected the city's application. Making its bias even clearer, the government also amended the Ontario Municipal Act, adding a clause that effectively prevented municipalities from competing with private companies that operated utilities (unless the municipality bought the company at a price fixed by arbitration — an expensive proposition). All this angered and re-energized the public power advocates, and provoked a string of newspaper editorials criticizing the government.

There were splits in the business community over the issue. Historian H.V. Nelles notes that public power "pitted the haute against the petite bourgeoisie of Ontario. The capital-intensive character of the hydro-electric industry necessarily allied agents of finance capitalism — the investors, brokers, banks, insurance companies — on one side against the consumers of power — merchants, manufacturers and ratepayers — on the other.... In the Ontario of the time the forces that separated these business groups were stronger than the ideology that united them."[2]

Walter Massey, president of the leading farm machinery firm Massey-Harris, was deeply concerned about the high rates charged by the private monopolies. Massey chaired a committee of the Toronto Board of Trade that produced a report indicating an openness to public power. And the Toronto branch of the Canadian Manufacturers'

Association unabashedly threw its support behind Toronto City Council, which had made clear it had no intention of abandoning the fight. Indeed, the city reapplied to the Ross government the following year, only to be rejected again. This triggered more anger, consternation, and pressure, and disapproving editorials in the press.

When a provincial election was held in 1902, public power was one of the issues reducing the popularity of the Ross government, which had its majority sliced to just one seat. Included among the newly elected members of the legislature were several sympathetic to the cause of public power. Indeed, the opposition Conservatives were increasingly vocal in their support of public power, seeing it as a vote-getter. They backed the efforts of Toronto City Council, and when the city was yet again rebuffed by the Ross government, the Conservatives put forward a motion in the legislature clearly endorsing public power.

Public power advocates in Toronto also soon realized that they had allies in other Ontario cities and towns, particularly those west of Toronto, where a transmission connection to Niagara Falls seemed to be a dream that was within reach. Like Toronto, these municipalities had had bad experiences with cutthroat private power operators, including the Syndicate. So when an all-day meeting was held in the town of Berlin (later renamed Kitchener) in June 1902, municipal officials, local activists, and small-business owners showed up from Toronto, Waterloo, Preston, Hespeler, St. Jacobs, and Galt. Out of that meeting emerged a more ambitious goal: a public system to serve the power needs of not just Toronto, but other parts of the province as well.

Meanwhile, the Ross government, fresh from its near defeat in the election, was sensing growing support for public power and softening its objections.

Even so, in January 1903, it showed it still sided with private power when it granted the new Niagara Falls power franchise to Pellatt's Syndicate. At the same time, the province announced that, with the addition of the Syndicate, the private franchise holders would generate sufficient power to ensure prices would be kept in line, and therefore it would not be necessary to grant any additional franchises.

The door to further franchises from Niagara Falls appeared to be closed, bringing the dream of public power to an end.

By contrast, Henry Pellatt's dream appeared to be just taking shape. As he contemplated a future of untold riches, he moved enthusiastically forward with his plans to build an estate fit for royalty, modelled on the kind of medieval European castles that had always intrigued him. He toyed with a Spanish name for his spectacular hilltop home: Casa Loma.

If the government thought it had put an end to pressure for public power, it was wrong. Its blatant favouritism toward the Syndicate prompted a storm of protest from the press and from business interests, as well as from the invigorated Conservative opposition in the legislature, led by James P. Whitney. Toronto City Council, angered by the Ross government's latest rebuff and refusing to abandon the cause, promptly approached the government yet again — only to be snubbed for a fourth time!

Undeterred, the public power forces sensed that the people were on their side and that the Liberals were more vulnerable on this issue than they realized, especially with their razor-thin majority. The advocates continued to organize, holding another meeting in Berlin in February 1903, this time at the YMCA, a larger venue, where delegations from ninety different Ontario communities crowded into the large hall. Among those attending was newly elected Conservative member of provincial parliament Adam Beck, who was also the mayor of London, the leading city in southwestern Ontario.

Beck had been born and raised in the small Ontario town of Baden, not far from Berlin. He had been given little formal education but had worked from a young age in the moulding room and machine shop of his father's foundry, where he took a keen interest in learning how things operated. At the age of seventeen, he had built a one-horse-power steam engine that worked. The Beck family was successful and prominent in the area, but the difficult economic conditions of the

1870s put his father's enterprise out of business, and the family lost everything. Adam moved to Toronto, where he worked in a foundry and a cigar factory. Anxious to run his own show, he borrowed five hundred dollars and, with a brother and cousin, set up a small business manufacturing cigar boxes. The Becks' company introduced a slight innovation: existing cigar boxes operated with metal hinges; the Beck boxes used simpler canvas strips instead. When the business proved successful, Adam Beck turned his attention to what he realized was his true interest: politics.

As a popular mayor of London, Beck demonstrated an early interest in public ownership. Although the city was ready to renew a thirty-year lease with a private operator to run the railway to Port Stanley, Beck vetoed the move; already, he had plans for the city to develop a publicly run rail line. After he was elected a member of the provincial legislature — while still retaining his mayorship — he discovered the issue that would animate the rest of his life: bringing public power to Ontario. At the 1903 Berlin meeting, he listened with fascination to the case for public power articulated by Alderman Spence from Toronto, as well as by dedicated local advocates such as Elias Snider from the town of St. Jacobs and Daniel Detweiler, a successful Berlin flour miller. But it was Beck who would soon emerge as an indomitable force in the public power movement.

That 1903 Berlin meeting attracted considerable attention, with the widely read Toronto weekly *Saturday Night* describing it as "a declaration of popular rights as opposed to monopolistic privilege" and interpreting the large turnout as clear evidence that the movement for "public franchises" was growing in popularity. "If the members of the Ontario government are wise," the publication warned, "they will no longer deaden their ears against the rising clamor of the multitude."[3]

Energized by the Berlin gathering, a delegation of municipalities asked for and received a meeting with the premier. Clearly somewhat intimidated by the "rising clamour of the multitude," Premier Ross promised at that meeting to introduce legislation that would allow municipalities to establish their own local public utilities to deliver Niagara power. This seemed like a significant concession. But in reality, it didn't bring the municipalities much closer to their goal, since the premier made clear that his government was unwilling to lend them money to help establish these public utilities, and the municipalities had limited borrowing powers on their own.

The premier increasingly understood, however, that he had to at least seem sympathetic to the public power movement and avoid appearing to be in the pocket of the Syndicate. Maintaining an appearance of distance became even more imperative when the Syndicate served up a flagrant example of its narrow self-interest and indifference to any broader public purpose. Proceeding with excavations for its new installation at Niagara Falls, Syndicate engineers had discovered a more powerful water flow than anticipated. Applying to the province for permission to generate additional energy, the Syndicate was reminded of a stipulation in the contract it had signed guaranteeing that half the power it produced be reserved for Canadian use. Aware of big opportunities for selling power south of the border, the Syndicate bristled at being held to such conditions and pushed to be free of them.

This brazen attitude was just the catalyst needed to bring to a head the long-simmering public resentment toward Pellatt and his partners, who were increasingly seen as a band of robber barons. As the government headed into another election campaign in late 1904, holding on to its majority by a thread, public power became a central issue and a rallying cry for the opposition, with Conservative leader Whitney declaring that "the water power of Niagara should be as free as air."[4] The Syndicate waged its own campaign with statements highlighting the fact that it was Canadian — the only Canadian firm involved in Niagara power generation! This shoddy appeal to patriotism did little to win over voters, who were well aware the company was manoeuvring to free itself completely of any requirement that it serve the Canadian market.

On election day in early 1905, the voters delivered a resounding victory to the Conservatives. In short order, James Whitney, the new premier, rejected the Syndicate's application for increased power generation rights at Niagara Falls. Signalling that there would be a new, very different approach at Queen's Park, Premier Whitney unabashedly proclaimed, "I say on behalf of the Government, that the water power all over the country should not in the future be made the sport and prey of capitalists and shall not be treated as anything else but a valuable asset of the people of Ontario."[5]

Within five months of the election, the Conservative government had created the Hydro-Electric Power Commission, with Adam Beck as its chairman — while Beck was also serving as minister without portfolio in the Whitney Cabinet. Beck moved quickly to develop a comprehensive overview of water resources and power throughout the province, a task made more difficult since the private electrical utilities mostly refused to co-operate, afraid of revealing the kinds of mark-ups they were charging. Beck pointed out, for instance, that Pellatt's Syndicate was selling its power from Niagara to its own Toronto street-car and lighting companies for thirty-five dollars per horsepower per year. Yet the municipally owned hydroelectric plant in Orillia was able to supply power to local manufacturers for half that rate, just sixteen dollars per horsepower per year. And Beck predicted that public power from Niagara Falls could sell in Toronto for roughly the same low rate, dramatically reducing power costs in the city.

When Beck called for a public meeting in Toronto in April 1906, some 1,500 delegates from seventy Ontario municipalities converged on city hall. Claiming to represent more than one million people in rural and urban parts of the province, they enthusiastically endorsed a resolution calling for legislation enabling the construction of new publicly owned generating plants — or the expropriation of existing private ones. Then the delegates marched en masse up University Avenue to Queen's Park, where they gathered in the legislative chamber, chanting in unison "We want cheap power, and we want it now!"[6]

A month later, the Whitney government responded with far-reaching legislation largely delivering what the public power advocates were demanding. But Whitney's strong declaration that water should not be "the sport and prey of capitalists" and now this sweeping legislation masked a deep division inside the ranks of his own Conservative Party, which had strong ties to the business community and roots reaching back to the Family Compact that had ruled Upper Canada in the early nineteenth century. Some influential Conservative Party members had connections to the Syndicate and to other financial interests and didn't want to see the party veer in what they considered a socialist direction. Even the province's own lieutenant governor, William Clark, speaking at the opening celebration of the Syndicate's new power plant at Niagara Falls, pointedly expressed his concern that the new legislation not prevent the Syndicate owners from being "permitted to enjoy the legitimate fruits of their enterprise."[7] There were stronger words from Byron Walker, president of the Canadian Bank of Commerce, who directly attacked the notion that government could own and operate something as complicated as a power generating system: "We know that this kind of public ownership, applied to a problem so intricate, is as useless as the breath of the politicians who advocate it."[8]

For that matter, Premier Whitney himself, for all his eloquent words, had close ties to the financial elite, including the Syndicate. Nelles reports that the premier was involved in behind-the-scenes efforts to protect the interests of the Syndicate: "Publicly it appeared as if a united government had striven with singular purpose toward public ownership; but privately, without Adam Beck's knowledge, the senior members of that government had been continuously exploring a whole series of compromises in the mutual interest of the province and industry."[9]

Ultimately, however, it would be up to the province's ratepayers to decide. They were to vote in municipal elections, typically held on New Year's Day, and the public power question was to be on the ballot on January 1, 1907. The debate raged for months leading up to the vote, with the private power interests rallying support in the business community and placing expensive advertisements in the press.

But they were badly outflanked by Adam Beck, who doggedly criss-crossed the province making the case against their coercive monopoly power at public meetings that attracted large crowds. Beck had become one of the best-known and most respected figures in the province, and public power had become his passion. Now fifty years old, he had educated himself thoroughly about every aspect of the issue and had become a skillful operator able to outsmart his many detractors and opponents as he shepherded his projects through political mine-fields. While many accused him of arrogance and bullheadedness, few doubted he had a genuine commitment to implementing his vision of affordable power for all.

When the votes were counted on election day, Toronto over-whelmingly endorsed public power, as did eighteen other municipal-ities: Berlin, Brantford, Galt, Guelph, Hamilton, Hespeler, Ingersoll, London, New Hamburg, Paris, Preston, St. Marys, St. Thomas, Stratford, Toronto Junction, Waterloo, Weston, and Woodstock.

It was a crucial first step, but the choice had to be ratified by muni-cipal voters in the following year's election, after the municipalities had negotiated contracts with Ontario Hydro. So the battle raged on for another year, gaining in intensity, even as Ontario Hydro began con-structing its new transmission lines with money borrowed from the province. The private power interests, organizing themselves behind the softer-sounding banner of the Anti-Hydro Citizens Committee of Business Men, made their case on roadside billboards and in news-paper editorials and advertising, as well as by hiring canvassers to go door to door warning of the dangers of Hydro debt. These costly efforts were more than matched by the large army of pro-Hydro canvassers — students, trade unionists, engineers, young married housewives, and members of the Canadian Women's Suffrage Association — who all voluntarily gave their time for what many had come to see as a vital crusade for equality and the betterment of society.

The municipal elections of 1908 produced the same resounding victory for public power. Realizing they had lost — or never enjoyed — public support, the private interests simply changed their strategy. They took to the courts, trying to throw legal roadblocks in Hydro's way. They also pushed Ottawa to intervene, claiming Ontario was stepping beyond its jurisdiction. In addition, they approached farmers along the proposed route for Hydro's lines, warning them that Hydro's plans for higher-voltage transmission was dangerous. (In fact, it was safe, and also turned out to be a technological innovation that soon became the new standard for electrical transmission throughout the world.) Most maliciously, the private power forces mounted a massive campaign to destroy Ontario's credit rating with foreign investors in Britain and the United States.

The financial press, at home and abroad, fell in line, happy to sound the alarm on behalf of private capital. In England, the *Economist* denounced the Whitney government, claiming its behaviour showed that "Provincial Legislatures cannot be trusted to deal fairly with the rights of property and ... they have given just cause of alarm to the English capitalist." London's daily *Financier and Bullionist* also weighed in harshly: "Well-wishers of Canada are grieved beyond measure that the British investor has been smitten in the house of a friend.... [I]f the Government of a Province like Ontario violates and rides rough-shod over property rights and declines to play the fair game, then anything may happen in Canada."[10]

Unfazed by the campaign and attempts at obstruction, Beck pushed forward with Hydro's plans, managing to outmanoeuvre the increasingly isolated and shrill private interests. Starting in October 1910, there were great public celebrations as power surged for the first time through Hydro lines from Niagara Falls to cities and towns more than 160 kilometres away, a feat that was still regarded as almost a miracle.

Indeed, the first such celebration — held, fittingly, in the town of Berlin, where public power had found some of its most ardent early advocates — drew a crowd of eight thousand people, including many who came by horse and buggy from nearby towns and villages. Berlin had been preparing for months for the occasion, and its freshly paved roads were dressed up with banners and garlands. A string of incandescent light bulbs spelling the words "For the People" had been hung over the town's main street, awaiting the turn of a master switch that would illuminate them for the first time. The Berlin *News Record* was full of breathless stories anticipating the event, beneath the banner headline "NIAGARA FALLS — BERLIN RISES."[11]

When the special train arrived from Toronto carrying the premier, Adam Beck, and other key members of the Cabinet, the crowd surged forward. The celebrities were then driven through the streets in open motor cars, smiling and waving to the wildly enthusiastic throngs.

With dusk arriving, the dignitaries gathered on a specially built podium at the local hockey rink, the biggest space in the town. Finally, the designated moment arrived. Premier Whitney reached over and, grabbing Adam Beck's hand, placed it on the master switch. "Gentlemen," he said (apparently ignoring the many women present, including Adam Beck's beloved wife, Lillian), "with this hand, tried and true, this hand which has made this project complete, I now turn on the power."[12] Although it hadn't been tested, so no one could say for sure whether the lights would come on, they did — thousands of them suddenly flooding the near-dark town with a shock of light brighter than the townspeople had ever witnessed after nightfall. The crowd roared with amazement and approval.

A special cheer went up when two local heroes on the podium shook hands: Beck, born in nearby Baden, and "Billie" King, born right there in Berlin and now the local member of Parliament (later Canada's longest-serving prime minister, William Lyon Mackenzie King). Beck delighted the heavily German-speaking crowd by speaking in both English and German, insisting that Hydro's work had just begun. "We must deliver power to such an extent that the poorest working man will have electric light in his home. No more oil and gas, and soon, I hope, no more coal."[13]

The party continued on into the night, with celebrants cavorting on the brightly lit streets as if in a dream. There were further electrical wonders that evening: at Market House, some five hundred guests sat down to a dinner cooked almost entirely by electricity. That was an occasion for more adulation of Adam Beck. A roar went up from the crowd as he rose to speak after dinner. The band played the rousing tune "See, the Conquering Hero Comes" — and then played it again three more times with wild cheering continuing to reverberate around the room. "Niagara power is free as air," Beck declared, savouring the moment. "You are not alone," he added. "The government is behind you until this power reaches the humblest hamlet and the smallest manufacturer."[14]

Meanwhile, back in Toronto, Henry Pellatt was proceeding to build for himself the least humble home on the continent. The prospects for his business empire had been somewhat diminished by the rise of the public power movement, but Pellatt was still a very wealthy man and more determined than ever to live like a king. By 1911, construction of his massive castle was underway; some three hundred workers were building the mansion's ninety-eight rooms, with its thirty bathrooms, secret passageways, and a kitchen equipped with an oven big enough to cook an ox. No expense was spared in an attempt to showcase Pellatt's wealth; there were gold fixtures in the bathrooms and the finest mahogany wood lining the walls of the enormous stables. Only a few miles to the south, newly arrived Irish and Chinese immigrants lived jammed together in filthy rundown shacks in the area known as St. John's Ward (now Nathan Phillips Square). But none of that was visible from the sprawling grounds of Pellatt's estate, where he and his wife, Mary, lavishly entertained Toronto's elite and even visiting royalty.

However, Pellatt's extravagant lifestyle concealed the fact that his days as a lordly financier were numbered. Certainly, he was losing the battle against Adam Beck and the public power movement, which went from one local victory to another. On May 2, 1911, it was Toronto's turn to celebrate the arrival of public power, and the switching-on ceremony at city hall attracted thirty thousand celebrants. Indeed, the crowd was so large and boisterous that some participants were injured as people scrambled in the near-darkness to enter the main foyer, where the ceremony was taking place. Once again, it was Beck's hand, guided by the premier, that turned on the dazzling display of lights, this time accompanied by water gushing over a symbolic Niagara Falls, which left many in the crowd soaking wet. As the band played in frenzied celebration, no one seemed to care.

Excitement about the new public power grew in the following years, prompting more and more municipalities to sign up with Ontario Hydro, with switching-on celebrations — usually attended by Beck himself — held in communities across the province. As William Plewman, a journalist who covered Beck and the early Hydro developments, later wrote, "The Hydro movement appealed to the imagination of the public and the services of Adam Beck as a speaker were demanded in every part of Ontario. He was the most sought after man in Canada."[15]

Beck's success did not go unnoticed south of the border, where Americans were grappling with the same problems caused by "water barons" — private monopolies gaining control of hydroelectric power. The water barons and their lobbyists went to great effort to discredit Ontario's experiment with public power, but there was sufficient curiosity about the Canadian innovation that Beck was invited to appear before a Congressional committee in Washington in 1917. In more than two hours of testimony, he set out the scope of what Ontario Hydro had accomplished: in seven years, it had become the world's largest transmitter and distributor of electrical energy. Whereas electricity had cost twelve cents per kilowatt hour in Toronto when the city was serviced by a private monopoly, Ontario Hydro had sliced that rate down to two cents per kilowatt hour, Beck told the committee. Some 225 municipalities had signed up, and the savings to Ontario households alone had amounted to $2.5 million the previous year.

However, Beck's resounding endorsement of public power failed to convince U.S. lawmakers to stand up to the mighty American water barons. The oligarchs remained dominant until President Franklin D. Roosevelt dared to take them on in the 1930s. Roosevelt had long been impressed with Ontario Hydro, and in the depths of the Depression, he copied aspects of it in creating huge publicly owned utilities like the Tennessee Valley Authority and the Rural Electrification Administration.

In 1921, when the thirty-year franchise for Toronto's street railway expired, the Syndicate found itself back in the spotlight. William Mackenzie was quoted in the Toronto press declaring he didn't give a damn about the public. After decades of public dissatisfaction with the private railway company, including its refusal to operate trains beyond municipal boundaries as part of its one-fare system, Mackenzie's dismissive arrogance was the final straw. With Torontonians fired up about the benefits of public ownership, city council declined to renew the Syndicate's private contract and instead set up the Toronto Transit Commission to operate a modernized railway system in the city. The following year, the Clean-Up Deal, finalizing Hydro's purchase of all Pellatt's remaining electrical interests in Toronto, was signed by both sides, signalling an end to the city's long and bitter struggle with the man who fashioned himself a king.

～◎〜

The quest to bring affordable public power to Ontario had triumphed, with Beck at its helm. Beck had devised a novel system in which municipalities owned and operated their own utilities connected to the province-wide Hydro grid. Canadian writer Merrill Denison observed in 1960 that Hydro was regarded, both by its friends and its foes, as "one of the most successful enterprises of its kind to be found anywhere in the world." Denison, who had also written radio plays for the CNR decades earlier, credited Hydro with being a pioneer of "large-scale hydro-electric development, standardization of equipment and appliances, utility management and rural electrification."[16]

Among Hydro's more notable technological achievements was the Queenston-Chippawa generating station, which involved diverting water from above Niagara Falls through more than twenty kilometres of open canals and tunnels, dug through solid rock, until the water plunged from a height almost twice as high as the falls — and generated roughly twice the power. With the construction supervised by Beck every step of the way, the Queenston-Chippawa station finally opened in 1925, amid controversy over its costs. Still operational today, it's been designated a national historic site as the world's first hydroelectric megaproject.

For all his accomplishments, Beck failed in achieving another key dream: creating a system of publicly owned, electrically operated trains throughout southern Ontario, with Toronto as the hub. Beck had worked tirelessly developing and pushing the scheme, which took his goals of public ownership and affordable electricity and applied them to the realm of public transportation. Although the scheme had many supporters, the growing use of the automobile by the mid-1920s seemed to point to a different sort of future built around highways and cars. After years of winning almost every political battle he had engaged in, Beck lost this one. In August 1925, at the age of sixty-eight, a deeply disappointed Beck died of anemia.

His arch-nemesis, Henry Pellatt, also suffered big setbacks, in addition to losing his electrical empire. Accusations of wartime profiteering dogged him, a fraudulent real estate scheme landed him in major financial trouble, and city taxes on Casa Loma left him unable to afford to live there. He moved out in 1924 and continued to downsize until, at the time of his death in 1939, he was living in a modest home with his former chauffeur.

The battle between Beck and Pellatt — two characters who strode flamboyantly across the Ontario political landscape in the early 1900s — was ultimately a contest between public and private ownership of a vital service. Public ownership emerged the winner, with Ontarians strongly supportive of the vast public power system that gave the province's industries access to reliable, low-cost power, enabling them to become highly competitive with their American rivals. The emergence of southern Ontario as the nation's industrial heartland was in significant part due to the work of Adam Beck, or the "Hydro Knight" as he was dubbed by his legion of admirers.

Even Beck's "failure" seems rather inspiring, suggesting perhaps that he was simply ahead of his time. The electrical rail system he envisioned would have created a vast public transportation network connecting southern Ontario, not unlike the commuter GO Train network introduced decades later in the 1960s. Long before he could have known about the threat of climate change, Adam Beck apparently had a gut instinct that a comprehensive, publicly owned transportation system was a worthy alternative to an increasing reliance on the gas-guzzling private car.

In another strangely prescient thought, Beck warned close confidants of his fear that those managing Hydro in the future would needlessly depart from his commitment to low-cost power rates. "Remember what I am telling you," he reportedly told a confidant shortly before his death. "They have no cause to raise Hydro rates. Watch what they do when I am gone."[17]

Beyond Beck's exceptional qualities, the tale of Hydro is the story of how a popular movement waged a fierce and successful political battle to create a publicly owned power system — a story that is unique to Ontario. Denison notes that the public power movement did not occur anywhere else. "The question arises, therefore: what impelled one Canadian province among all the states of North America — or elsewhere for that matter — to embark on such a novel experiment?... [N]othing in the previous Canadian experience had indicated the virtues of public ownership." Denison observes that Canadian governments had intervened financially to build canals and railways, but had done so due to necessity rather than because of a belief in collective ownership; indeed, the government-owned Intercolonial Railway had been widely ridiculed for patronage and inefficiency. "Against such a background," writes Denison, "it is the more remarkable that 'White Coal' and 'The People's Power' should have become the rallying cries of a political struggle which had its inception in Western Ontario and kept the province in a state of constant emotional turmoil for the better part of a decade."[18]

Remarkable indeed. The key question isn't why this extraordinary development happened, but rather why have we forgotten about it?

∼ଲ∼

In the decades since Adam Beck presided over Ontario Hydro, many big mistakes have been made. Perhaps the biggest mistake — the one that arguably led to so many others — was the decision not to copy the successful Hydro model and create a similar publicly owned system for natural gas.

By the early years after the Second World War, Hydro's transmission lines had brought electricity to every corner of the province. But while electricity was a superb power source for lighting and for small motorized functions, it was not nearly as efficient as natural gas in providing heat, something clearly essential in the Canadian cold. With natural gas abundant in Alberta, there was growing interest in the 1950s in the idea of building a pipeline to bring western gas to

Ontario and Quebec. And, given Hydro's popularity, many Ontarians saw merit in making it a publicly owned, non-profit pipeline and distribution system, which, according to estimates, would reduce the cost of gas to the consumer by 30 to 40 percent.

Conservative premier Leslie Frost weighed the possibility of developing a publicly owned gas system, realizing that this would fit well with his party's much-lauded creation of Hydro decades earlier. However, there were private interests in the gas business keen on expanding their market. "It was the public versus private power contest all over again," notes energy analyst and author Bill Reno. "Although this time, the private interests weren't a huge entrenched force like the earlier private power interests, and Ontarians were already aware that a public system could work very well."[19]

But even if the private gas interests weren't the formidable force the Syndicate had once been, they still had influential friends inside Frost's Cabinet. Provincial treasurer Dana Porter, for instance, argued that it would be unfair to oblige private oil and gas companies to compete with a publicly owned gas company, which would be able to deliver gas cheaply. With this logic, Porter turned Adam Beck upside down: instead of regarding lower prices resulting from a public system as a *benefit* to the public, it was seen as an *injustice* to private interests.

In the Ontario legislature, the CCF — forerunner of the NDP — strongly pushed for a public gas system, but in the end the Conservative Cabinet decided to hand the lucrative gas distribution business over to private companies. "Half a century after private power monopolies were dismantled by popular vote, here was a Conservative government creating new private power monopolies — without holding any votes," said Reno in an interview.

Meanwhile, in Ottawa, the Liberal government of Louis St. Laurent was taking steps to ensure that the pipeline delivering the gas would also be in private hands. C.D. Howe, the federal minister of trade and commerce, went to Texas and negotiated a deal with powerful U.S. oil interests who, along with some minor Canadian partners, had formed a consortium called TransCanada Pipelines (TCPL). When TCPL was unable to raise all of the $375 million needed to finance the 925-kilometre pipeline, the consortium asked Ottawa to guarantee its debentures. Even though this meant putting public money at risk, Ottawa agreed, in exchange for shares giving it a voice in the company. The Canadian players in TCPL accepted these terms, but the U.S. oilmen sharply rejected them, insisting they weren't willing to give a "foreign" government influence in their company!

This could have been the cue for Ottawa to take over the project itself, using its excellent credit rating to raise the funds at more favourable rates. But C.D. Howe, despite his wartime experience developing strong Canadian Crown corporations, was now trying to unwind much of the public ownership he had overseen in the interests of advancing the war effort. In peacetime, he and the St. Laurent government were instead focused on using the power of government to strengthen the private sector. So, in the spring of 1956, they proposed that the government take over construction of the most difficult stretch of pipeline, the section north of Lake Superior. This problematic section — and it alone — would be owned by a Crown corporation. Ottawa agreed to later sell this section, at below cost, to TCPL, after the whole pipeline was up and running, when the private oil interests could easily come up with the money out of the handsome profits they would be making.

Then, bending over backwards still further, the St. Laurent government offered the U.S. oilmen an eighty-million-dollar loan to help them overcome their financing problems. It was an incredibly generous offer, since the government would be providing crucial upfront financing during the risky stage of the project. Even so, the oilmen responded by arrogantly insisting that the Canadian Parliament fully approve the arrangement within two weeks, by June of 1956. With the Co-operative Commonwealth Federation and the Conservatives determined to block the deal by stalling its progress through the House of Commons, a massive parliamentary showdown — known as the Great Pipeline Debate — erupted. After six raucous days in Parliament, the deal passed. But it was widely seen as a betrayal of Canadian interests, and was almost certainly the main cause of the Liberals' whopping electoral defeat the following year.

The creation of a private set of interests in the gas delivery business set the stage for a showdown over control of the energy market between the privately owned gas interests and publicly owned Ontario Hydro. "It didn't have to happen," insists Reno. "If both forms of energy had been publicly owned, government could have divided up the energy market in a rational fashion — electricity for lighting and motors, and natural gas for heating and cooking." Instead, Hydro, bent on ensuring it won the contest for market share, embarked on an extensive, needless, and counterproductive campaign to increase consumer consumption of electricity. With its already dominant position and its catchy "Live Better Electrically" campaign, Hydro managed, unfortunately, to greatly drive up the demand for electricity, paving the way for nuclear energy to be seen as a necessary supplement to hydroelectric power.

Of course, Hydro would have likely explored the nuclear option anyway, as did utilities in other jurisdictions. But Reno has a point that the surging demand for electricity in Ontario — prompted by Hydro's misguided campaign to beat out the private gas interests — encouraged Hydro planners in the early postwar years to see the vast potential of nuclear energy as a sensible option. With nuclear power still in its infancy, there was a widespread belief that it offered the promise of virtually limitless energy at little cost.

For decades, Hydro planners and successive Conservative governments in Ontario embraced the nuclear option with zeal, building huge nuclear generating stations at great cost and ignoring the obvious but unsolvable problem that there was no safe way to dispose of nuclear waste. The other obvious problem — the possibility of nuclear meltdowns — was vividly demonstrated in 1986 when the Chernobyl nuclear explosion in Ukraine led to an ongoing death toll, estimated today at up to four thousand people. Finally, in 1990, the NDP government of Bob Rae put an end to Hydro's reckless and foolhardy nuclear expansion, but not before David Peterson's Liberal government had decided to finish building the enormous Darlington nuclear station, leaving Hydro with a crushing $14.3 billion debt for the project that still reverberates through Hydro bills today.

The resulting rise in electricity rates made Hydro an easy target for the privatizers in the Mike Harris government. In December 2001, they announced plans to sell Hydro One, the key transmission arm of the original utility. But despite Hydro's wasteful and costly nuclear investments, there was little public appetite for selling the utility. Facing mounting opposition over a number of controversies — particularly the seven deaths resulting from water contamination in Walkerton, Ontario — the premier resigned in 2002 and was replaced by Ernie Eves. In early 2003, Eves retreated from the unpopular Hydro privatization plan before going down to electoral defeat at the hands of Liberal Dalton McGuinty.

That seemed like it might be the end of the Hydro privatization issue. But in 2015, the Liberal government of Kathleen Wynne brought it back from the near-dead. Although Wynne lacked Harris's passion for privatizing public assets, she found the province short of funds (after years of deep tax cutting) and bought into the logic that selling off part of Hydro One would enable her to "leverage" that public asset to pay for other badly needed new assets, particularly public transit. Accordingly, she decided to sell 60 percent of Hydro One in order to raise nine billion dollars — five billion for public transit investments and four billion for deficit reduction.

But the logic was deeply flawed. While the public transit investments were clearly needed, it would have made more sense for the government to borrow the money or raise taxes, or both. And the deficit reduction was clearly just a one-time, pre-election ploy to make her government look fiscally responsible. The province's own financial accountability officer noted that the financial benefits from the privatization would be short term, since the provincial treasury would lose hundreds of millions of dollars in ongoing annual revenue from the utility, leaving the province worse off financially in the long run. Even the pro-corporate *Toronto Sun* saw the faulty logic, with columnist Lorrie Goldstein noting that "you can only sell the furniture once."[20]

Apart from financial short-sightedness, the Hydro sell-off meant the government was surrendering to the corporate world important levers over energy and environmental policy. While this consequence of the privatization was rarely discussed, it should have been a central concern. Our collective ability to take steps to address the approaching catastrophe of climate change is surely one of the most pressing issues we'll face in the future. Yet one of the first actions of the newly privatized Hydro One was to negotiate the $6.7 billion takeover of giant U.S.-based Avista Utilities, which owns a large coal-fired power station in Montana. So, after Ontario had closed the last of its coal-fired plants in 2014 in the interests of fighting climate change, Ontarians had to watch from the sidelines as the privatized version of their former public utility decided to get back into the coal business. (In December 2018, the Avista takeover was rejected by Washington state regulators, citing political interference after newly elected Ontario premier Doug Ford fired the board and CEO of Hydro One.)

In an attempt to put a positive spin on the Hydro privatization, the Liberals often insisted that it was about "broadening the ownership" of the utility. Kathleen Wynne even made this preposterous claim in the final leaders' debate leading up the June 2018 election. But how does privatization broaden ownership of an asset, when that asset was already owned collectively by *all* the province's people? On the contrary, by selling off 60 percent of it, the government diluted Ontarians' collective ownership and transferred control of this vital asset from the people of the province to a small number of investors.

For the financial community, there was much to like about Hydro's privatization. The fees involved in marketing the shares added up to at least one hundred million dollars, split among the dozens of brokerage houses that handled the share issues.

But outside the boardrooms of Bay Street, the privatization was never popular. Polls showed some 75 percent of Ontarians were opposed — even before revelations that the privatized Hydro One board members had voted themselves pay raises, bringing their personal compensation to $185,000 a year for part-time work.

Many factors contributed to Kathleen Wynne's devastating rout in that June 2018 election. Certainly a key dissatisfaction was Hydro, with its high rates and outrageous executive pay.

And, although few Ontarians knew the whole story, there might well have been a lingering collective memory of how people in dozens of communities across the province had organized decades ago to remove the power system from the hands of avaricious private monopolies. Perhaps Wynne's crushing electoral defeat was in part punishment for her decision to take the hard-won achievement of public power and hand it back to private interests.

Five

From Horse Barn to World Stage: The Connaught Story

T he large hypodermic needle was full of poison. As he prepared to inject it into the neck of a horse, John Gerald FitzGerald was well aware of the risks. If the horse jerked and his hand slipped, the needle could penetrate his own flesh, poisoning him and leaving him in the throes of an excruciating death.

It was a cold December day in Toronto in 1913, and FitzGerald, a medical doctor, was not indifferent to the danger. Apart from his own fears, he had others to think of. At the age of thirty-one, he was anticipating becoming a father for the first time, and he felt tremendous love and responsibility toward his pregnant wife and future child. He was putting so much at risk — without any clear idea that his experiment would work.

Still, FitzGerald felt deeply motivated to proceed. The stakes were enormous. His goal was nothing less than to produce a serum that could effectively treat diphtheria, a disease striking thousands of Canadian children each year and killing many of its victims. Indeed, it was the leading killer of children under fourteen.

With a colleague holding the horse firmly by the halter, FitzGerald took a deep breath, steadied his hand, and then stabbed the sharp point of the needle into the animal's neck.

The needle went in smoothly, which was a great relief to FitzGerald and his dedicated colleague, laboratory technician Billy Fenton, who had helped set up the small horse barn behind his house on Barton Avenue in Toronto for this very purpose. But this was only the beginning. There would be another four months of these injections with the goal of developing diphtheria immunity in the horse's blood, from which they hoped to derive a serum that would treat diphtheria in humans.

Diphtheria struck terror into families. It typically started with a sore throat and was often mistaken for a mere cold. But if it was diphtheria, it could quickly turn deadly, with the throat becoming swollen and inflamed, leaving the feverish child struggling to breathe. As parents watched helplessly, the child slowly and painfully suffocated to death. And that could be just the beginning of the family's nightmare, since the disease was highly contagious. Great efforts were taken to contain it; infected children were typically quarantined in a bedroom, behind a disinfectant sheet strung across the doorway, and every item the child had touched was carefully boiled. Still, the disease would often spread to brothers and sisters. In some cases, there were multiple deaths in a household, all happening in quick succession, leaving a family incredulous and shattered.

What made this child carnage particularly heartbreaking was that many of these deaths did not need to happen. A medication capable of treating a child with diphtheria — often saving the child's life — already existed and could be purchased through Canadian pharmacies. But that did nothing to help the thousands of Canadian families who simply couldn't afford the cost of the treatment.

Although diphtheria had been a scourge of humanity for centuries, scientific advances late in the nineteenth century had led to the development of an antitoxin in the 1890s. When taken in adequate doses and administered early, it had proved fairly effective in treating the disease. But the cost of the medication, manufactured in New York, was exorbitant. A full dose of treatments cost about eighty dollars, the equivalent of several weeks' wages for most workers, who rarely had any savings to draw on or wealthy relatives to turn to. Unable to come up quickly with such an enormous sum, desperate families purchased as much as they could. But without sufficient serum immediately, the treatment was rarely effective.

The situation was clearly devastating for those without resources. In one case recorded by a Toronto physician, a family had to choose which of two infected children to treat. The treated child lived; the other died. In some cases, doctors, deeply moved by the plight of their patients, contributed their own resources to the cost of the medication. But in most cases, despite the existence of a treatment, children from poor and middle-class families simply died. "The children of any but the wealthy are left to die of diphtheria," noted Dr. John McCullough, who was Ontario's chief medical officer of health at the time.[1]

It was this stark, deeply troubling situation that had prompted Dr. FitzGerald to act. With his horse experiment, he sought to prepare a diphtheria treatment that could be produced and sold cheaply. Indeed, his real goal, as he spent countless hours in the cold, crude laboratory-barn in the winter of 1913–14, was to develop a treatment that would be distributed for free to any Canadian who needed it.

Although he had no way of knowing it at the time, FitzGerald's vision — and the work he undertook to make it happen — was the seed for the development of a key part of Canada's public health care system. Long before Tommy Douglas, Dr. John G. FitzGerald had unwittingly become an early father of Canadian medicare.

In fact, the dream that all Canadians should have free access to medically necessary drugs is a goal that has not yet been achieved, despite efforts over the years that have resulted in growing pressure to introduce a national pharmacare program, similar to ones that exist in other advanced nations. More on this later.

Despite this significant failing, Canada has achieved an impressive public health care system. Although both federal and provincial governments have allowed aspects of the system to be privatized, the fact remains that Canada has an excellent overall public system. Paid for by Canadian taxes, the system provides doctor and hospital services at no extra cost to all Canadians.

FitzGerald contributed to this significant development by advancing the notion that free access to life-saving medication should be universal — a notion that was novel and radical in Canada prior to the First World War. Crucially, his vision of universality relied on a key role for government. Right from the beginning, he envisioned that a public system would be the vehicle for delivering his diphtheria treatment to Canadians. Rather than trusting private delivery, FitzGerald understood that only a public system could ensure that the vital life-saving products he was preparing would be made available to all Canadians, rich and poor alike.

To help him in his quest, FitzGerald had sought the support of the University of Toronto (U of T). As the university's board of governors pondered his entreaty, the impatient young physician and bacteriologist had embarked on his experiment in the Barton Avenue stable. The university soon approved the minimal request, granting FitzGerald a small space for a laboratory in the basement of the medical building.

By the middle of March 1914, only three months after FitzGerald had carried out the first of many injections into the horse's neck, he was ready to move on to the crucial next stage in his experiment. Using a small surgical knife, he cut open an artery on the animal's neck and, with a rubber hose, drew out ten litres of blood, which he then poured into small, sterilized bottles. After sewing up the neck of the stoic horse — his name was Crestfallen — FitzGerald carefully stacked the bottles into the trunk of his car and drove the precious cargo straight to his rudimentary basement lab at the university.

In the dingy, lamplit lab, FitzGerald continued the experiment over the next few weeks, applying techniques he had learned a few years earlier while studying at the Pasteur Institute in Paris and the University of Freiburg. He had the help of his twenty-seven-year-old sister, Hazel, as well as his heavily pregnant wife, Edna, who had already shown her dedication to the project by donating money from her dowry to help pay for the construction of the Barton Avenue horse barn. With this key assistance from his family, FitzGerald filtered the vials of antitoxin, testing its potency on guinea pigs until he got the dosage just right.

Less than three weeks later, he had prepared the first batch of serum. He sold it to Ontario's board of health — for one-fifth of the commercial rate. It quickly showed effectiveness in treating diphtheria, prompting a flood of orders from across Canada in the weeks and months that followed.

FitzGerald had succeeded brilliantly in preparing and distributing a low-cost treatment for diphtheria. Now he wanted to see if he could replicate his method and produce low-cost treatments for other diseases that were killing large numbers of Canadians, including typhoid fever, tetanus, smallpox, and meningitis.

The model FitzGerald had in mind was simple. He would sell his products — mostly biologics, particularly preventative vaccines — to provincial boards of health, which would provide them free to doctors to administer to patients at no cost. Even at the very low prices FitzGerald charged the health boards, his lab would make a small profit. For instance, he sold his diphtheria serum to health boards for thirty-five cents per thousand units, ten cents more than it cost his lab to produce a thousand units. That ten cents of profit would be invested back into the lab, enabling it to carry out further research to develop products to fight other infectious diseases.

Excited by the prospects for his antitoxin lab, FitzGerald returned to the university's board of governors, seeking six thousand dollars to really get things going. In front of the sober, grey-haired governors, FitzGerald brimmed with excitement as he made his pitch for a lab that he confidently predicted would be self-supporting "within three to six months, probably less."[2]

While the idea seemed to offer great social benefit, getting the money was by no means assured. Essentially, FitzGerald was asking the university to participate in the operation of a commercial drug company — something that there was no precedent for in the world, and that would likely encounter opposition from the private sector. Indeed, FitzGerald's diphtheria treatment had already provoked antagonism from pharmacists and drug manufacturers who disliked the price competition. Robert Defries, who was involved in the early days of the lab, later recalled that druggists sometimes refused to carry a supply.

Nonetheless, despite potential controversy, the university board decided to back the project, with board member Sir William Osler providing five hundred dollars of his own money. FitzGerald enthusiastically began building his lab which, as he'd predicted, was soon self-supporting. The innovative young doctor had begun to realize his dream — a dream that, as Dr. Gordon Bates observed at the time, would put life-saving medication "within reach of everyone."

Although FitzGerald's not-for-profit lab involved a bold step into uncharted territory, it fit well with rising concern at the time over public health conditions. Scientific advances in the nineteenth century had shown that infectious diseases were transmitted through germs or micro-organisms and that sanitation could play a key role in stopping the spread. This had drawn attention to the dangerous living conditions in rapidly growing cities.

In Toronto, the infamous St. John's Ward near city hall was home to thousands of impoverished, newly arrived immigrants from southern and eastern Europe who lived in filthy, crowded, broken-down shacks. Infectious diseases were rampant and spread quickly. In addition, widespread sexual abuse and prostitution had turned venereal disease into a major problem. Many in Toronto's white, Protestant middle class simply sought to keep this unwashed horde at a distance and resisted the idea of spending tax dollars to build public water-treatment systems.

Others in the Anglo elite pushed for action. There was an emerging reform movement composed of doctors, including Gordon Bates, as well as clergymen and other prominent citizens who understood that any hope of human betterment for these struggling masses

— and for society at large — started with adequate public sanitation. "Sociology did not yet exist as a social science, but if it did, it would be called *bacteriology*," comments writer James FitzGerald in his intriguing book, *What Disturbs Our Blood*, about his grandfather, Dr. John Gerald FitzGerald.[3]

The push for improved sanitation had been reflected in the appointment of Dr. Charles Hastings as the city's medical health officer in 1910. Hastings, whose own daughter had died from typhoid due to infected milk, was relentless in his campaign to reduce the disease outbreaks in the city, imposing quarantines on infected areas and ordering the demolition of thousands of filthy outhouses in the ward. He also fought feisty battles to ensure city water was chlorinated and milk pasteurized. Hastings and the growing public health movement were enormously pleased with and supportive of FitzGerald's efforts at treating communicable diseases, which fit perfectly with their own efforts.

FitzGerald's lab also got a big boost during the First World War. Soldiers were highly vulnerable to tetanus, or lockjaw, if bacteria got into their wounds, so the war created a pressing demand for large quantities of a serum to treat the disease. With the federal government providing funds, FitzGerald and his expanding laboratory team churned out a huge supply of tetanus antitoxin and smallpox vaccines.

The scope of products required for the war effort was enormous. To help, Colonel Albert Gooderham, heir to a large distillery fortune, donated a fifty-seven-acre farm north of the city where FitzGerald and his crew were able to develop immunity in a large number of horses as a step to developing human treatments. Gooderham's gift included the construction of a well-equipped laboratory at the farm. It also came with a request for the right to choose an honorary name for the lab. Unlike so many of today's philanthropists who demand their own names be plastered on the facilities they fund, Gooderham wanted the new lab to be called Connaught Laboratories, in honour of his friend and Canada's governor general at the time, the Duke of Connaught. (Another option would have been to name the lab after FitzGerald.)

Operating in overdrive throughout the war, Connaught Laboratories contributed significantly to the dramatic reduction in disease-related deaths. It produced more than 250,000 vials of tetanus antitoxin, helping to virtually eliminate deaths from tetanus. In earlier wars, roughly eight soldiers died of infection or disease for every one who was actually killed in battle. In the First World War, that pattern was dramatically reversed on the Western Front, where just one Canadian soldier died of disease for every twenty killed in battle.

In addition to helping with the Canadian war effort, Connaught Labs produced fully one-fifth of all the serums used by the British army, gaining international recognition for its contribution to wartime medicine. With the end of the war, Connaught's products were in high demand in places as far away as China, New Zealand, and the Caribbean. And at home, its antitoxins and vaccines were available free to Canadians, distributed through provincial health authorities across the country.

~◎~

Connaught Labs also played an important role in one of the most exciting and dramatic medical breakthroughs of the twentieth century.

In October 1920, Fred Banting, a twenty-eight-year-old doctor who lectured part-time at the University of Western Ontario, was reading medical literature to prepare notes for a class when he came up with a concept for a possible treatment for diabetes. The disease, which had sentenced millions of victims around the world to tortured lives and deaths over the centuries, continued to baffle scientists. Banting knew little about diabetes or the extensive medical research into it. But he had a gut instinct that he might be onto something with his simple idea, which was based on developing an ingredient that could be extracted from the pancreas of dogs.

Although he had grown up on a farm and had little experience with scientists, Banting approached a leading authority on diabetes, Professor J.J.R. Macleod, chairman of U of T's physiology department. Nervously, Banting, the unsophisticated farm boy, outlined his concept to the distinguished professor, who was not at all impressed. Banting left the meeting feeling so humiliated he was tempted to abandon the idea. But his landlady urged him not to give up, noting that it was worth risking further patronizing comments from the professor on the chance that his idea had merit. Fortunately, he listened to her.

Macleod was still not convinced when he heard the idea again, but decided to allow Banting to use a dingy, modest space on the second floor of the medical building to carry out some experiments. Within a few months, Banting, assisted by twenty-one-year-old medical student Charles Best, had demonstrated that a crude extract from a dog's pancreas could be used to lower the blood sugar level of a diabetic dog. If the extract could do the same in humans, they might be close to coming up with a treatment for this infuriating, little-understood disease. Macleod remained skeptical.

By Christmas 1921, Banting and Best were aided by James Collip, a talented twenty-nine-year-old biochemist on leave from the University of Alberta. It was Collip who came up with a key piece of the puzzle, figuring out how to purify the pancreatic extract, dubbed *insulin*. Even Macleod was now obliged to acknowledge that the trio seemed to be on the cusp of something big. FitzGerald enthusiastically jumped in, offering the team lab space at the Connaught facilities in the same building and providing five thousand dollars from Connaught's budget to help them with the cost of preparing enough extract for clinical trials.

Working at a frantic pace, the team prepared a batch of experimental insulin and took it to the grim ward at Toronto General Hospital where patients with advanced diabetes lay dying. A sickly, withered fourteen-year-old boy was injected with the extract and showed some signs of improvement — but not enough. So Collip returned to his lab. After more days of frenzied scrambling, Collip realized in a blissful moment late one night that he had stumbled on a formula that allowed him to produce a significantly more purified extract.

The new batch was rushed over to the hospital and administered to the dying fourteen-year-old diabetic. Fairly quickly, his face brightened, his eyes focused, and, in front of the stunned hospital staff, the boy managed to get up and walk.

For Banting and Best, the thrilling development was accompanied by some devastating news. Back at the lab, Collip informed his partners that he intended to cease collaborating with them and instead take out a patent for the purer extract under his own name. Enraged, Banting planted a fist in Collip's face, knocking him to the floor, where the strapping farm boy continued to pummel the traitorous biochemist.

Best managed to separate the two men, but it fell to FitzGerald to come up with a workable solution that would ensure the insulin project went forward and remained under public control. Building on the arrangement already established between the inventors and Connaught, FitzGerald convinced the volatile inventors — now including Macleod — to sign a contract pledging not to take out any private patents while they were working with Connaught.

FitzGerald and the inventors then approached authorities at the U of T. At their request, the university oversaw the signing of a patent arrangement that would prevent any company or individual from gaining a monopoly over the life-saving drug. Under the deal, insulin had to be tested for purity by Connaught Labs, with the testing fee going toward future insulin research as well as toward other research projects conducted by Banting, Best, or Collip. Connaught worked closely with U.S. pharmaceutical company Eli Lilly to ensure large-scale insulin production.

Meanwhile, as news spread of the incredible powers of insulin, diabetics flocked to Toronto for treatment. Toronto became known as the place where three young, inexperienced Canadian researchers had come up with a miraculous treatment for a disease that had bedevilled scientists for centuries — and the Canadians had done so in only a year and a half with almost no resources. Connaught creator FitzGerald had played a pivotal role in advancing the project and, crucially, in ensuring control of it remained in the public domain, where it would be "within reach of everyone." The discovery of insulin, which has saved countless lives in the past nine and a half decades, is a remarkable, truly Canadian story.

After the insulin breakthrough, Connaught Labs continued for the next half century to make a major contribution to the advancement of health, both in Canada and globally. Connaught became part of the U of T, and FitzGerald remained in charge of it for the next two decades. He also established the U of T's School of Hygiene, an innovative, forward-thinking institution that advanced the ideas of public health reformers, providing a much broader view of health care than the standard medical perspective. Not just concerned with treating disease, the school focused on improving the population's overall health, which included considerations like living conditions and social structures. With FitzGerald overseeing both the school and the lab, the two institutions worked closely together, sharing an impressive roster of cross-appointed staff. Connaught and the School of Hygiene soon became a hub of scientific experimentation, academic inquiry, education, and public health advocacy.

Connaught's innovative approach and effectiveness attracted the interest of the Rockefeller Foundation, which had earlier supported the establishment of schools of public health at Johns Hopkins and Harvard Universities in the United States. So impressed were the Rockefeller health experts by FitzGerald and his Connaught Labs that the foundation contributed $650,000 in 1924 to pay for the construction of a large four-storey building to house the School of Hygiene and to cover costs of expanding its academic scope. More money was to follow over the next two decades, as the U of T public health school became one of three North American institutions heavily funded by the foundation.

And although the focus of public health went beyond the standard emphasis on disease control, Connaught also went on to score a number of stunning achievements in disease control — and eradication. After FitzGerald's advances with a diphtheria antitoxin before the First World War and into the 1920s, Connaught was pivotal in developing and testing a vaccine against diphtheria in the 1930s. Working with city health officials, the lab conducted a trial involving fifty thousand schoolchildren. Connaught doctors gave speeches and radio interviews to overcome pockets of fear and resistance to the trials. When the vaccine was demonstrated to be safe and 90 percent effective against

diphtheria, Connaught gained further public respect and growing recognition as an international leader in preventative medicine.

Connaught researchers also played a key role in making a blood
anticoagulant called heparin widely available. Although heparin had
been discovered in 1916 at Johns Hopkins University, it was never used
due to its cost and concerns about its safety. A team at Connaught,
headed by Charles Best of insulin fame, set out to change that in the
early 1930s. By 1937, his team had come up with a safe, effective,
affordable version of the drug, which was not only useful in treating
internal blood clots but also opened the door to advanced new proced-
ures like open heart surgery and organ transplants.

Similarly, Connaught was part of a collaborative scientific effort
that led to the development in the 1950s of a vaccine against polio,
which could kill children or leave them permanently disabled from
paralysis.

It was Jonas Salk, an American virologist at the University of
Pittsburgh School of Medicine, who made the initial medical breakthrough, coming up with a method of stimulating the immune system
so that it would develop antibodies to the polio virus. He tested his
vaccine on monkeys, but it wasn't sufficiently safe to test on children.

At the same time, however, Connaught scientists, led by zoolo-
gist Raymond Parker, came up with a synthetic solution that could be
used for growing the polio virus. They contacted Salk and, using the
synthetic solution developed at Connaught, Salk was able to develop a
vaccine safe to test on children.

However, in order to test it on enough children to make the testing
viable, large amounts of the vaccine were needed, and it was not known
how to produce it in sufficient quantities. Once again, the answer came
from a Connaught scientist — in this case, Leone Farrell, one of the
few women at the time with a Ph.D. in biochemistry. Farrell developed
a complex technique involving rocking a solution in large bottles,
which became known as the *Toronto method*. She and her team were
able to produce three thousand litres of the precious liquid, which was
used to conduct a massive polio vaccine trial involving more than a
million children.

Although Connaught was central to the development of the polio vaccine, its role was not widely known, partly because there was a deliberate attempt at the time to keep it secret, according to Canadian medical historian Paul Bator. Research into polio was heavily funded in the United States by the National Foundation for Infantile Paralysis, which had been established in the 1930s by U.S. president Franklin D. Roosevelt, one of the world's best-known polio victims. The foundation's annual March of Dimes campaign raised large sums for research, and starting in the early 1940s, some of those funds had been directed north to Connaught, which was known to be carrying out relevant, top-quality research. The directors of the U.S. foundation feared they would be criticized for sending research dollars outside the country. So, at their request, Connaught kept quiet about the hundreds of thousands of dollars in grants it received from the March of Dimes' fundraising efforts.

Connaught also played a little-known role in the global eradication of smallpox, a role that has been documented by another Canadian medical historian, Christopher Rutty. Throughout history, smallpox had struck terror into populations around the world, leaving victims covered in small disfiguring blotches and causing blindness and death. Although a vaccine against smallpox was first developed in England in 1796, the highly infectious disease, dubbed the "speckled monster," continued to kill large numbers of people well into the twentieth century. The World Health Organization (WHO) estimated that there were some fifteen million new cases in 1967 alone.[4]

It was in that year that the WHO, the public health arm of the United Nations, launched a major campaign to wipe out the disease. Interestingly, the WHO turned to Connaught, assigning it the task of helping to improve standards and testing for smallpox vaccine producers throughout the western hemisphere. (Responsibility for the eastern hemisphere was assigned to the National Institute of Public Health in the Netherlands.)

Connaught had been producing smallpox vaccines for decades, and its high-quality vaccines had succeeded in eliminating the disease in Canada by the 1940s. The lab now jumped at the chance to contribute to the global eradication effort. Two scientists overseeing the Connaught smallpox program, Paul Fenje and Robert Wilson, visited labs in twelve Latin American countries and brought scientists and technicians from Latin America back to Toronto to further instruct them on improving production quality. Fenje and Wilson were also instrumental in developing and codifying WHO's international standards for smallpox vaccine production.

By 1971, the global program to eliminate smallpox had made great strides, with progress particularly notable in Latin America. But there was an unexpected smallpox epidemic in Bangladesh in 1972, as well as a smaller but deadly outbreak in Yugoslavia. At the request of WHO, Connaught produced a stockpile of twenty-five million doses in case of an emergency in Latin America.

The WHO's vaccination program continued with vigour until the last case of smallpox was recorded in Somalia in October 1977. In only ten years and at a cost of merely $112 million, one of history's most feared and lethal diseases had been wiped out. In December 1979, the WHO celebrated victory, officially declaring that smallpox had been eradicated from the face of the earth, thereby saving an estimated one billion dollars a year in global health costs, not to mention sparing countless people untold suffering.

Connaught had played a central role in that victory. Donald Henderson, an American epidemiologist who oversaw the WHO's campaign, later acknowledged the pivotal contribution made by the two Connaught scientists. "I appreciate only too well how many of the concepts in the execution of the smallpox program saw the first light of day over a glass of beer with Bob [Wilson] and Paul [Fenje]," Henderson later recalled. "Directly and indirectly, the ammunition for the campaign bore the indelible stamp — 'made in Canada.'"[5]

◦≈◦

While Connaught focused on fighting disease around the world, it paid less attention to fighting some forces threatening its own survival back in Canada. As an institution that had openly championed the virtues of public health and non-profit medicine, it had irritated some influential players in private medicine and the business world.

As noted, there had always been tension between supporters of private medicine and the reformers who were drawn to the broader public health model advanced by Connaught Labs and the School of Hygiene. But the tension between the two approaches became particularly pronounced in the early 1960s, as pressure built for Canada to adopt public medical insurance.

The tension had broken into the open first in Saskatchewan in 1960, where the socialist-leaning government, led by Premier Tommy Douglas, tried to establish the first government-controlled single-payer medical insurance system in North America. Douglas's bold move was met by an incredibly fierce local opposition led by doctors, the business community, and the media. Backing these elite local groups was the Canadian Medical Association, representing doctors nationwide, as well as the powerful American Medical Association, which contributed one hundred thousand dollars to the battle, seeing it as part of the larger struggle against the forces of public medicine in North America.[6]

The 1960 Saskatchewan election was fought almost entirely over the medicare issue, and was comfortably won by Douglas's Co-operative Commonwealth Federation, which was then emboldened to press forward with its plan. But the anti-medicare forces refused to accept defeat. In particular, Saskatchewan's College of Physicians and Surgeons, the provincial licensing body for doctors, used its power and influence to scare the public about "socialized medicine" and to intimidate any doctors tempted to break rank with the medical establishment over the issue.

The situation exploded into a bitter battle when the province's doctors waged a dramatic strike in July 1962. A small band of brave physicians broke with the rest, risking their medical licences by setting up community clinics to serve the public. They helped swing public opinion against the rebellious doctors. After three weeks of acrimony, the striking doctors succumbed, accepting the terms of what became known as the Saskatoon Agreement, which backed the provincial government's plan for a government-run, universal, comprehensive medical insurance plan. Medicare, after a difficult delivery, had been born in Canada.

The Saskatchewan drama had pushed the medicare issue onto the national stage. Seeing the potential danger if the federal government adopted the idea, the Canadian Medical Association had pressed Conservative prime minister John Diefenbaker to appoint a royal commission, assuming that an inquiry panel selected by a Conservative government would deliver a stringing rebuke of the medicare idea. But Diefenbaker appointed his old law school classmate from Saskatchewan, Emmett Hall, who was chief justice of the Court of Queen's Bench in Saskatchewan. Hall turned out to be independent in his thinking. As he got deeper into the issue, holding hearings across the country, he became convinced of the merits of a public system. Three years later, in 1964, Hall produced his landmark report. Although he'd been elevated to the Supreme Court of Canada by this point, he became a dedicated and eloquent advocate for medicare. By 1966, with the public strongly supportive, the House of Commons voted — by a stunning margin of 177 to 2 — in favour of a national public health care system.

While the medicare battle had raged throughout the early 1960s, the Connaught crowd had thrown its support solidly behind the pro-medicare forces. This created further discord with the private medicine advocates prominent inside U of T's Faculty of Medicine. They derided the School of Hygiene, with its cross-appointed Connaught faculty, as "the little red schoolhouse" and as "a hotbed of radicalism." In the corridors of the medical building, the tension between the two factions was palpable.

And, while the private medicine model had been losing public support, it was a different story among senior university officials, who were more closely aligned with the Faculty of Medicine than with the "little red schoolhouse." The advocates of private medicine also drew on support from elements in the business community, particularly in the drug industry, which had long chafed over Connaught's tax-free status.

Ken Ferguson, Connaught's director at the time, noted in 1968 that, over the years, critics had often asked what the justification was for the university to be running a manufacturing enterprise like

Connaught. "Then comes the next question," wrote Ferguson, "'why shouldn't Connaught Laboratories, which competes with Canadian taxpayers, pay taxes too?' Frankly, I have never been able to think of really satisfactory answers to either question."

Ferguson's response was surprisingly weak for someone supposedly championing Connaught! It apparently didn't occur to him that Canadian taxpayers are not simply business owners but also, for the most part, citizens with an interest in their own health and that of others. Surely, Connaught's tax-free status could be easily justified, given its enormous contribution to treating deadly diseases and promoting initiatives that improved the public's overall health.

For that matter, Connaught's lack of a profit motive made it a highly unusual — and useful — player in the health business, focused on health benefits, not on gaining market advantage or pushing up its stock price. While private firms manoeuvred to corner the market on a lucrative drug, Connaught shared its advances with other producers in order to make needed treatments more widely available. Connaught scientists had, for instance, developed methods for the purification and mass production of penicillin. Instead of using these advances to further its own market dominance, Connaught distributed its top-quality strain of penicillin yeast to other laboratories at no charge, enabling them to mass-produce it. Connaught also made its staff available to assist in setting up penicillin production facilities around the world, just as it had helped with the establishment of insulin plants worldwide.

While business critics were attacking Connaught for its tax-free status, others were complaining that Connaught's public-interest orientation reduced its viability as a business. Paul Bator notes that after Connaught had developed the means for the large-scale production of penicillin, the commercial drug companies stepped in and exploited it to the fullest: "The penicillin story at Connaught was an example of how commercial competitors took advantage of Connaught's generosity to drive the Toronto Laboratories out of the marketplace."

By the late 1960s, Connaught's non-profit status had come to be regarded as an anachronism by a business elite with a waning interest in the public good and an increasing focus on bottom-line profits. The changing nature of the corporate world was reflected in the business-men who sat on U of T's board of governors. The Connaught committee, which oversaw Connaught for the board of governors, was now headed by John E. Brent, president of IBM Canada. With the mindset of an executive employed by a large U.S.-based multinational, Brent favoured selling Connaught — even though the lab had paid its own way from the beginning and had even contributed funding to research conducted by the School of Hygiene and the Banting and Best Institute. Still, Brent saw the sale as a lucrative opportunity for U of T at a time when it was faced with considerable expansion costs as baby boomers were arriving at the university in large numbers.

In June 1972, U of T sold Connaught for twenty-six million dollars to the Canada Development Corporation, an agency that had just been established by Pierre Trudeau's Liberal government to develop and maintain Canadian-controlled companies in response to public concerns about foreign ownership of the economy. Under this new arrangement, Connaught became a profit-driven company and shares were sold to the public.

Only a few years later, in 1975, the university also dismantled the School of Hygiene. Its departments were absorbed by the university's powerful medical school, thereby ending the long rivalry between the two schools with their sharply different approaches to health care.

❧

The increasingly aggressive attitudes on the part of the business elite, which had been a factor in the sale of Connaught and the dismantling of the School of Hygiene, have also played a role in preventing the expansion of Canadian public health care to include a national pharmacare program. Opposition from private insurance and drug companies has been particularly potent. As a result, Canada today is one of the few advanced nations (along with the United States) that lacks a national drug program, and so Canadians are forced to pay more, per capita, for pharmaceuticals than citizens in most advanced nations (other than the United States).

There was fresh hope in February 2018 that a national drug program might finally be under serious consideration when the Trudeau government appointed Eric Hoskins, a former Ontario health minister and long-time pharmacare advocate, to head an advisory council on implementing pharmacare. Hoskins's final report is expected before the end of June 2019.

Certainly, numerous investigations and public inquiries, starting with Emmett Hall's 1964 royal commission, have advocated pharmacare as a way to ensure universal access to needed medications and to lower drug prices. Recent studies estimate that pharmacare could save Canadians more than seven billion dollars a year of the twenty-two billion dollars we spend annually on prescription drugs. These savings would result from the fact that multinational companies would be forced to bargain with a single national agency in order to get their drugs on the insurance-covered national drug formulary, notes Dr. Joel Lexchin, professor emeritus at York University's School of Health Policy and Management.[7]

Lexchin also believes that, if Connaught had remained a public enterprise, it could have gone on to play a useful role in today's pharmaceutical market. He notes that one of the serious problems in recent years has been the shortage, from time to time, of a generic substitute for a brand-name drug. Such shortages occur, he says, because generic manufacturers may decide, for business reasons, not to produce a particular generic, leaving the public obliged to pay the much higher cost of a brand-name drug. If Connaught were still operating as a public entity, it might have branched out and stepped into this role, producing key generic drugs when needed.

Instead, Canadians — without a national pharmacare program or a publicly owned pharmaceutical company — have little protection against the powerful and notoriously greedy multinational drug industry.

While it's impossible to know exactly what contribution a publicly owned Connaught could have made in recent decades, it's a question worth briefly pondering.

Let's consider the story of a wonder drug called Glybera, developed by a team of medical researchers at the University of British Columbia. The UBC team spent almost two decades developing Glybera before the drug was eventually produced and marketed by an Italian pharmaceutical company, along with a Dutch biotech firm. Glybera turned out to be remarkably effective, capable in a single dose of treating a rare, deadly genetic disorder known as lipoprotein lipase deficiency, which happens to be particularly prevalent among people living in the area around Saguenay, Quebec. Yet, in April 2017, for purely business reasons, Glybera was withdrawn from the market and is no longer available anywhere in the world.

The Glybera saga helps illustrate much of what is terribly wrong with today's pharmaceutical industry, which is dominated by multinational corporations that make decisions with life-and-death consequences for reasons that are related exclusively to their corporate profitability.

Glybera was marketed at the astronomical price of one million dollars for a single dose, clearly putting it well beyond the reach of just about every potential customer and discouraging insurance companies and government agencies from covering the cost. But why was Glybera so expensive? Was it derived from some incredibly rare plant or was it particularly costly to develop or produce? No. Rather, the extraordinary price was due purely to business considerations — financial calculations made by the companies that marketed it, as CBC-TV correspondent Kelly Crowe revealed in extensive reporting about the drug. An executive from the Dutch biotech firm involved explained to Crowe that the company compared Glybera to other drugs on the market that are used to treat rare disorders and concluded the one-million-dollar price tag was reasonable. "It's not a crazy price," the biotech executive said, adding that the treatment cost would end up lower than the cost of providing ongoing alternative drug therapies that add up to three hundred thousand dollars per patient per year.[8]

But hold it right there. Why are these purely business considerations the only ones being factored in, when we're dealing with a life-saving drug? The answer, of course, is that business considerations are the only ones that matter in the corporate world. But why is this decision left exclusively to the corporate world, when the drug was originally developed at the expense of Canadian taxpayers? The eighteen years of research done by the UBC team in developing Glybera was paid for by Canadians, through the Canadian Institutes of Health Research, a government agency that funds basic medical research in Canada.

In fact, it is usually public money that funds the development of a new drug, even in the United States. U.S. economist Mariana Mazzucato points out that most important new drugs — as opposed to copycat variations of existing drugs — are developed in labs funded by the U.S. government. "While private pharmaceutical companies justify their exorbitantly high prices by saying they need to cover their R & D costs," Mazzucato writes in *The Entrepreneurial State*, "in fact most of the really 'innovative' new drugs, i.e. new molecular entities with priority rating, come from publicly funded laboratories."[9]

The same is true in Canada, where roughly one billion dollars of Canadian public money is spent each year on basic medical research. Yet, Canadians have no ownership of the products that result. Instead, the university researchers are permitted to take out patents on the products they develop (with our money), and then sell or license those products to corporations that market them, often at great profit. These corporations, as we've seen in the case of Glybera, can simply decide to stop selling a drug, even if it serves a valid and important medical purpose. Despite our public investment that initiated the whole process, we have no say in the matter.

Even in this crazy system, where no recognition is given to the public's financial contribution, a publicly owned Connaught Labs might well have made a difference. "A version of Connaught Labs might have enabled Glybera to be produced and sold at a lower price," says Lexchin, the York University health policy expert. "The decision to price it at one million dollars was clearly a business decision. As a publicly owned company, Connaught would likely have made a very different pricing decision." Certainly, based on its history, Connaught would have taken the public interest into account, thereby giving major consideration to patients unable to afford treatment for a deadly genetic disorder — just as Dr. FitzGerald did when he established Connaught in order to make unaffordable diphtheria treatments available to needy patients.

Furthermore, the UBC team that developed Glybera would have almost certainly been willing to deal with Connaught; they had no financial stake in the drug. "The reason for doing this is to have some impact on patients," said Dr. Michael Hayden, one of the UBC researchers.

There is every reason to believe, then, that if there had still been a publicly owned Connaught, this saga would have had a very different ending. Connaught would have undoubtedly put considerable effort into ensuring that Glybera — "a genuine made-in-Canada medical breakthrough"[10] — was available for those who needed it, many of whom are Canadians.

Lexchin goes a step further, insisting that any medical product developed with Canadian taxpayer funding, such as Glybera, should be publicly owned, so that the government would have some say in who markets it and how. It's such a simple idea, and it makes so much sense. But it's wildly out of sync with the corporate-dominated world we live in. And, sadly, the chances of this changing any time soon seem slim.

❧

In 1985, the Conservative government of Brian Mulroney completed the privatization of Connaught, selling off the remaining shares held by the Canada Development Corporation. Brian King, Connaught chairman and president at the time, noted that there was little interest from the Canadian investment community. "If they can't dig it out of the ground, pump it out of the ground, chop it down, or throw up a building, they are not interested."

Since then, Connaught has had several different owners but has ended up in the hands of Sanofi, a giant French multinational pharmaceutical company, headquartered in Paris, which operates in one hundred countries. The old Connaught horse farm — now within the confines of the expanded city of Toronto — remains the site of a sprawling biotech operation run by Sanofi Pasteur, the vaccines division of Sanofi. This Toronto operation is part of Sanofi Pasteur's global empire, which produces a billion vaccine doses a year, making possible the vaccination of more than five hundred million people around the world.

So, a happy ending to the story?

Connaught seems to have ended up in a useful corner of the biotech health industry, with a viable Toronto operation employing some nineteen hundred people, about half of whom have scientific training. Sanofi Pasteur is currently building a five-hundred-million-dollar new vaccine facility as part of its Toronto operation, with seventy million dollars in support from the federal and provincial governments.

Even so, was this the best option, from a public-interest point of view? Ottawa's hope of maintaining Connaught as a Canadian-controlled company clearly failed — perhaps because, as Brian King explains, the Canadian investment community has always been reluctant to invest in anything beyond resource extraction, a sad commentary on Canadian business. Still, was it necessary to turn Connaught into a private company? Another option would have been for Ottawa to purchase it from U of T and continue to operate it as a Crown corporation. As noted above, a publicly owned Connaught could have, among other things, produced some needed generic drugs as well as abandoned drugs like Glybera, thereby counteracting some of the serious problems that result from the dominance of the multinational pharmaceutical industry.

Furthermore, as FitzGerald had promised, Connaught had always been self-sustaining, even profitable. Undoubtedly, significant investments would have been needed to keep its facilities up-to-date. But there's no reason to believe that Connaught would have become a burden to taxpayers. As a Crown corporation, it could have continued its tradition of operating in the public interest and investing its profits back into its own medical research.

Certainly, Connaught had established an impressive record on the research front. "Unlike its commercial counterparts in the Canadian pharmaceutical business, Connaught Medical Research Laboratories devoted an unusually large percentage of its expenditures to research and development (R & D)," notes Bator. In 1968, with sales of $8.8 million, it was investing $2.1 million of that — 24 percent — in R & D, far more than the private drug companies were investing. In fact, although Connaught had only 2.5 percent of all pharmaceutical sales in Canada, it was carrying out roughly 20 percent of the R & D performed by the entire industry in Canada, which was made up mostly of foreign-owned multinationals. Connaught was clearly more than carrying its weight on the R & D front. (The multinationals, with head offices in the United States or Europe, largely did their research back in their home countries.)[11]

Indeed, despite its small size, Connaught made a very significant contribution over the years to global medical research. It played a role that was, in many ways, unique — certainly very different than the role played by pharmaceutical giants with far greater resources. They typically spend their research dollars on clinical trials, after the basic research has been performed at public expense in hospital or university laboratories.

Connaught, on the other hand, was engaged in basic research, sometimes funded by government and sometimes funded out of its own profits. It carried out a wide range of research projects based on what its scientists considered important, not what promised to be lucrative. It had no sales agents out flogging its products. Its research contributed to a number of key medical breakthroughs of the twentieth century: insulin, the Salk polio vaccine, penicillin, heparin, and many others. Often, basic research carried out by Connaught scientists was coordinated and matched up with basic research being carried out by scientists elsewhere, and the combination led to an important medical advance, as in the case of the polio vaccine.

"Connaught was the engine of innovation," Rutty observed in an interview. "Especially when it was closely connected to the School of Hygiene and the university, it was a unique, fluid environment with the ability to meld research and production, in a way that was public-service oriented."[12]

Rutty also contends that the dynamic combination of Connaught and the School of Hygiene helped lay the groundwork for Canada's support for public solutions to health care, putting us on a very different path than our southern neighbour. In the United States, for instance, polio research and treatment had been funded largely by the voluntary sector, notably the March of Dimes campaigns. In Canada, Connaught and the School of Hygiene had managed early on to encourage a publicly funded approach to dealing with polio, as well as tuberculosis, venereal disease, and cancer, which were all treated through programs run by provincial governments. This common approach among the provinces is perhaps not surprising, since virtually all provincial deputy ministers of health had been trained at the School of Hygiene, notes Rutty. "They were all part of the same culture," he adds.

So, thanks to Connaught and the School of Hygiene, that public-spirited culture pervaded the higher levels of governments across the country.

When Connaught was sold to the Canada Development Corporation in 1972 and then fully privatized in 1989, there were dire warnings that Canada would lose impressive laboratories and high-level researchers. Rutty says that, while he regrets that Connaught is no longer in public hands, the dire predictions have not come true. He points out that Sanofi Pasteur is continuing Connaught's legacy as a leading global producer of vaccines. The company's recent major investment in its Toronto location — still officially known as the Connaught Campus — shows that it has kept the Connaught tradition alive, in reality and in spirit.

True. But the head office of Sanofi Pasteur is located in Lyons, France, and much of its ongoing research is now carried out there and in other countries where it operates. Sadly, Connaught, in its incarnation as the Toronto branch of Sanofi Pasteur, is no longer the "engine of innovation" or the hub of scientific energy that for decades enabled it to make crucial contributions to global public health initiatives and disease eradication.

To think that we had a homegrown, uniquely Canadian enterprise, one that dazzled and triumphed on one of the world's most important stages, developing life-saving treatments for the benefit of humanity — in bold contrast to the rapacious pharmaceutical industry — and our political leaders sold it!

Unbelievable.

~ *Six* ~

Driving Out the Loan Sharks:
The Case for Public Banking

When Canada Post announced in December 2013 that it would be ending door-to-door mail delivery in urban areas across the country, it seemed like this was just one more service Canadians would have to learn to live without. Although mail delivery had existed since before Confederation, Canada Post explained that it had no choice but to end home delivery for the remaining one-third of Canadians still receiving it, in order to deal with the Crown corporation's anticipated financial problems.

What the post office did not say in its announcement was that this cutback was completely unnecessary. There was another solution to its future financial problems — a solution that had been favoured by senior executives running Canada Post. In fact, Canada Post's management had been studying this other option with considerable interest for several years. Instead of cutting back mail service to Canadians, the option involved creating a significant new service for Canadians: banking, through the post office.

The Canada Post executives had put together extensive files on postal banking, documenting that it was highly successful in a number of

European countries. The files also showed that online banks in Canada, like ING and Canadian Tire Bank, were averaging healthy profits of 20 percent a year. One report in the files, *Banking: A Proven Diversification Strategy*, concluded that there was no obvious risk in undertaking postal banking and that the "size of the prize" was substantial.

The Canada Post executives had been sufficiently interested in the idea that they had drafted a "vision for Canada Post financial services." And they had ordered polling and focus groups, which showed considerable public interest in having postal outlets across the country offer retail banking services. All this led Canada Post senior officials to conclude that the idea would be a win-win strategy — earning significant profits for the post office while offering a popular new service for consumers.

But their enthusiasm apparently ran into a wall of resistance from Stephen Harper's Conservative government. This wasn't surprising; for years, right-wing business interests, led by the Fraser Institute, had pushed for the privatization of the post office, dismissively labelling it a "monopoly protected by government" — ignoring the fact that it is *our* monopoly and therefore can be used to serve our interests.

The die-hard market conservatives in Harper's Cabinet had no interest in an innovation that would make a Crown corporation stronger and better able to serve the public. Rejecting the intriguing possibility of postal banking, the Harper team instead instructed Canada Post to deal with its anticipated financial problems by cutting door-to-door mail delivery and dramatically increasing the cost of stamps. So, in place of a win-win, Harper came up with a lose-lose: Canadians would get less service from the post office and would pay more for it. Never mind that this was a worse deal for Canadians; it was in keeping with the fierce ideological commitment — of those in the Harper government and other right wingers — to diminish and dismantle Canada's public services.

The Harper team no doubt figured it could get away with imposing this unappealing lose-lose solution since Canadians had become resigned to government cutbacks. Even so, it clearly wanted to prevent the public from knowing that there'd been another option and that the other option had been keenly supported by senior officials at Canada Post. All of this came to light as a result of an Access to Information request filed by *Blacklock's Reporter*, an Ottawa news service that closely covers government administration issues. *Blacklock's* obtained Canada Post's confidential file of 811 pages on postal banking, but only after 701 of those pages had been censored by the Harper government.[1]

Clearly, the last thing Harper wanted was a public debate about the merits of postal banking. Such a debate would have inevitably stirred interest in the prospect of what amounted to a public bank. It also would have drawn attention to problems with Canada's private banking sector, which happens to be one of the most concentrated, least competitive banking sectors in the world, with some of the highest banking fees. Then there are the problems faced by countless Canadians who are underserved by our banking sector, either because they live in rural or remote communities where banks have closed their branches, or because their incomes are low and they don't qualify for a bank account, leaving them easy prey for payday loan operators who typically charge triple-digit interest rates.

For these underserved people — and it's not an exaggeration to say they number in the hundreds of thousands, if not the millions — postal banking could have been a godsend, making basic financial services available at affordable rates through postal outlets across the country. For that matter, public banking would have likely also appealed to many ordinary city dwellers, who have access to Canada's Big Six banks but are annoyed by their greed and arrogance. Indeed, postal banking might well have injected something into the Canadian banking industry that our major banks would definitely prefer to avoid: *competition*.

And, given their immense wealth and power, straddling the very heart of the Canadian establishment, the big banks have tended to get what they want and to eliminate what they don't want. Indeed, although it's a little-known story, Canada has a long history of creating public banks, directly operated by government or by the post office, and then shutting them down in the face of pressure from the private banks.

Private banking interests have long been closely connected to political power in Canada. In theory, Parliament is tasked with overseeing the banking industry, which involves granting charters to banks and then regulating them in the public interest. In reality, however, there has been more coziness than oversight. As financial historian R.T. Naylor observes, "The political power of the larger banks and of the Bankers' Association can hardly be exaggerated."[2]

The Big Six banks that dominate our economy today all have deep roots dating back to Confederation or earlier. The oldest of them, the Bank of Montreal, was established back in 1817, when it operated a single branch out of a rented house. The early banks were affiliated with the commercial interests of the day, having been established largely to provide short-term loans enabling these commercial interests to move staple products, such as fur, grain, and wood, to market. The Bank of Montreal, for instance, had been set up by fur traders, the Bank of New Brunswick (later merged with the Bank of Nova Scotia) by timber merchants, the Bank of Toronto by grain dealers, and the Dominion Bank by railway entrepreneurs. The National Bank was created in 1859 by a group of francophone businessmen who felt the need for a bank under francophone control.

By obtaining a bank charter, commercial interests could not only finance the transport of their products but also become very rich. They were essentially able to create money, since they had the power to make loans and collect interest on more money than they took in as deposits. Gustavus Myers, a chronicler of American and Canadian wealth in the nineteenth century, notes that a set of commercial interests could "wheedle or bribe a certain entity called a legislature to grant them a certain bit of paper styled a charter, and lo! they were instantly transformed into money manufacturers."[3] By the 1880s, there were some three dozen banks operating under charters granted by the Canadian government, and many of the men who owned the banks were growing very rich.

In the early decades after Confederation, bank directors and bank presidents frequently sat in Parliament and in the Senate. According to a surprisingly honest contemporary account written by George Hague, general manager of the Bank of Toronto in the early 1870s, key decisions about the industry and the new country's financial direction were made by what amounted to "a joint committee of Parliament and banks." Hague notes that the banks were actively involved in writing the 1871 Bank Act, and describes in detail how closely involved bankers were in writing all parts of that legislation: "Representatives of the [chartered banks] ... sat in conference day by day discussing the clauses of the proposed act one by one."[4]

These chartered banks, closely connected to successful commercial interests, had little inclination to accept deposits from working-class people, presumably because the amounts involved would be small and considered inconsequential. A Halifax banker testifying before a royal commission in 1889 was asked, "Do you receive deposits from the working classes?" He curtly replied, "No, I don't care to do that sort of business."[5]

This left an opening, and the government stepped in. As early as the 1820s, just shortly after the Bank of Montreal started operating out of that rented house, the British colonial authorities established government-run banks that were specifically aimed at collecting deposits from the working class. These "savings banks" were modelled on government-run savings banks in Britain, where a strong social reform movement had pushed for them as a way to counteract the extreme poverty and suffering produced by the Industrial Revolution. Reformers on both sides of the Atlantic saw the savings banks as a way for workers to improve their financial situation, and to reduce the need for public and private charity. There was a fair bit of moralizing among the reformers about how savings banks could encourage "working-class thrift," which would help mould labourers into responsible members of society. By enabling workers to reap the benefits of their labour through savings, it was argued, the banks would discourage them from spending their meagre earnings on wayward activities, in bars and brothels.[6]

An 1826 article in the *Novascotian*, an influential Halifax newspaper, reveals how reformers saw savings banks as a tool for keeping workers productive and sober. The article described the case of an industrious Irishman who worked on Halifax's wharves and had managed, through "parsimoniously saving," to accumulate twenty-five British pounds (about four thousand Canadian dollars today). The worker entrusted this nest egg to a Halifax merchant for safekeeping, a fairly common practice at the time, given the absence of banking services for working people. But the merchant absconded with the money to the United States — also a fairly common practice. Devastated by the loss of his savings, the distraught worker became a drunkard, according to the article, "and is now one of the most degraded and worthless of our labourers."

Such a dismal fate could be averted, according to the article, with a government-run savings bank, which would offer workers security and an opportunity to earn interest on their savings. It pointed out that, at 4 percent interest, a worker who set aside two shillings a week — a significant amount of his income — would be able to save a sum of 157 pounds (about twenty-five thousand dollars today) in twenty years. This, along with regular church attendance, according to the article, would help create a prudent, sensible working class. In a subsequent essay in the *Novascotian* the following week, another author made the point that savings banks would allow workers to become free of government support, thereby "making them independent and moral beings, in place of the mean pitiful applicants for public bounty."

Along with reformers, members of the financial and political elite became interested in setting up government savings banks. They wanted government to be able to accumulate capital that could be used to fund infrastructure development. In Halifax, for instance, Charles Fairbanks, a local politician keen on getting funds to build the Shubenacadie Canal, linking Halifax and the Bay of Fundy, put forward a bill in 1826 proposing the establishment of a government savings bank.

The colonial authorities in Nova Scotia followed through in 1832 and opened the Halifax Savings Bank. The official announcement stated that this public bank would accept deposits from "Tradesmen, Mechanics, Servants, Labourers, and others of the Labouring Classes, Seafaring Men, Non-Commissioned Officers, and Privates in the

Army, and Charitable Societies." The announcement clarified that the bank would be open only on Mondays and that withdrawals would require a week's notice.

The Halifax Savings Bank proved very popular. By 1844, it had attracted 825 depositors, principally domestic servants, mechanics, and labourers, but also fishermen, truckmen, widows, minors, and mantua makers (who made women's clothing), as well as two customers identified only as "Indians." The bank could have been even more popular, but it was under instruction to turn away depositors who didn't belong to the working class. "I have refused to receive the deposits from persons of middling classes, such as Clerks in offices and stores," explained general manager Edward Duckett, "and a great number of others who did not come under the restrictions as laid down in printed rules." Just why the bank was restricted from accepting deposits from outside the working class was not stated, but it is likely that local bankers insisted upon it as a way to ensure they didn't lose affluent customers.

In 1868, only months after Confederation, the new Canadian government created the Post Office Savings Bank as one of its first major orders of business. Within a year, the post office bank had opened up 213 offices, mostly in Ontario and Quebec. Previously, nine separate government-run savings banks had been established in New Brunswick and six in Canada East and West. In the following two decades, there was considerable further growth in these publicly owned savings banks, operated directly by the federal government or through the post office. Finance Minister John Rose, known to be Prime Minister John A. Macdonald's closest friend, insisted in Parliament that the Conservative government maintain the savings banks as part of its moral obligation to promote and encourage working-class thrift.

By 1885, the Post Office Savings Bank was flourishing, particularly in Ontario, where it boasted 355 branches holding accounts worth more than fifteen million dollars on behalf of seventy-three thousand depositors. And there were forty-eight outlets of the Dominion Government Savings Bank operating across the country, mostly in the Maritimes. Among them was the very successful Halifax Savings Bank, which continued to prosper and was apparently no longer restricting its business to the working class. According to one Halifax business publication of the time, the savings bank was "daily thronged with depositors of all classes, from the poor labourer and artisan to the highest classes of the city."[7]

While the Conservatives highlighted their commitment to promoting working-class thrift, it is clear that the Macdonald government was also interested in its savings banks as a source of capital for railway construction in the late nineteenth century. The railways were mostly privately owned, but they were heavily subsidized by government, and a significant part of that government money came from public savings banks. As historian Dan Bunbury notes: "The readily accessible pool of capital held in the savings banks was essential to the completion of the Canadian Pacific Railway. Indeed, the savings banks' role in the construction of the CPR has been largely overlooked in the economic history of Canada."[8]

The success of the government savings banks also meant they ended up in competition with the private chartered banks. There had always been some tension between the public and private banks, but that tension started boiling over in the 1880s as a result of the lingering economic depression that followed the financial panic of 1873. Competition had intensified among the chartered banks, which numbered close to four dozen, and their profit margins were falling. Some of the larger chartered banks now envisioned an ambitious future for themselves as nationwide banks, and they were therefore determined to expand beyond their traditional role dealing exclusively with commercial interests and the wealthy. Suddenly, they were eagerly eyeing the savings of small depositors across the country, which they had previously shunned. The public banks were holding some thirty million dollars in small deposits, and the chartered banks now actively sought to poach some of this lucrative business.

One difficulty the private banks faced in attracting small depositors was the more attractive interest rates offered by the public banks. The private banks certainly didn't want to get into a costly bidding war where they'd have to raise their rates in order to woo customers from the public banks. Instead, they went on the offensive, pressuring the government to lower its interest rates. The chartered banks complained that the government savings banks were improperly interfering in the marketplace and were offering their depositors overly generous interest on their accounts.

To this end, Thomas Fyshe, general manager of the Bank of Nova Scotia, already one of the leading chartered banks, wrote a feisty article in the *Montreal Herald* in 1886 entitled "Government Savings Banks and the Mischief They Are Working in the Lower Provinces." Fyshe insisted that capital was being drained from the chartered banks, where it belonged, into the government savings banks. Elaborating in a memo to the finance minister, Fyshe claimed that the public banks enjoyed an unfair advantage with potential customers — not just because of their higher interest rates, but also because of the greater security they offered depositors, due to the government backing that the public banks enjoyed. Pointing to the demise of seventeen private chartered banks in the Maritimes, he complained that it was impossible for the private banks to compete because each "additional [private] bank failure ... hastens the flow of deposit to the government coffers and out of the channels of productive industry."[9]

Among themselves, the chartered banks had mostly eliminated the pesky problem of competition by entering into an "informal cartel arrangement" under which they maintained an agreed-upon interest rate, according to Naylor, the historian. This cartel arrangement was facilitated by the establishment of the Canadian Bankers' Association (CBA) in 1891, which became a formidable, highly centralized organization representing the large private banks.[10]

Having eliminated competition among themselves, the chartered banks turned their attention to eliminating the competition they faced from the public banks. It certainly helped that the chartered banks enjoyed close ties to the highest levels of government. And their influence was further strengthened by the coordinated lobbying efforts of the CBA, which proved to be extremely effective.

Indeed, the CBA, which remains a powerful lobby today, exerted an astonishing degree of influence over government and the banking sector right from its establishment. Byron Walker, president of the Canadian Bank of Commerce and head of the CBA, crowed about how the CBA's chief lobbyist, Zebulon A. Lash, managed to get his way in Ottawa. Commenting to CBA members at an 1895 meeting, Walker observed that "some private bills containing clauses objectionable to the banks were introduced into the Dominion Parliament, and the attention of the proper authorities being called by Mr. Lash to these features they were removed."[11]

The CBA also came to enjoy the extraordinary power of determining who should have the privilege of operating a bank, notes Naylor. Applicants for bank charters had to have their fitness approved by the CBA, thereby enabling the banking lobby to block applicants it opposed — a power it was happy to exercise in order to keep out potential competitors.[12] So influential did the CBA become that, in 1913, Walker unabashedly boasted that every significant change in banking legislation since the passage of the 1871 Bank Act had been instigated by the bankers themselves.

Given their exceptional power and influence, the private chartered banks and the CBA were in a strong position when they decided they wanted to encroach on the small-deposit business of the public banks. Both directly to the finance minister and through the business press, the private banks complained that the 4 percent interest rate offered by the public banks amounted to unfair competition, making their own 3.5 percent rate unattractive to potential customers. They also objected to the three-thousand-dollar annual ceiling on deposits at public banks, arguing that this was too high a ceiling for a bank that was supposedly aimed at encouraging thrift among the working class. They insisted that the public banks were also attracting more affluent customers, who were the rightful clientele of the private banks.

In June 1886, the finance department responded to the private banks' concerns by offering to lower the deposit ceiling at public banks to one thousand dollars a year. But the private banks weren't satisfied. They urged instead that the deposit ceiling at the post office bank be lowered to three hundred dollars a year, with an interest rate of 3 percent, and that the other government-run banks be shut down entirely. Although the government-run banks were not shut down, Ottawa obligingly reduced their interest rates to 3 percent.[13]

However, as noted, the public banks had proven popular not just because of their higher rates, but also because of their greater stability and security. In the late nineteenth century, the private banking industry in Canada was highly unstable and was rocked by charges of corruption and criminality. It included rogue figures like Samuel Zimmerman, who founded his own bank to finance railway swindles, as well as the banker Francis Hincks, who became finance minister and was implicated in the Pacific Scandal that led to the fall of John A. Macdonald's government in 1873. Between Confederation and the outbreak of the First World War, Canadian chartered banks failed at a rate of 36 percent — even higher than the U.S. rate of 22 percent at the time. And many of these Canadian bank failures resulted in criminal charges against bank officers or employees. The greater stability of Canada's public banks was a key factor in their popularity, and it enabled them to maintain their customer base even as the private banks cajoled Ottawa into cutting their interest rates.

After two such interest rate reductions, the public banks had lowered their rate to 3 percent by 1898, but the private banks wanted it lower still. They had reduced their own interest rate on deposits to 2.5 percent, and they pushed Wilfrid Laurier's Liberal government to cut the rate offered by government-run banks to the same level. Once again, Ottawa obliged, bowing to the pressure from the muscular chartered banks. Finance Minister William S. Fielding made a feeble attempt to justify this capitulation, maintaining in Parliament that the working class no longer needed special government outlets for their savings, even though they seemed to still want them. The Conservative opposition protested that the move would push the country's small savers toward unstable private banks — which it did.

Public banking reached a high-water mark in 1901, with small deposits totalling fifty-six million dollars. After that, the private banks steadily gained ground, winning over customers from the public banks. Among the chartered banks themselves, there was a consolidation of power, with stronger banks buying up or pushing out weaker ones. While there were thirty-six chartered banks in 1901, that number fell to just eight by the First World War, with five of those emerging after the war as truly national banks. Those five had branches across the country, but financial power was increasingly concentrated in Montreal and, to a lesser extent, Toronto. The once-influential private chartered banks in the Maritimes had been mostly wiped out, with capital drifting out of the region.

As the five national banks extended their dominance, the public banks were increasingly pushed to the margins. With the completion of the CPR, Ottawa was less concerned about having a reliable source of capital to draw on for costly railway financing, and evidently had lost interest in encouraging working-class thrift. In 1929 Ottawa abolished its government savings banks, and in 1968 the remaining banking operations of the post office were finally shut down. Public banking — a financial vehicle that had been popular with ordinary Canadians for decades while providing a pool of capital for government infrastructure developments — had effectively been killed, eliminated by an immensely powerful private banking sector that didn't like the competition.

Amazingly, public banking stayed alive — and remains alive today — in a corner of the country where it would be least expected.

By the early 1930s, the Alberta economy was struggling through the depths of the Great Depression. After the buoyant years of the 1920s, the '30s brought financial hardship and ruin to farmers in the province, as the price of wheat fell below the price of seed. In addition to the crash in world grain prices, there was a brutal decade of drought and dust storms. In his book *Men Against the Desert*, James H. Gray describes the prairie drought of the '30s as "the longest siege of atrocious weather since, in all probability, the times of Joseph in Egypt." With the double whammy of collapsing grain prices and terrible weather, farmers faced a third foe: the eastern banks.

Farmers who had borrowed from the banks in the booming 1920s found themselves unable to keep up with the interest payments. With grain prices plummeting, farming income in the Prairies dropped from

$363 million in 1928 to a negative $10.7 million in 1931. Section 88 of the federal Bank Act allowed banks to seize cattle or tractors in lieu of payments. But such items had little market value, since no one had money to buy them. As banks foreclosed on farm mortgages, many farmers lost everything and were forced off their land, leaving a deep bitterness toward the big, faraway banks with their godlike powers.

The Royal Bank, which had already established itself as Canada's largest bank by the 1930s, became a favourite target. The feeling that the eastern power elite was lined up against the West was reinforced with the 1930 election of Prime Minister R.B. Bennett, who was a former Royal Bank director and solicitor and remained a prominent bank shareholder.

Even the Royal Bank's official history, *Quick to the Frontier*, acknowledges how unpopular the bank became in the West, to the point that Prairie bank managers were instructed to scrape the gold letters advertising the size of the bank's assets off their branch windows. Author Duncan McDowall recounts how the Royal Bank's branch in the once-booming central Alberta community of Lavoy largely ceased to function. Even with its grain elevator, Lavoy had turned into a financial ghost town. "The real banking day began when the branch closed," writes McDowall. That's when the bank manager and his assistant headed out on the back roads to visit desperate, impoverished farm families, who often barely spoke English but clearly understood the bankers were there to collect money — money they didn't have.[14]

All this created fertile soil, if not for grain, at least for politics. Radio airwaves on the Prairies were full of denunciations of the banks and the eastern "big shots." In 1933 several Regina parliamentarians, led by J.S. Woodsworth, established the Co-operative Commonwealth Federation — forerunner of today's NDP — which produced a manifesto calling for the nationalization of Canada's banks. A different, but equally radical, anti-bank message took hold in Alberta. William Aberhart, a golden-voiced radio evangelist, advocated salvation through a mixture of religion and "social credit" economics that would pump money into the stricken economy. Unable to interest the provincial political parties in his ideas, Aberhart entered Social Credit candidates in the 1935 Alberta election and, to everyone's surprise including his own, won a landslide victory.

The politically inexperienced Aberhart struggled as premier. He followed through on campaign promises to issue Albertans "prosperity certificates," but the vouchers weren't even accepted at provincially owned beer stores. The Social Credit government also passed the Accurate News and Information Act, which gave Cabinet the power to preview press articles and demand space to refute articles it didn't like. Also, under pressure from Social Credit members of the legislative assembly, Aberhart introduced laws to heavily tax and regulate private banks, effectively bringing them under the control of the provincial government. The bank bills played well with many angry Albertans, but the measures brought the province into a power struggle with Ottawa.

The Supreme Court of Canada ended up resolving the skirmish, striking down the bank bills on the grounds that only the federal government had the power to legislate banking. Aberhart's aspiration to create a provincial zone free of domination by the eastern banks was further thwarted when Ottawa refused to grant the province a licence to operate its own bank.

Undeterred, the Social Credit government effectively established its own bank without a licence from Ottawa. Creating a special program, the province opened what amounted to bank branches, but deemed them "branches of the Provincial Treasury." The program's popularity was enhanced by a system of bonuses paid to depositors. And, in an attempt to increase its popularity by serving remote communities abandoned by the private banks, the program permitted banking facilities to be set up in gas stations, grocery stores, and insurance agencies. Albertans approved of their government's deft defiance of Ottawa's control over banking. Within a few years of operation, the Alberta Treasury Branches (ATB) boasted thirty-four thousand accounts and $4.9 million in deposits.

The Aberhart government's solutions largely failed; the prosperity certificates and the press freedom restrictions were struck down by the Supreme Court of Canada, along with the attempt to control private banks. But its public bank survived.

In fact, the ATB has prospered. Despite the hostility to public ownership among many in the province's economic and political elite, the ATB today has assets of fifty billion dollars and 750,000 customers. It operates like a chartered bank but remains publicly owned by the people of Alberta. Its vast network of rural outlets and its 100 percent government guarantee on deposits has made it extremely popular, protecting it from the zeal of would-be privatizers. While public banking is common around the globe, particularly in developing countries, there are only two public banks in North America — the Bank of North Dakota, founded in 1919, and the ATB. (Ontario also had a public bank, the Province of Ontario Savings Office, established in 1922, but it was privatized by the Conservative provincial government in 2003.)

Bob Ascah and Mark Anielski, two Alberta-based public policy researchers, note that public banks weathered the 2008 financial crisis better than private banks. "Public banks have an inherent competitive advantage over private banks in that they can operate with a no-profit motive," they write in *Alberta's Public Bank*, a report they prepared for the Parkland Institute at the University of Alberta.[15] (Ascah formerly worked for the ATB as a strategic planner.)

The authors argue that, in addition to providing basic financial services to Albertans, the ATB can perform key functions advancing the public interest. They note, for instance, that a public bank typically has the advantage of being able to borrow at lower rates, which means that it can make long-term public investments at lower cost. And, like private banks, a public bank can create money by loaning out more than it collects in deposits. As Ascah and Anielski point out, "The majority (97 per cent) of our modern money supply is created when private banks issue loans."[16] Instead of this money-creating feature being used just to enrich shareholders of chartered banks, there's no reason it can't also be used to benefit the people of Alberta.

The ATB has been able to perform some highly useful public functions, such as providing low-cost personal and agriculture loans, according to Ascah and Anielski. But, they argue, it could expand its services to include providing mortgages at-cost for low-income households. It could also play a strategic role in helping the province transition to a greener energy future by providing low-cost loans for renewable energy and energy efficiency programs.

"We believe money and its creation should be seen as a form of a public utility," they write, "whereby the creation of money through credit benefits the greatest number of people at the least possible cost to society."[17]

Instead, our society delegates that money-creation role — with its enormously lucrative returns — exclusively to private banks, where it benefits a tiny number of people at considerable cost to the rest of us.

———— ∞ ————

It is hard to think of a corporate sector that wields more power or reaps more wealth in Canada than the private banking industry. And while the Big Six national banks — RBC, Scotiabank, BMO, TD, CIBC, and National — are lauded in business and political circles for their stability, there is surprisingly little political debate or inquiry into how well they are serving the interests of Canadians. Certainly, their charters grant them the right to effectively create money by lending out far more than they collect in deposits and then charging interest on those loans. In addition, they are protected by legislation and foreign-ownership restrictions that give them a privileged position at the top of the Canadian economy.

These rules, backed up by the effective lobbying of the CBA, have allowed the Big Six to become among the world's most profitable banks. In 2018, they accumulated staggering profits of forty-five billion dollars, more than double the profits they enjoyed in 2010, according to the Ottawa-based group Democracy Watch. Finance Canada acknowledges the Big Six's exceptional reach over the Canadian financial scene and their remarkable profitability: "The large banks have proven profitable through strong and weak economic periods. While there are several ways to measure this profitability, since the financial crisis, the large banks' return on equity exceeds their international peers, smaller Canadian banks and the corporate sector overall." Duff Conacher, a law professor and co-founder of Democracy Watch, argues that the big banks have achieved at least some of this extraordinary profitability in recent years by firing thousands of their employees, cutting bank services dramatically, and hiking banking fees.[18]

Certainly banking fees seem to have risen needlessly. The average monthly fee on chequing accounts rose by 13.6 percent between 2005 and 2013. It's not unusual now for Canadians to pay $360 a year for basic banking services, notes Ottawa-based researcher and postal banking advocate John Anderson.[19] The high cost of banking fees is striking, considering that up until a few decades ago, the banks usually didn't charge fees for personal banking. They were satisfied to get personal deposits, which allowed them to increase their pool of lending funds. But that changed, according to Carleton University business professor Ian Lee, when the banks went digital, since they faced enormous costs for hardware, software, and security. Really? Lee's explanation, in a CBC interview in 2016, strains credulity.[20] Going digital has generally enabled businesses to become more profitable — and banks are certainly no exception, as noted above. So why the need to add fees for personal banking? One possibility is that, while the banks certainly didn't need to do so to remain profitable, their dominant market position allows them to do so.

Lee also defended banking fees on the grounds that the big banks face more competition these days from smaller institutions, like credit unions, and that increased competition shrinks profit margins. Again, this explanation strains credulity. Far from facing increased competition, the big banks have actually taken over more of the Canadian banking market in the past decade, so that they almost completely dominate it. As even Finance Canada notes, "The large banks' share of all assets in the banking sub-sector has increased since the financial crisis, and they now represent 93 percent of all banking assets, compared with about 90 per cent in 2007."[21] Nor are their profit margins shrinking. Far from it! As noted above, their profits have more than doubled since 2010. Indeed, three of Canada's Big Six banks — RBC, TD, and Scotiabank — ranked in the top ninety *most profitable companies in the world*, according to *Fortune* magazine in 2016.

Of course, the banks are often defended on the grounds that they've produced financial stability for the Canadian economy and, notably, that they did not collapse like some of the big U.S. banks in the 2008 crisis. This is true, but it was at least partly because of the considerable government support they got at the time, support that is rarely acknowledged by those keen to promote the reputation of our banks as responsible and stable.

As the Canadian Centre for Policy Alternatives (CCPA) has documented, our major banks were effectively bailed out to the tune of about $114 billion.[22] No, that wasn't the same as the seven-hundred-billion-dollar bailout given in cash to U.S. banks from the U.S. Treasury following the 2008 financial crisis. Those funds came direct from the U.S. taxpayer.

The Canadian bailout was different. Here's what happened:

The financial crisis of September 2008 left global credit markets in chaos, creating problems for major Canadian banks, which rely on these markets for roughly one-third of their funding, according to the CBA (yes, the same CBA that lobbied for the banks in the nineteenth century). In a response to the CCPA allegation of a bailout, the CBA notes that in 2008 "due to the crisis of confidence in global credit markets, some funding sources that banks normally relied upon *became unavailable*" (italics added).[23]

The CBA's wording tends to downplay the seriousness of the situation that faced Canadian banks during the 2008 crisis. The truth is, for Canadian banks to suddenly lose access to one-third of their funding amounted to a potential liquidity crisis for them. But that crisis never developed to the point where it threatened the solvency of the banks because the Canadian government stepped in and took measures through the Bank of Canada and the Canada Mortgage and Housing Corporation (CMHC).

In order to improve the balance sheet of the banks, the CMHC purchased sixty-nine billion dollars' worth of mortgages from the banks. The bankers' association acknowledged that this sixty-nine-billion-dollar purchase happened, but insisted that it did not amount to a bailout of the banks because the mortgages were safe investments. Why were they safe? The CBA explained that there were safe because they were insured — by the CMHC!

Daniel Tencer, senior business editor for the *Huffington Post*, comments on the absurdity of the CBA's logic: "If the mortgages default, presumably the CMHC will be fine, because it'll pay out the insurance policies to itself.... [T]his turns the CMHC into a financial snake eating its tail."[24]

The purpose of the CMHC purchase, however, was clear: to provide the Canadian banks with liquidity, therefore keeping them out of the sort of trouble the U.S. banks found themselves in.

In addition to the CMHC actions, the Big Six Canadian banks were protected by government measures taken by the Bank of Canada — and by the U.S. Federal Reserve Bank. Our banks were able to dip into a fund established by the Federal Reserve to help banks stay afloat in a crisis. According to public data released by the Federal Reserve, the Canadian banks drew a total of thirty-four billion dollars from the U.S. fund at the time of the financial crisis. The banks also got forty-one billion dollars in special funds from the Bank of Canada, according to the CCPA, although the Bank of Canada does not release such information.

CCPA senior economist David Macdonald concludes that the Big Six got tens of billions of dollars in government support during the crisis: "The federal government claims it was offering the banks 'liquidity support' but it looks an awful lot like a bailout to me."

Tencer agrees. "That the government called it 'liquidity support' is irrelevant; this wasn't ordinary, day-to-day banking. These were emergency measures ... meant to keep Canada's banks and financial system running in the face of an imminent standstill in global lending. They would only have happened if there was a significant threat to Canada's banks."[25]

Tencer also notes that the measures Ottawa took to protect our banks didn't require parliamentary approval, so there was little public debate about them. This was in sharp contrast to the situation that existed in the United States, where Congress had to approve the seven-hundred-billion-dollar bailout of the banks, prompting outrage from Americans, particularly those who were getting no government support as they lost their homes in the same financial crisis.

The ability of the Canadian government to deliver its support quietly, out of the public spotlight, meant that the bailout of our banks — or whatever you want to call it — went largely unnoticed here. As a result, our banks emerged looking like stand-alone success stories, free-market institutions that didn't have to rely on government for support; it seemed like they weathered the world financial meltdown all on their own. This furthered their image as stable, responsible, and secure. Prime Minister Stephen Harper rarely missed an opportunity to praise them. "We have, I think, the only banks in the Western world where we're not looking at bailouts or anything like that," he said in a CNBC interview in February 2009.

The image of our banks as stalwart and reliable in the tumultuous world of global finance is certainly useful to those who'd like us to turn a blind eye to the uncompetitive nature of our banking industry and the enormous profits the big banks make in the captive Canadian market. It seems almost churlish to complain about banking fees or bank profits when it's the Big Six who, bold and free, apparently stand between us and financial ruin.

⌒◍⌒

Once we get beyond the mythology, it's clear that our major banks are thriving — in part because of the warm cocoon of government support, which is quietly but promptly and generously available in an emergency.

But while government is there for our banks as needed, our banks are increasingly not there for Canadians as needed. In recent years, as the Big Six have turned their focus to overseas expansion and catering to the wealthy, they have closed branches across the country. In many parts of rural Canada today, you're no more likely to see a bank than a buffalo. In 1990, there were 7,964 bank branches in Canada. By 2018, that number had dropped to 6,190 — a loss of almost 1,800 branches. Credit unions, which provide financial services to roughly ten million Canadians, particularly in Quebec, have also shrunk, with their branches declining from 3,603 to 2,831. As a result, there are hundreds of small

165

communities across the country today that have neither a bank nor a credit union, with many lacking even an automated teller machine.

This lack of banking facilities is a particularly difficult situation for anyone trying to operate a small business. John Anderson notes that in some remote areas, small-business operators must travel hundreds of miles to the nearest bank. Of a total of 2,620 communities surveyed across the country, he observes that an astonishing 1,178 — 45 percent — had neither bank nor credit union. (The rate was more than 60 percent in British Columbia and Nova Scotia, more than 80 percent in Newfoundland, and more than 90 percent in Indigenous communities.)[26]

One thing most of these small communities do have, however, is a post office — a remnant of the days when mail was the only form of long-distance communication and the federal government considered post offices essential to knitting the country together. Today, even with cutbacks, Canada Post still operates a network of 6,200 outlets, more than all the bank branches in the country combined. This vast postal network, operating in small towns and remote communities, as well as in major cities, could become the infrastructure for a national public banking system.

In fact, this would not involve that much of a leap, since Canada Post already sells money orders and prepaid credit cards for travel, as well as a form of certified cheque. These financial offerings could be extended so that customers could also open savings and chequing accounts and pay bills at a post office outlet. Eventually, postal outlets could offer mortgages, business and personal loans, investment services, and insurance. After all, the post office had experience offering a range of banking services until 1968, and the legislation for it to do so is, interestingly, still in place. Furthermore, the staff at postal outlets — represented by the Canadian Union of Postal Workers (CUPW) and the Canadian Postmasters and Assistants Association — are strong supporters of postal banking and are keen to be trained to offer a more extensive range of financial services.

In addition to people in remote or rural communities, there is another constituency that has been badly served by the Big Six: the poor and near-poor, including those in urban areas. This low-income crowd is of little interest to Canada's major banks, which are increasingly focused on the business of "wealth management." As a result, many low-income Canadians, particularly those with poor credit ratings or without identification, are unable to qualify for a bank account. Spurned by the banks, they often turn in despair to payday loan companies, like Money Mart or Cash 4 You, which will cash their cheques but charge notoriously high rates of interest.

Provincial governments have tightened the rules somewhat on the industry in the last few years, but payday operators are still able to charge interest rates that, on an annualized basis, are ten times higher than the high rates banks charge on their credit cards. For instance, in Ontario and Alberta a one-hundred-dollar loan from a payday operator carries an interest cost of fifteen dollars for a two-week period, which works out to an annualized interest rate of 391 percent. That's an improvement from the annualized rates of 500 and 600 percent that were permissible only a few years earlier, but it's still a punishing interest rate. Even so, business is booming in the payday industry, which caters to people desperate for cash in order to pay rent, avoid a Hydro shut-off, or cover an essential car repair. And the problem is that one loan can quickly lead to another if the borrower is unable to come up with the money to cover the first loan. The bill can quickly skyrocket, leaving the borrower paying hundreds — if not thousands — of dollars in excess interest costs.

The Financial Consumer Agency of Canada, the federal government's consumer protection watchdog, observes in an understatement that payday loans are "an expensive way to borrow money" but that the demand for them is growing: while one in fifty Canadians turned to payday loans in 2009, that number rose to one in twenty-five in 2014. According to the Canadian Payday Loan Association, almost two million Canadians resort to payday loans each year.[27]

All this points to the crying need for a banking system that isn't based on exploiting the desperation of financially vulnerable people. A public banking system, operated through the post office, could fill that ticket. And it could do so without financial risk to taxpayers. Payday loans are offered only to individuals with a reliable source of income, either from an employer or from the government. This means a postal bank could safely offer a payday loan — but at a dramatically lower interest rate, notes Anderson. For example, with an annualized rate of 29 percent, similar to what the banks charge on their credit cards, a borrower would pay $1.11 for a two-week loan of one hundred dollars, rather than fifteen dollars. The postal bank could still make a profit, while the low-income borrower would be spared explosive interest charges.

Indeed, the potential for earning profits is another reason that Canada should adopt a public banking system through our post office. As the managers at Canada Post learned, the financial success of postal banking has been amply demonstrated in a number of countries, including the United Kingdom, France, Germany, Switzerland, Italy, and New Zealand. France's Banque Postale, for instance, has ten million customers and earns 55 percent of the profits in the French post office system. New Zealand's Kiwibank, with eight hundred thousand customers, is so profitable that it subsidizes national mail delivery — a model that should attract the attention of Canadians wanting to maintain home delivery here.

Interestingly, there is also growing pressure to revive postal banking in the United States, where it operated from 1911 to 1967. The renewed interest was sparked by a 2014 report from the U.S. Postal Service's inspector general, which suggests that the post office could offer much cheaper banking services than payday loan operators while earning nine billion dollars a year for the cash-strapped national postal service. The report notes that an estimated sixty-eight million Americans are not served by the traditional banks. Many of these people are vulnerable, low-wage workers who turn with anxiety to payday lenders. In the state of Arizona alone, there are 650 payday loan businesses, some so busy they operate twenty-four hours a day. The American Bankers Association slammed the inspector general's report, dismissing postal bank loans as the "worst idea since the Edsel." But the cause of postal banking — dubbed "a central bank for the poor" — has gained ground among influential progressives.

It could become an issue in the 2020 election campaign, since it's being championed by a number of potential Democratic presidential contenders, including Senators Bernie Sanders, Elizabeth Warren, and Kirsten Gillibrand.[28]

If the notion of the Canadian government running a successful bank sounds overly ambitious, it shouldn't. Not only do we have the example of the ATB in Alberta, but our federal government also already owns and operates a number of successful banks for special purposes. These include Farm Credit Canada ($33 billion in assets), the Business Development Bank of Canada ($25.3 billion in assets), Export Development Canada ($63 billion in assets), and the Bank of Canada (over $1 trillion in assets). These federally owned banks made profits totalling $3.2 billion in 2016. They operate out of 242 offices nationwide and have a long track record of providing various financial services to Canadians. Farm Credit Canada, for instance, provides loans and mortgages to some hundred thousand farmers, while the business and export development banks provide loans to thousands of Canadian businesses. These publicly owned banks employ more than seven thousand civil servants. So there would be plenty of banking expertise, already paid for by the taxpayer, to draw on as Canada Post moved to establish banking services in postal outlets across the country.

~⊘~

When the Harper government announced its plan in 2013 to shut down what remained of home mail delivery, it fell to Deepak Chopra, Canada Post CEO, to put a positive spin on the cutback in service to Canadians. "We can't build a network, looking forward 20 or 25 years, based on what we did in the last 50 or 100 years," he told the *Globe and Mail*, as he pointed to the exciting e-commerce opportunities for the post office. When asked about postal banking, Chopra had little encouraging to say: "There is really no room to operate as a bank.… The battle of banking took place in 1967 when the decision was made by Canada Post to exit the banking business, and since then we have no institutional knowledge, no expertise and no infrastructure."[29]

No infrastructure? Chopra pointedly ignored the fact that Canada Post has an enormous infrastructure of 6,200 retail outlets — more than five times the 1,209 branches of the Royal Bank, the biggest financial institution in the country. No institutional knowledge or expertise? Chopra obviously ignored the significant banking expertise that would be available from the seven thousand public servants already employed by federally run banks. And, of course, he failed to mention the fact that his own executive staff had put together an extensive file pointing to the extremely profitable opportunities of offering banking services and how they would amount to a win-win strategy for the post office.

The Harper government's plan to end home delivery became a hot issue during the 2015 federal election campaign, with both the Liberals and NDP vowing not to proceed with the cut. And, in office, the Liberals have kept to their promise. The Trudeau government has been less keen, however, on venturing into public banking through the post office. While not shutting that door, the Liberals joined the Conservatives in March 2018 in voting against a parliamentary motion to study postal banking.

Indeed, while the Liberals aren't hell-bent on cutting public services the way the Conservatives are, they do appear to be locked into the austerity model, vigorously promoted by business interests, that depicts any expansion of public services as unaffordable. Accordingly, when the Liberals appointed a task force to study prospects for Canada Post, they stacked it with business people: three high-level figures from the business community and one private consultant with a background in the federal public service. There were no representatives from labour, low-income, or consumer groups.

Not surprisingly, in its review of the possibility of postal banking, this business-dominated task force drew heavily on the advice of the Canadian Bankers Association, despite the fact that the banks obviously have a vested interest in blocking competition from the post office. Based on this input from bankers, the Liberal task force found that the only viable option for postal banking would be "partnering with 3 to 5 large banks or credit unions to provide a low-cost extension to the branch network in less profitable locales." But the task force went on to scuttle even this option by suggesting that it might be hard for the post office to find banks or credit unions agreeing to such a partnership.[30]

As for the serious problem of payday loan operators, the task force saw little help the post office could offer. The task force reached this surprising conclusion again due to the extensive input of the bankers' association, which "indicated that many users of payday loan lenders choose the service because of the relative anonymity it affords." Really? Apparently, the bankers' word on this was enough to dismiss reports that hundreds of thousands of low-income Canadians pay the punishing interest rates demanded by payday loan operators, not because they want to be anonymous, but because no other banking option exists for them. With the help of the bankers' association, the task force was able to put those concerns to rest, and conclude that Canada has a "well-established banking market that serves Canadians well."[31] Amen.

And so it was that the Liberal-appointed task force stomped all over the idea of public banking. While Canada Post would be reshaped for the digital age, it wouldn't be reshaped in a way that would provide a basic service badly needed by Canadians, particularly low-income ones or those living in remote communities. That sort of reshaping doesn't fit with the plans of our big banks. And that appears to be enough to kill the idea. What is striking is the way the Trudeau government, which likes to think big when it comes to partnering with the private sector for its new infrastructure bank, seems determined to think small when it comes to an initiative the public sector could do entirely on its own.

Meanwhile, the fifty thousand postal workers represented by CUPW are full of faith in what the public sector can achieve — *if it would only try*. By the fall of 2018, CUPW, along with the Canadian Postmasters and Assistants Association, the union representing eight thousand rural postal workers across the country, were locked in bitter negotiations with Canada Post. In addition to the usual issues of pay, benefits, and job security, the unions were pushing for an ambitious plan aimed at turning Canada's vast postal network into a hub of outlets aimed at advancing the public interest.

The centrepiece of the plan is adopting postal banking, thereby providing basic financial services to potentially millions of Canadians — both those unable to get service from our major banks and those who would prefer not to pay their exorbitant fees.

But the plan goes beyond banking. Teaming up with environmentalists such as The Leap director Avi Lewis, the unions argue that post office outlets could and should be used to help Canadians transition to a cleaner energy future. They note that the post office is the largest retail network in the country, with more outlets even than Tim Hortons. And they envision a future where post offices would have roofs covered in solar panels while, out in front, there would be public, high-speed charging facilities for electric cars. Among those vehicles would be made-in-Canada electric postal delivery vans.[32]

Certainly, the network of postal outlets that dot every nook and cranny of this country represents a significant opportunity to make a positive contribution to the lives of Canadians. Rather than regarding this network — built up over more than a hundred years — as something to be ignored, slowly dismantled, or privatized, it should be seen as an immense and valuable public infrastructure that could be doing a lot more to serve the public good.

∽ *Seven* ∾

Oil and the Search
for Our Inner Viking

For many years, commentators in Alberta have crowed about how the province demonstrates the merits of free-market capitalism. While most provinces struggled with deficits, Alberta was deficit-free — and its media commentators and politicians clearly enjoyed lecturing other provinces on how to cut taxes and make other pro-market reforms so that they, too, could be successful like Alberta. Typically downplayed in all this commentary was the fact that the gush of oil revenues pouring into Alberta's coffers made it easy for the provincial deficit to melt away, like ice cream left in the hot sun.

Then came the reckoning. The stunning collapse in global oil prices, starting in the summer of 2014, brought about a sea change. Alberta suddenly faced significant deficits and an uncertain future. Surprisingly, the province had saved only seventeen billion dollars in its rainy-day savings account, the Alberta Heritage Savings Trust Fund. It was noted at the time that this amount would quickly be eaten up if the oil price slump persisted or if the world got serious about switching to clean energy.

The declining outlook for oil also affected Norway — a nation that, like the province of Alberta, is endowed with generous oil reserves and a small population. Norway had also saved for a rainy day. But, strikingly, its heritage fund was full to overflowing with more than *one trillion dollars*, ensuring a future for its citizens free from austerity and full of possibilities.

In another interesting difference, Norway had created a state-owned oil company, Statoil (recently renamed Equinor), which is the eleventh largest oil company in the world. With assets of more than one hundred billion dollars, Equinor is majority-owned by the Norwegian people, adding yet more to their collective wealth. In the 1970s, Alberta created Alberta Energy Company, which was half-owned by the province. Today, Alberta Energy Company is the second largest oil and gas producer in Canada, but the province privatized it in 1993, leaving Albertans with no ownership stake in their oil industry, or the corresponding wealth that goes with that.

With the 2014 oil price collapse, the sharply diverging prospects facing Norwegians and Albertans suddenly became a focus of attention, in a way that didn't reflect well on Alberta. Reports and commentaries began appearing in the *Globe and Mail* and on the CBC suggesting there were lessons Albertans could learn from semi-socialist Norway.

That suggestion enraged Gary Lamphier, business columnist for the *Edmonton Journal*. In a frothy column headlined "Norway Offers Few Lessons for Alberta," he dismissed the proposition that Alberta had anything to learn from Norway and angrily attacked "media cheerleaders in Toronto" for floating such an idea.[1]

But as satisfying as Lamphier no doubt found it to rail against Toronto, he was unable to get around a simple fact: Norway had somehow managed to build up a rainy-day fund that was an astounding sixty times larger than the Alberta fund. Lamphier notes that Norway's state oil company controls most of the country's oil production, while Alberta's oil industry is dominated by "domestic and foreign players" that are "expected to generate a decent return for their shareholders…. It's called capitalism. Norway embraces a very different socialist model." Lamphier's argument is an odd one. He seems to think that merely pointing out that Alberta embraces capitalism while Norway embraces a more socialistic model is enough to put an end to the argument. But this should not be the end of the argument; rather, it should be the logical starting point.

Indeed, surely the debate should boil down to a simple question: Which model works better? Unless we are captives of ideology, we should want to know the answer to this basic question. Rarely has there been a more clear-cut divergence in economic strategies, enabling us to compare the merits of Alberta's free-market private ownership approach with Norway's model of public ownership and control.[2]

Lamphier can stomp his feet all he wants. What's needed, however, is not emotion or ideological conviction, but rather a fair-minded assessment of which approach best manages a key resource for the benefit of the people.

～◎◇〜

Alberta's inclination toward a market approach was evident in its politics following the Great Depression. With the death of Social Credit leader William Aberhart in 1943, the Alberta government moved away from attacking eastern banking interests and adopted a more clearly pro-business stance under the new Socred leader, Ernest Manning. That pro-business orientation intensified after 1947, when an Imperial Oil exploration crew discovered oil in Leduc, near Edmonton, launching Alberta's development as a major oil producer.

The province was quickly caught up in the hoopla of a new petro prosperity — a thrilling change for many people still haunted by the dark days of the Depression on the Prairies. By the time the long-reigning Socreds were finally swept from office in 1971, Alberta was already heavily under the influence of the private oil industry, which was mostly foreign owned. The leading company, Imperial Oil, although established by Ontario refiners in 1880, had been taken over in 1898 by Standard Oil of New Jersey (now ExxonMobil). By 1971, the mainly American-owned multinational oil companies accounted for fully 79 percent of the oil and gas revenues in Alberta and 84 percent of the industry's profits, with half of the province's oil output exported to the United States.

The newly elected Progressive Conservative premier, Peter Lougheed, was a businessman and lawyer who came from a very prominent Alberta family. His grandfather, James Lougheed, had been an influential senator in Ottawa and a former law partner of Prime Minister R.B. Bennett. Following the family tradition, Peter Lougheed was a Conservative and was certainly pro-business. But that didn't prevent him from recognizing that Albertans were not getting a good deal from the oil companies. And, unlike the earlier Alberta premiers the companies had faced, Lougheed did not see his role as simply one of keeping the industry happy.

The new premier broke sharply with his predecessors in vigorously asserting that Albertans owned the oil and gas in their ground and that they had to start "thinking like owners." He showed what he meant by that when, in one of his first acts as premier, he announced plans to significantly increase the share of oil wealth going to the province by raising the royalties the companies had to pay. Accustomed to a sweetheart deal that limited royalties to 17 percent, the companies fought back when Lougheed pushed the rate up to 25 percent on newly drilled wells. *Oilweek*, the Calgary-based magazine that functioned as a mouthpiece for the industry, hinted that the premier had lost his mind, running a cover photo of Lougheed beneath the heading "This Man Needs Help." Another *Oilweek* cover featured a desolate abandoned farmhouse with the caption "What Would Alberta Be Like Without the Oil Industry?"

The industry didn't hesitate to revive memories of Depression-era Alberta, attempting to stoke fears that the royalty hike risked "killing the goose that laid the golden egg." At public hearings, the companies openly threatened to take their rigs elsewhere. Calgary-based Hewitt Oil warned Albertans: "We can certainly start spending our funds in Saskatchewan, which we have in the past avoided.... Within the past two weeks, however, Alberta has worried us to the extent that we have acquired 400,000 acres of land in Saskatchewan.... Do not implement any program that will increase the cost of doing business."

But Lougheed persisted and prevailed. The oil companies, apparently concluding (correctly) that there was still profit to be made in Alberta, simply adjusted to the new royalty regime. More broadly, they found themselves obliged to adjust to a new regulatory framework in which provincial civil servants were actively involved in planning and overseeing the exploitation of the province's resources.

In an effort to counter the dominance of the multinational oil companies, Lougheed established the above-mentioned Alberta Energy Company, half-owned by the provincial government with the other half owned by members of the public purchasing shares at affordable prices. The notion of Albertans investing in the province's resources — privately and through public ownership — proved wildly popular. Alberta Energy Company was given some attractive oil properties to develop and was touted as a vehicle for diversifying the province's economy beyond oil, including establishing a spinoff petrochemical industry. Lougheed was keen to push Alberta out of its past pattern of exporting raw resources for processing elsewhere. He insisted that shipping unprocessed oil out of Alberta made no more sense than farmers selling their topsoil.

Lougheed's determination to secure a better deal for Albertans was helped by the quadrupling of world oil prices in the early 1970s, due to the rise of the Organization of Petroleum Exporting Countries. With Alberta awash in oil revenues beyond anyone's wildest dreams, there was plenty to go around, easing the way for Lougheed as he pushed royalties up to 40 percent, providing the province with an annual ten-billion-dollar boost in revenues. Realizing that the heady oil prices wouldn't last forever, he also established the Alberta Heritage Savings Trust Fund, with an initial investment of $1.5 billion in 1976, to hold a portion of the province's resource revenues as a nest egg for the future.

It was Lougheed who launched the development of Alberta's massive tar sands, or oil sands, as they've been renamed to soften their image. He saw the gigantic oil sands deposit as pivotal to the long-term prosperity of the province, as well as offering a chance to break the dominance of foreign corporations. A 1972 document produced for his government describes the oil sands as "a unique opportunity to change the historical trend of ever increasing foreign control of non-renewable resource development in Canada."[3] From its early days, the Lougheed government invested heavily in advancing the oil sands, funding government agencies that developed key technologies to extract bitumen from the gooey, tar-like sands, as well as creating a regulatory framework to supervise the development. When the privately owned Syncrude consortium seemed on the verge of abandoning its oil sands project in 1975, the Lougheed government stepped in with a two-hundred-million-dollar investment. Ottawa and the Ontario government also invested, and the three governments became partners (for a while) in oil sands development.

Lougheed's time as premier, from 1971 to 1985, represented the high-water mark for assertive public control and management of the province's oil reserves. In the later years of Lougheed's premiership, with a sluggish world economy producing falling oil prices in the early 1980s, his government retreated somewhat. It allowed petroleum companies to keep a larger share of revenues, and it made smaller contributions to the province's heritage fund. (The contributions were phased out entirely by 1987.) Lougheed also switched his prime focus to fighting Ottawa for control over oil, after Pierre Trudeau's Liberal government introduced the sweeping National Energy Program (NEP) in 1980.

The NEP proved a godsend for the multinational oil companies, since Ottawa moved into the hot spot as Alberta's chief adversary, accused of interfering with the province's quest to control its oil. The multinationals were delighted to line up with the Lougheed government in battling Ottawa's attempt to increase Canadian ownership of the oil patch and to grab a bigger piece of oil revenues for the federal government. The foreign-owned oil companies took full advantage of the resulting bad blood between the warring Canadian factions, helping Lougheed whip Albertans into an anti-Ottawa frenzy.

Ed Shaffer, a University of Alberta economist, has noted how the industry benefits from splits between provincial and federal governments: "In general, the oil companies would prefer to deal with a host of relatively weak provincial or regional governments than with a strong federal government. In this way they can play one province against the other and the provinces against the federal government. Through such a policy they can prevent various governments from extracting the maximum possible economic rents."[4]

The close alliance between the Alberta government and the oil industry in fighting the NEP became a far cozier alliance, however, in the era of Ralph Klein, the folksy former Calgary mayor who served as Progressive Conservative premier from 1992 to 2006. Klein fully privatized the Alberta Energy Company in 1993, undoing Lougheed's attempt to provide Albertans at least a partial ownership stake in the province's key industry and to give the government some involvement in shaping Alberta's economic development. With slogans like "Get government out of the business of business," Klein abandoned any notion that Albertans were running the show and behaving, in Lougheed's words, "like owners" of their valuable resources. In doing so, he surrendered a stunning degree of wealth and control to the multinationals.

The break with the Lougheed approach was most evident in the handling of the oil sands. The industry wasted no time in its efforts to rip down Lougheeed's regulatory framework, which had ensured a measured pace of development. An industry-sponsored task force, almost completely dominated by corporate players, recommended massive changes that would lower royalties, lower taxes, and speed up project approvals. And industry got almost exactly what it wanted from the acquiescent Klein government. The new royalty rate was set at a piddling 1 percent; only after every penny of capital costs had been deducted would that rate rise to a modest 25 percent. With all caution and restraint stripped away and oil sands properties sold at bargain-basement prices, development flew into overdrive, with much of the wealth draining out of Alberta. The province lacked the capacity to process the massive amount of bitumen being produced, and industry was happy to simply ship it unprocessed to refineries elsewhere.

This "rip and strip" approach got so overcharged that in 2006 Peter Lougheed came out of retirement to express alarm. "What is the hurry?..." he asked in an interview in *Policy Options* magazine, insisting that development was way too fast and the royalty rate way too low.

"It is wrong in my judgement, a major wrong, and I keep trying to see who the beneficiaries are.... It is not the people of the province."[5]

Kevin Taft, a Liberal who served as leader of the opposition during the later years of Klein's premiership, describes how the multinational oil companies essentially captured control of Alberta, limiting its ability to function as a meaningful democracy. In *Oil's Deep State*, Taft documents Big Oil's enormous influence over the province's democratic institutions — the premier's office, the legislature, the civil service, the media, and academia. He describes how Klein's energy minister, Patricia Nelson, openly acknowledged that she relied almost entirely on her weekly consultations with important industry players who formed what she called her "kitchen Cabinet." Big Oil's dominance was particularly pronounced under Klein, but Taft maintains that, in the years since his departure as well, the industry has maintained effective control over the Alberta government — and over Ottawa.[6]

Certainly, the drastic lowering of oil royalties under Klein and his successors has had an enormous impact on the province's finances. Andrew Nikiforuk, a respected journalist who has long covered Alberta's petroleum industry, puts it bluntly when he says that the lower royalties "cheated the citizens of Alberta, the owners of the province's hydrocarbons, of tens of billions of dollars."[7] The public share of oil revenues dropped from an annual average of 27 percent in the Lougheed years to an annual average of just 15 percent under Klein. When he was criticized over the low royalties, Klein famously said that he didn't give "a tinker's damn" about royalty reviews or whether Albertans were getting their fair share. Instead, he sent a Cabinet minister to speak to oil executives about the rates and was reportedly satisfied that the executives felt they were paying enough. Case closed.

Klein's successor, Ed Stelmach, acknowledged that the industry was getting too sweet a deal and, invoking the spirit of the Lougheed years, set up a royalty review in 2007. Headed by forestry executive Bill Hunter, the review was by no means aimed at carrying out an assault on corporate interests. Still, after studying the evidence, it found that the public's share of oil revenues was notably small in Alberta compared to other petroleum-producing states; in fact, it was among the smallest.

The review minced no words in calling for industry to pay more for a resource that, after all, belongs to the people of Alberta: "Albertans do not receive their fair share from energy development and they have not, in fact, been receiving their fair share for quite some time."[8]

But, even coming from a corporate-friendly review panel appointed by a Conservative government, these words aroused the fury of the oil multinationals. They flew into action with an aggressive campaign to sink the review's conclusion that royalties should be raised. In fact, the proposed royalty increase would only raise Alberta from the bottom to the middle range of petroleum producers, in terms of public share. Economist André Plourde, then at the University of Alberta, calculated that, given reduced federal and provincial tax rates, the proposed changes would simply bring the public share of oil revenues back to the level where they'd been in 1997, during an earlier stage of the Klein years.

The industry campaign was aided by the 2008 financial crisis and general economic slowdown, which amplified fears that the multi-nationals might make good on their threats to pack up and leave Alberta, should they face higher royalties. Although the Stelmach government largely backed down, the fact that it had toyed with the idea of higher royalties angered the petroleum giants, which reduced their financial support for the Conservatives and redirected their largesse to a new, even more wildly pro-corporate party called Wildrose.

By the time the Conservative dynasty finally fell, knocked out by Rachel Notley's NDP in 2015, the public's share of oil revenues was projected to fall to a devastatingly low level of just 3.6 percent — a huge slide from Lougheed's record of collecting 41 percent in 1978. Notley, who had long argued in opposition that Albertans were not getting a fair deal, freshly invoked the spirit of Lougheed and moved quickly to establish a new royalty review.

The timing was, of course, bad. The collapse of world oil prices was causing economic hardship in the province, enabling the oil companies and their Wildrose associates to maximize fears that higher royalties would lead to deeper job losses in the oil patch. In the end, Notley's review panel recommended essentially doing nothing. "The collective sigh of relief in downtown Calgary was probably audible last week," noted a report on the CBC's website, "as Alberta's royalty review panel decided against asking the energy sector to pay more."[9] The panel report won quick endorsement from the Canadian Association of Petroleum Producers and a number of other industry heavy hitters.

The sheer size of the share that Big Oil has managed to grab for itself has been calculated in research done by the Parkland Institute, which is affiliated with the University of Alberta. In in a report entitled *Misplaced Generosity: Update 2012*, the Parkland Institute found that the public had never received more than 20 percent of the rent from the oil sands.[10] It's worth pausing for a moment to clarify the meaning of the word *rent* in this context. An economic rent is the value of what's left over after deducting all the production costs and a normal rate of profit (typically 10 percent). Bill Hunter, the forestry executive who chaired Stelmach's 2007 royalty review, notes that "[a]s Albertans we own 100 percent of the resource, and we should expect nothing less than 100 percent of the rent."[11] In other words, after all costs and a reasonable profit have been paid to the producing company, everything else should go to the people who own the resource.

Yet, according to the Parkland study, Albertans have never received anywhere near the "100 percent of the rent" that Bill Hunter says is their due. In fact, as noted, they've never received more than 20 percent of annual rent from the oil sands, and they have received far less in some years, as little as 2 percent. Business observers point out that oil from the oil sands is extremely expensive to produce. But when we are measuring economic rent, we are talking about the gain left over *after* all costs — however enormous — and a normal rate of profit are deducted. The Parkland study concludes that, since 1997, although Albertans were entitled to receive 100 percent of this annual rent (or leftover gain) from the oil sands, they've averaged just 9 percent. Here's another way to look at it: after being paid for all expenses and a normal rate of profit, the industry has managed to *also capture fully 91 percent of what's left over* — even though the oil belongs to the people of Alberta.

The extraordinary share of oil wealth captured by private industry presumably reflects its power to scare Albertans into believing that if they try to claim a larger share for themselves, companies will abandon the province, presumably taking the oil with them. Whether or not the industry's threats are credible, Albertans apparently believe them. Norwegians, on the other hand, have managed to ignore Big Oil's constant huffing-and-puffing attempts at extortion, without paying a price.

The ability of Norway, a tiny nation of just five million people, to successfully stand up to and stare down the most powerful set of corporate interests in the world is so remarkable that one is tempted to conclude this sort of defiance is rooted somewhere in the Norwegian DNA. Vancouver-based journalist Mitchell Anderson pursued this theme in a lively series of articles on Norway's oil development, describing how Norway channelled "its inner Viking" to take on Big Oil.[12]

The famously fearless Vikings mounted raids during the eighth and ninth centuries aimed at warding off invasion and occupation by the legendary Charlemagne as he expanded the Holy Roman Empire through Western Europe. The Vikings' reputation as brutal, uncompromising warriors apparently paid off, and Charlemagne bypassed Scandinavia in search of easier conquests. As a result, Norwegians never experienced the top-down system of feudal domination that prevailed elsewhere in Europe. Instead of being serfs working for a landed gentry, Norwegians became yeoman farmers managing their own small homesteads, drawing freely on local water and timber resources. They developed a less hierarchical culture than existed in the rest of Europe, becoming the first, for instance, to establish legal equality for women.

In the early 1900s, this independent culture came into conflict with European industrial interests that were keen to create dams for generating hydroelectric power in Norway's coastal fjords. As the Europeans tried to buy up rights to their waterfalls, Norwegians reacted angrily. Norway had just separated from Sweden, and there was strong resistance in the newly independent country to succumbing to control by foreign capitalists. In 1906 the Norwegian parliament passed legislation, known as the Panic Laws, which slowed down approval of foreign purchases of natural resources, with the aim of buying time for Norwegian business interests to assemble the capital necessary to carry out the resource development.

In the following years, a more left-leaning government went further, placing restrictions on Norwegian business interests as well. Under a radical law introduced in 1917, capitalists — both foreign and domestic — were required to develop natural resources in socially beneficial ways, such as using Norwegian materials and workers, and providing cheap electricity to local communities.

Another far-reaching aspect of the law stipulated that waterfalls and hydro dams would revert to public ownership after a period of sixty to eighty years, without any compensation being paid. Prime Minister Gunnar Knudsen proudly defended this "right of reversion," noting that public ownership of waterpower would give "the Norwegian people ... the conditions necessary for a material success enjoyed almost nowhere else in the world." (In fact, as mentioned earlier, one other place where the people benefited from a strong political commitment to publicly owned waterpower was Ontario, where the premier famously vowed in 1906 never to allow waterpower to become "the sport and prey of capitalists.")

This commitment to protecting the public interest was well established in Norway by the time oil was first discovered in the North Sea off the country's coast in 1969. By this point, Norway had evolved into a highly equitable society — one of the most equitable in the world — with a tradition of public trust in government. It also had a strong tradition of civic engagement and co-operation, with established practices for bringing together business, labour, farmers, and other interested parties to find a consensus.

Accordingly, following a robust national discussion about the implications of the North Sea discovery, the parliamentary industry committee produced a report in 1971 that became known as the "Ten Oil Commandments." Number One: "There should be national governance and control of all petroleum operations." The commandments also called for the establishment of "a state oil company" and the involvement of the state "at all levels in the coordination of Norwegian interests, including an integrated oil industry." The sweeping report, endorsing an approach to oil development dramatically different from Alberta's industry-dominated model, won broad support from the Norwegian public. And it was unanimously adopted by the Norwegian parliament.[13]

In 1972, another unanimous act of parliament established the state oil company, Statoil. The Norwegian government made no bones about giving priority to this publicly owned entity. Private corporations would also be allowed to participate in the oil patch, but preference would be given to the people's own company. In offshore concessions, where Statoil partnered with foreign interests, Statoil was granted the largest ownership shares in areas considered the most promising. And its foreign partners were required to cover most of the exploration costs, again providing an advantage for Statoil. Even so, it turned out that foreign companies were eager to participate.

Norway's finance ministry produced a white paper in 1974 that further proclaimed the country's commitment to public ownership and control. The paper set out clearly that the goals were to get the largest possible share of oil rent for the public and then to ensure that that bounty would be shared equitably among Norwegians, and with future generations. The paper also asserted the importance of establishing government control over the oil industry. That control was considered as important as maximizing the public's share of the rent; in fact, the two goals were regarded as integrally connected. To achieve control, it would be necessary, the report said, for the Norwegian state to develop its own technological expertise, so that Norway's political leaders would have an independent source of information about the oil industry. Accordingly, Statoil was given a mandate to be involved in all stages of petroleum production, from exploration to refining to retailing.

Clearly, right from the outset, the Norwegians recognized the importance of establishing public control over the petroleum industry, thereby minimizing the influence of Big Oil and its potential leverage over the country. By developing independent technological expertise through Statoil, Norway ensured that it would have detailed and reliable knowledge of costs related to every aspect of the business, putting itself in a strong and informed position to negotiate aggressively with foreign multinationals over how oil revenues would be divided. And, should the multinationals try to squeeze out a bigger share for themselves by threatening to leave, such threats would ring hollow. Statoil would be poised to step in and take over.

It's interesting to note that Norway was taking control of its oil resources in the early 1970s, at roughly the same time Peter Lougheed was toughening up Alberta's relationship with its petroleum industry. Alberta had more experience with Big Oil, and Lougheed's moves to strengthen the government's control over the industry were studied in Oslo. One expert with considerable knowledge of Alberta is Rolf Wiborg, a Norwegian who did his degree in petroleum engineering at the University of Alberta in the early 1970s and later headed the Norwegian Petroleum Directorate. Wiborg was impressed by Lougheed's focus on regulating the industry more tightly and getting a better deal for Albertans.

But while there was some overlap in approach in the early days, Norway was always more radical than Alberta — more adamant about establishing strong public ownership, and more determined to be dominant in its relationship with the multinationals. In 1974, when the dramatic rise in global oil prices emboldened Lougheed to raise royalties, Norway went considerably further in increasing its share of the exploding oil wealth. Based on Statoil's insider information about the true extent of the extraordinary profits the oil companies were earning, Norway passed a new petroleum law that dramatically increased taxes on the industry, pushing them up from 50 percent to almost 90 percent. The law also specified that the taxes would be calculated on numbers determined by the Norwegian oil authorities, not the companies, thereby diminishing opportunities for the companies to juggle their books.

Exxon, Shell, and the others were enraged and launched a media campaign protesting that it was impossible to carry on business successfully in a "socialist country."[14] But their efforts had little traction, partly because Norwegians largely stuck together and the political parties declined to use the issue for political gain. Einar Lie, a professor at the University of Oslo, notes that there was little divergence among the political parties. "Business interests have really never been integrated into Norwegian political life. It's really unthinkable that the oil sector interests would intervene in the political debate by trying to have spokesmen among the political parties," observes Lie. "Everyone was in favour of the Norwegian society prospering and that we should get the maximum benefit from the oil resource."[15]

Oddly, Albertans have been less adamant about getting the maximum benefit from their petroleum and have allowed Big Oil to walk away with most of the benefit. And, as noted, the clash between Alberta and Ottawa allowed the multinationals to play the factions off against each other. After Lougheed left politics in 1985, Albertans became much more susceptible to corporate threats of departure if the industry didn't get the terms it wanted. By contrast, Norway never allowed the multinationals to get very far playing that game. Although internal documents reveal that Norwegian authorities wanted the multinational industry to participate in Norwegian oil development and sometimes feared its departure, they reverted to Viking mode when actually dealing with demanding foreigners.

Wiborg recalls attending a meeting between Norway's oil minister and a group of powerful foreign oil executives in the late 1980s, after Norway had toughened its terms considerably and the multinationals were once again threatening to pull their capital out of the country. The oil minister, Arne Øien, listened to the bellicose foreign executives complain that the new rules would make their Norwegian operations unprofitable. After all the executives had had their say, Øien looked at his watch and commented simply, "I have to leave, but I recognize that nobody has left the table." Then, turning to the Norwegian officials in the room, Øien added in a voice loud enough for all to hear, "So, you guys didn't take enough." Years later, Wiborg still marvels at the oil minister's "Viking chutzpah."[16]

In truth, a strain of Viking chutzpah has been evident at times in Canadians, particularly back in the Lougheed years. David G. Wood, communications director for the Lougheed government, recalls then energy minister Don Getty negotiating the terms for tar sands development with high-level members of the Syncrude consortium in 1973. When it became clear the consortium wouldn't budge on their demands, Getty announced that he was ending the meeting, which he did, prompting the consortium to become more flexible in the following days.[17] For that matter, Lougheed's insistence on standing up to the industry made him sufficiently unpopular that his membership in the Calgary Petroleum Club was revoked.

A similar Viking spirit was evident in Danny Williams, the former Progressive Conservative premier of Newfoundland and Labrador, who publicly battled oil giant Chevron over an offshore deal in 2006. Williams demanded a "super-royalty" and a government ownership stake in the oil development, which promised to finally bring some wealth to the long-deprived province. But Chevron refused and, assuming it could push around a desperate province, countered with demands for five hundred million dollars in government subsidies. Williams responded with an emphatic no: "I would say to those companies that are not interested, to simply move on. The oil is not going anywhere. And neither are we." Williams's feisty defiance proved enormously popular in the province. In the end, Chevron agreed to a 4.9 percent government ownership stake, a super-royalty, and no provincial subsidy.

But the boldest Canadian attempt to stand up to the multinationals actually came from an unexpected place: Ottawa. Faced with Mideast turmoil and shortages in global oil supplies in the fall of 1973, Pierre Trudeau's minority government agreed to an NDP motion calling for the creation of a national, publicly owned oil company. In 1975 the Trudeau government, then holding a majority, followed through and established Petro-Canada, despite strong opposition from the Conservatives and Big Oil. That opposition only intensified with Trudeau's 1980 National Energy Program.

The NEP is mostly remembered for the fury it provoked in the western provinces, where it was seen as a naked grab of power and money by the federal government. And it was those things. The NEP did increase the federal share of oil revenues and it did assert new federal authority in creating an overall energy strategy for the country, rather than leaving so much up to the whims of the multinationals and to global political developments. These changes were far-reaching, and the Trudeau government made the mistake of springing the new program on the country with little preparation or consultation with the provinces.

So, much of the rage was understandable, if not reasonable. Still, for all its flaws and the Trudeau government's clumsy management of its delivery, there was much about the NEP that was worthy and even inspiring, reminding Canadians that an inner Viking might be buried somewhere deep in the Canadian psyche.

The NEP set out to establish greater Canadian control over a vital industry that was almost completely dominated by foreign multi-nationals. It sought to significantly increase Canadian public owner-ship, through Petro-Canada, as well as to increase private ownership of the country's energy resources by Canadian companies. The NEP also aimed to raise the public's share of oil revenues, to ensure Canadian energy self-sufficiency, and to spread the benefits of oil wealth more broadly across the country. These goals were largely popular and, before an orchestrated campaign got underway, the NEP was initially well received across the country, including in the western provinces. Certainly, the attempt to increase Canadian ownership in the oil patch was a goal many Canadians would have supported — and did support.

Gordon Laxer, a political economist and founding director of the Parkland Institute at the University of Alberta, recalls helping organize a 1981 meeting in Ottawa between an influential group of progressives and Prime Minister Trudeau. The group included prominent former Liberal finance minister Walter Gordon, former NDP leader Tommy Douglas, and Ottawa mayor Marion Dewar, as well as labour and farm leaders. The group held a press conference on Parliament Hill to express their support for the NEP's Canadian ownership initiative before going on to the private meeting with the prime minister.

At the private session, Walter Gordon, a Bay Street accountant who had long been an outspoken advocate of economic nationalism, kicked things off by suggesting that if the prime minister was serious about increasing Canadian ownership, he should start by buying Imperial Oil. After all, it was the country's biggest oil company and, as a subsidiary of the world's biggest petroleum company, Exxon, it was a symbol of the dominance of Big Oil. "Trudeau appeared sympathetic to the idea, and asked how it would be paid for," recalls Laxer.[18]

Today it is hard to imagine such a meeting, or a program as ambitious as the NEP — not to mention the prime minister calmly mulling over the possibility of buying up one of the bastions of world capitalism.

Laxer points out that, while you'd never know it in the contemporary Canadian political climate, public ownership of the oil industry is common throughout the world. "Canada is one of the few countries to shun public ownership," he says. (Petro-Canada was privatized in the 1990s.)

The heyday of private oil was back in the 1920s, when the heads of the three leading companies (now called Exxon, BP, and Shell) met at Achnacarry Castle in Scotland under the guise of a grouse-hunting vacation. In reality, they were there to work out a formal agreement that carved up the world's oil market among themselves. Today's private oil giants are still fabulously rich and powerful, but the vast majority of the world's oil reserves are actually held by nationally owned oil companies, such as Saudi Aramco, Kuwait Petroleum, Gazprom (Russia), National Iranian Oil Company, and Pemex (Mexico). Exxon-Mobil, with the largest reserves among the private companies, has twenty-five billion barrels — an amount dwarfed by the massive stash of 307 billion barrels held by Saudi Aramco.

Interestingly, there is plenty of government ownership in Canada's oil industry. "The problem is that none of it is Canadian," observes Laxer. National oil companies owned by China, South Korea, Thailand, and Abu Dhabi have all been allowed to buy stakes in the oil sands. But the Alberta government's opposition to Canadian public ownership in the oil patch led to the privatization of the Alberta Energy Company in 1993, denying Albertans yet another chance to get collectively rich.

Amazingly, the biggest failure on the part of Alberta and Ottawa when it comes to oil isn't the failure to amass the one trillion dollars in oil wealth that little Norway somehow figured out how to capture for its people. Bad as that failure is, it's just money. The bigger failure, the one with truly devastating consequences for all of us, is environmental.

As virtually everyone now acknowledges, the production and burning of oil is one of the major culprits causing climate change, which directly threatens the viability of the planet. And producing bitumen from the oil sands is a particularly significant contributor to climate change.

So, in our comparison between the public and private models of oil development, let's not leave out the environmental impact. Both Norway and Alberta have produced and consumed huge amounts of oil over the last fifty years, so both bear significant responsibility for contributing to climate change. Still, there are important differences in their approaches to dealing with the climate problem, and these variations seem integrally tied up with the bedrock difference between public and private models of development.

Under the free-market model, the corporate goal of generating a profit for shareholders is paramount. Corporations have no commitment to the environment; typically, they resist as much as possible attempts by government to impose environmental restrictions or penalties that reduce their profitability. By contrast, under the public model there is no profit motive. The goal, at least in principle, is to advance the public interest which, under any reasonable definition, includes protecting the environment, as well as generating wealth and employment.

It's not surprising, then, that Norway has been much more co-operative with international efforts to tackle climate change than Alberta and Canada have been. For that matter, Norway has long been in the forefront of global environmental action; former Norwegian prime minister Gro Harlem Brundtland is credited with developing and popularizing the concept of sustainable development in the 1980s, when she chaired a pivotal UN inquiry leading up to the 1992 Earth Summit in Rio de Janeiro.

Even as Norway has been a major oil producer for the world market, it has sought to diminish the reliance of Norwegians on oil. It has set targets to reduce its own carbon emissions by 40 percent, thereby exceeding the targets set by the European Union. In this spirit, it has enthusiastically embraced the electric car, waiving taxes on it, allowing it to travel in lanes reserved for buses, and providing free recharging stations in parking lots and along highways. The goals are for only electric cars to be sold in the country by 2025 and for Norway to be carbon neutral by 2050 or sooner.

There's definitely something of a contradiction, however, between Norway's proactive approach in weaning its own citizens off fossil fuels and its eager production and sale of oil to the rest of the world. Greenpeace Norway has gone to court to stop the Norwegian government from issuing permits to drill in the Arctic, insisting that this amounts to a violation of Norway's obligations under the Paris climate accord. So Norway's environmental record is far from perfect.

Still, even as an oil producer, Norway takes steps to be responsible, imposing an activist safety regime that empowers workers to shut down any practice they deem unsafe, thereby reducing the risk of oil spills as well as protecting workers. Norwegian officials also include environmentalists in political consultations on important issues, and sometimes even listen to them. Pressure from environmentalists was a factor in Statoil's decision to abandon its investment in Alberta's oil sands in December 2016. Indeed, Statoil has prided itself on being ahead of the curve in seeing and accepting an end to fossil fuels. "A lot of fossil fuels will have to stay in the ground, coal obviously ... but you will also see oil and gas being left in the ground, that is natural," Statoil CEO Eldar Sætre said in November 2017, a week after Norway's heritage fund announced plans to cut its investments in oil and gas companies.[19] Under Statoil's new name, Equinor, the company now describes itself as "a petroleum and wind energy company."

Norway's climate efforts are significant when compared to those of fellow petro-giant Canada. Over the years, politicians in Alberta and Ottawa, most notably Ralph Klein and Stephen Harper, sided with the oil industry in failing to acknowledge and take meaningful steps toward dealing with the looming climate crisis. More recently, Justin Trudeau has embraced the climate cause, fashioning himself as a leader at the 2015 Paris talks and supporting a national tax on carbon in Canada, despite strong opposition from several provinces. In practice, however, Trudeau has accomplished little on the climate front and has supported the Trans Mountain pipeline expansion, which would enable the tripling of oil sands production, making it virtually impossible for Canada to meet its international climate targets.

Norway's per capita carbon emissions are a third smaller than Canada's. If we zero in on just Alberta, the numbers become worse. "If Alberta were a country it would have the highest per capita emissions in the world, on par with Qatar," notes Bruce Campbell, former executive director of the Canadian Centre for Policy Alternatives.[20]

A 2018 study published in the journal *Nature Communications* ranked Canada among countries with the world's least effective climate measures. It found that Canada's current policies, if adopted throughout the world, would push up global temperatures by a disastrous 5.1 degrees Celsius by the end of the century. By comparison, the study found that Norway's current policies would push global temperatures up by 2.2 degrees Celsius by century's end — a result still above the 2-degree-Celsius limit set in the Paris talks, but obviously something much closer to that limit.[21]

Of course, producing oil from the oil sands is a more carbon-intensive process than producing oil from the North Sea. If anything, that should have made political leaders in Alberta and Canada more cautious. But there's been virtually no caution in Canada, as the lucrative oil sands have been developed with reckless abandon in the last twenty-five years, turning large swaths of Alberta into terrain resembling moonscape. And, despite claims to the contrary by Alberta politicians, there's been little improvement over time in the amount of carbon emitted in oil sands extraction. It remains one of the most carbon-intensive operations in the world.

There's also no willingness to slow things down, even as the evidence of climate change becomes more unmistakable with each passing year. Instead, political effort now goes into assuring the public that the necessary steps are being taken, even though this clearly isn't the case. Premier Notley, for instance, assured us that her government has put a "hard cap" on the oil sands in order to allow Canada to meet its climate targets. But this "hard cap" turns out to be really soft. Rather than cutting back oil sands emissions, it permits them to grow another 60 percent. At that rate, the oil sands will use up roughly 78 percent of the overall emissions budget for all of Canada in 2050, forcing the rest of the population and all other industries to reduce their carbon footprint to virtually zero. "Instead of being part of a climate solution for Canada, Alberta's 'hard cap' allows just one industry to consume our nation's climate goals and obligations," observes Barry Saxifrage, climate reporter for the *National Observer*.[22]

$$\sim\!\!\mathcal{Q}\!\!\sim$$

This national subservience to the development of the oil sands becomes even more incomprehensible when it becomes clear that the sands are not even a major job creator. Even at the peak of the boom in 2006, when the media gushed about high-paying jobs in the oil sands, oil, gas, and mining accounted for only 6.7 percent of total Alberta employment. With the 2014 oil price drop, employment has declined considerably. "If Canada is going to be forced to abandon our climate hopes and commitments to support job creation in one of Alberta's industries, then shouldn't that industry at least be required to crank out some amazing job growth?" asks Saxifrage. Nationally, the oil sands account for less than one-half of 1 percent of employment. And a 2018 Parkland Institute report found that while the five major oil sands companies had remained incredibly profitable throughout the oil price slump, that didn't prevent them from cutting almost twenty thousand jobs from the Alberta economy in 2015.[23]

The capacity of these companies to protect their own interests even as they fail to deliver jobs underlines the extent of their "capture" of the Canadian political system — and this poses immense danger on the climate front. In *Oil's Deep State,* Kevin Taft primarily focuses on how the extended tentacles of the petroleum industry over our democratic institutions have enabled it to block Alberta and Ottawa from taking any meaningful action on global warming. In other words, the unbridled power Big Oil has come to enjoy under Alberta's free-market model of development hasn't allowed it just to grab an enormous share of the oil wealth, but also to seriously jeopardize our collective ability as humans to survive.

～⊙～

Although that might seem to be the ultimate damning indictment of Alberta's free-market model, there's one more matter worth mentioning.

As the world inevitably faces up to the reality of climate change, the fossil fuel party is, sooner or later, coming to an end. For Alberta, this means not only a wind-down of its major industry but also a massive cleanup of the destroyed terrain caused by fifty years of petroleum production. In 2018, a senior official with the Alberta Energy Regulator estimated that the cleanup will cost a staggering $260 billion. The good news is that the industry is on the hook for these cleanup costs. The bad news is that the province has collected only a paltry $1.6 billion from the companies in security payments to cover these costs. One doesn't have to be overly cynical to believe that once the companies have pumped out all the oil they want, they will simply cut and run, leaving behind a massive and wildly expensive mess that the public will have to deal with.

The cleanup fiasco ahead is yet another example of how Big Oil has effectively captured control of the democratic process in Alberta, leaving the public interest hopelessly unprotected. The shocking $260-billion estimate of cleanup costs was revealed by Rob Wadsworth, vice-president of closure and liability for the Alberta Energy Regulator, at a private meeting with industry representatives in February 2018. Prior to this revelation, the provincial regulator had led the public to believe that the cleanup costs would be in the range of $58 billion — a stunning number in itself, but about $200 billion less than the estimate Wadsworth gave in private. The public would have remained in the dark about the true higher costs if it hadn't been for the work of a team of investigative journalists who, using freedom of information legislation, obtained copies of speaking notes from Wadsworth's presentation.[24]

And it gets worse. Wadsworth told the closed-door meeting that his $260-billion estimate was "likely less than the actual cost." So what are we really going to be faced with: $280 billion, $300 billion, $400 billion?

When the story was published, appearing on the front page of the *Toronto Star*, the response of Alberta's NDP government was to muddy the waters. There was an "apology" from the Alberta Energy Regulator, not for failing to alert the public about the true scale of this looming problem but for creating "concern and confusion" by allowing this information to leak out. There was also an attempt to downplay the accuracy of the estimate, without actually denying it. In fact, it is the accuracy of the lower $58-billion estimate that should be questioned, since it's based on numbers provided by the oil companies themselves — making it almost useless, since they have a vested interest in downplaying the true costs of what they will be responsible for cleaning up. The higher $260 billion estimate is based on internal assessments done by the regulator and has clearly been kept secret to not alarm the public.

But alarming the public is exactly what is needed! A trumpet should be blaring. As Wadsworth notes in his presentation, in something of an understatement, the $1.6 billion in security funds collected from industry is "insufficient." Indeed, that leaves almost a quarter of a trillion dollars in cleanup costs that may have to be covered by the province — and inevitably by the rest of Canada. How could that be characterized as anything but alarming?

Wadsworth also understated the situation to an absurd extent when he observed that Alberta has a "flawed system" of industrial oversight. Allan Warrack, a former minister in the Lougheed government, stated things more clearly in an interview in 2011: "There is going to be a thousand years of carnage left up there.... I mean this is crazy, just crazy."[25]

It's not hard to imagine why the oil sands cleanup bill is going to be so high. The scope of the scrubbing will be monumental, given the scale of the environmental devastation over the sprawling nine hundred square kilometres of oil sands development, including 220 square kilometres of tailing ponds full of toxic sludge. Then there's the eleven-million-ton sulphur pile that is bigger than the Egyptian pyramids.

Beyond the oil sands, cleaning up the waste from the conventional oil industry, after fifty years of operation, is another overwhelming task. More than 450,000 oil and gas wells — one for every ten Albertans — have been drilled across the province. About 330,000 of these wells are already exhausted and ready for clean up now or in the near future.

But who will pay for properly shutting down all these operations? A 1991 court case established that oil companies are responsible for cleaning up exhausted wells and that such payments take precedence over payments to creditors. But a 2016 Alberta court decision allowed bankrupt Redwater Energy, a junior oil and gas company, to pay off its creditors first, enabling it to abandon its environmental liabilities, including its responsibility to clean up seventy-one inactive wells. That ruling was overturned, however, in a decision with wide ramifications, when the Supreme Court of Canada declared in January 2019 that Redwater, despite its bankruptcy, couldn't just walk away from the cleanup costs. Whether this leads the industry-friendly Alberta Energy Regulator to adopt a tougher stance remains to be seen.

Certainly, Alberta's cleanup rules are inadequate and desperately in need of reform. One place to begin would be requiring companies to make full security deposits to cover the eventual cleanup costs of abandoned wells so that the provincial regulator would have more than the $1.6 billion in corporate down payments to deal with a soon-approaching $260-billion cleanup tab. Another common-sense reform would be enacting a regulatory regime, similar to ones in Colorado, North Dakota, and Texas, that imposes specified timelines for companies to clean up abandoned operations. Alberta regulators have strongly proposed such regulated deadlines, but the province — ever fearful of offending the oil industry — has failed to act.

It would be hard to find a starker contrast between the public model of oil development pursued by Norway and the private model pursued by Alberta. Through rigorous public management, Norway has taken charge of its petroleum industry, made the multinationals subservient to the state, and fully milked the oil benefits for its people. By contrast, Alberta has largely allowed the multinationals to call the shots and to make off with the lion's share of the oil wealth — and then some. The resulting difference in financial outcomes can only be described as staggering, especially since Albertans had a two-decade head start.

Their methods of collecting oil rents are different: Alberta relies more on royalties, Norway on taxes and public ownership. As the Parkland Institute has calculated, Albertans have collected an average annual oil rent of just 9 percent in recent years. By comparison, Norway's annual rent is in the 82 to 86 percent range. Whereas Albertans have left about 91 percent of the rent on the table for the oil industry to scoop up, Norwegians have scooped up the major share for themselves, leaving less than 18 percent for private industry.

That explains how Norwegians have managed to save up about one trillion dollars more in their rainy-day fund than Albertans. In addition, Norwegians collectively own one of the world's largest oil companies, with assets exceeding one hundred billion dollars. Unless Albertans are indifferent to money, this gigantic shortfall in the benefits they've derived from their oil can only be regarded as unconscionable, and as a mega-tragedy for the province.

What makes this shortfall so galling is that it clearly didn't have to be this way. If Alberta had adopted at least some of the principles used in the public model, it would have fared far better. Lougheed was a full-blooded capitalist, but he believed in asserting government control, including some public ownership, over a resource that belonged to the province's people, in order to maximize benefits for the people.

In an article written after Lougheed's death in 2012, Andrew Nikiforuk noted that western politicians were effusively praising Lougheed but failing to acknowledge how sharply his approach diverged from theirs: "Unlike the current libertarian 'strip it and ship it' crowd that governs most of the West, Lougheed stood for something different. He offered a far-sighted vision that was both progressive and altogether conservative. Although everybody from Saskatchewan's Brad Wall to Alberta's Alison Redford now praise the famously competent premier, none walk his talk." Nikiforuk summarized Lougheed's radical legacy, which has been largely abandoned by his political successors: "Behave like an owner.... Collect your fair share.... Save for a rainy day.... Add value.... Go slow.... Practice statecraft."[26]

And on the environmental front, Alberta has also fallen sadly short of Norway. Norway has taken some serious steps to deal with the environmental damage its oil production generates and is among the world's leading nations in promoting global action on climate change. Alberta, siding with the oil industry, has mostly resisted action on climate change and has pressured Ottawa to do likewise. Furthermore, to keep the multinationals happy, Alberta has largely allowed them to devastate the province's physical environment. And, since they haven't been required to make a serious down payment, the oil companies may be able to walk away once the costly cleanup begins.

Nikiforuk has succinctly described Alberta's situation today: "The low fruit has been picked and nobody saved anything for the future."[27]

Surely, in any fair-minded contest between the merits of Alberta's free-market model of oil development and Norway's public ownership approach, Norway wins. It's not even close.

✑ *Eight* ✎

The Triumph of the Commons

In 1968 U.S. ecologist Garrett Hardin penned what became a highly influential academic article entitled "The Tragedy of the Commons." He argued that, since humans are self-interested, they will inevitably take more than their share when resources are communally available. A similar argument had been expounded in an 1833 pamphlet by an English economist who speculated about the danger of cows overgrazing in the commonly shared fields. The solution to this depletion problem seemed to point to private ownership.

But the solution doesn't have to be private ownership. Another solution is regulation. Indeed, throughout centuries of English history, the common fields were effectively regulated by the people themselves; villagers who snuck an unauthorized extra cow onto the shared pasture were punished by the community. As Nobel Prize–winning economist Elinor Ostrom notes in her 1990 book, *Governing the Commons*, humans can collectively manage their use of shared resources by creating rules, and have done so throughout human history.

Still, the notion that the commons — or, more broadly, commonly held property — is problematic has persisted. It's been advanced by economists using mathematical models of decision-making, known as game theory, which illustrate why two rational individuals might not co-operate, even if it appears they would both benefit by doing so. With this apparent confirmation, the notion that common property is inherently unproductive, or at least less productive, has spread through the social sciences and been picked up with enthusiasm in the business and political worlds, where it has been seen as helping make the case for private ownership. Among other things, it has served as a useful, ostensibly scientific justification for stripping Indigenous Peoples of their commonly shared land so that it can be worked by more "productive" private interests.

Another tragic aspect of its success has been the general pall it's thrown over the very idea of collective solutions, redirecting attention relentlessly instead to the private sector. This ignores the observation of the economic historian Karl Polanyi that humans are, first and foremost, social animals. As social animals, we are likely hard-wired to work together to devise collective solutions.

Polanyi argues that the "free-market" economy that emerged in sixteenth- and seventeenth-century Britain — with its focus on the individual and its rejection of collective solutions — was so unnatural that its rules had to be forcefully imposed on the people, who vigorously fought the "enclosure" of the common land by private interests.

Those who defend private interests argue that the government should leave economic affairs to be sorted out by the free market, which, they insist, will ensure the best result. This approach is often called laissez-faire economics (roughly translated, *let act* or *leave alone*). The label is, in fact, highly misleading: it implies that the free-market economy is something that would naturally occur, if only government would get out of the way. That narrative has things backwards, insists Polanyi. The free-market economy is actually *unnatural* and it had to be constructed through laws; what is natural is for people to seek the protection of society, through some sort of collective body or government, to shield them from gluttonous private interests.[1]

Working out collective solutions is not only natural to human societies, it's also beneficial to them, even in today's advanced societies.

Rather than being a tragedy, the commons can be a triumph, and reviving the spirit of it — enhancing our public programs and enterprises — is our best hope for the future. Individually, we often struggle. Collectively, we are strong and wildly rich!

This book has focused mostly on Canada's impressive tradition of public enterprise. Equally important in the public domain, of course, are social programs that cover our basic needs: health care, education, pensions, unemployment insurance, social assistance, child care, and pharmaceutical drugs.

Corporate interests have pushed for reductions in government spending on these programs, insisting the private sector can provide many of these services. They argue that the cost of government social programs leads to higher taxes, which discourage business investment in the economy.

There is little evidence, however, to back up the assertion that tax levels have a significant impact on business investment. In recent years, for instance, Canada has significantly cut taxes — particularly taxes on corporations and high-income individuals — yet business investment levels have declined. Similarly, in the United States, Nobel Prize–winning economist Paul Krugman has observed how little impact tax-cutting has had on the American economy. "President George W. Bush's tax cuts didn't produce a boom; President Barack Obama's tax hike didn't cause a depression. Tax cuts in Kansas didn't jump-start the state's economy; tax hikes in California didn't slow growth," Krugman writes in a 2018 column in the *New York Times*. Krugman points out that Donald Trump's massive tax cut for the rich has failed to produce investment; instead, corporations have been using the savings to buy back their own stock, enriching their shareholders.[2]

While there's paltry evidence of the benefits of tax cuts, there is a lot of evidence of the benefits of high taxes. Yes, *high taxes*. The beneficial effect of high taxes was a central finding of *The Trouble with Billionaires*, a book I co-authored with Neil Brooks, professor of tax law and policy at Osgoode Hall Law School in Toronto. In the 2013 U.K. edition, we compared extensive data for two sets of countries in the developed world: the low-tax Anglo-American nations (including Canada) and the high-tax European nations (including the Nordic nations). These two groups have adopted very different approaches, creating what could almost be considered a laboratory for testing the impact of high and low taxes.[3]

The results of this thirty-year experiment amount to a staggering repudiation of arguments that have dominated public discourse in the Anglo-American countries about the negative effects of high taxes and big government. In particular, the Nordic countries, which epitomize high taxes and big government, have pulled dramatically ahead in achieving greater social well-being and equality, better health, and stronger economic security for all their citizens. Tax-cutting advocates have tended to ignore or downplay these achievements — or, when they do acknowledge them, to insist that they have come at great economic cost. But this is simply not true. Strikingly, these high-tax countries have enjoyed just as good and often better economic results and material prosperity as the low-tax countries.

The strong economic results of the high-tax countries are clearly visible even when the standard growth measure of GDP per capita is used. However, this is a flawed measure for any meaningful assessment. GDP per capita is simply the figure arrived at by taking the total income of the country and dividing it by the total population. The figure would be the same whether all the income went to one person or was distributed equally to everyone in the country. The U.S. GDP per capita is high largely because there are some extraordinarily rich Americans whose enormous incomes bring up the national average. Surely, a more important measure of a country's economic success is the material well-being of its ordinary citizens.

For instance, if we compare income growth in France and in the United States between 1975 and 2006, we see that the growth in GDP per capita was stronger in the United States (32.3 percent) compared to France (27.1 percent). However, if we remove the richest 1 percent of citizens in both countries from the calculations, the results are reversed: income growth was stronger in France (26.4 percent) than in the United States (17.9 percent). This shows that, although the United States had higher growth of overall GDP per capita, France's bottom 99 percent experienced much bigger growth in their material well-being than did the bottom 99 percent in America.

Certainly, when it comes to social well-being, the accomplishments of the high-tax countries are remarkable. The richness of their social welfare systems, not to mention their practice of mandated five-week or even six-week vacations for all workers, would leave North Americans full of envy — if we heard much about it. But we don't. It's odd that our "progressive" political parties here in North America spend so little time referencing the social achievements of the Nordic and European countries. Clearly these nations offer a much more inspiring alternative to our tax-cutting agenda — an alternative that isn't pie-in-the-sky speculation but tried-and-true results recorded over many decades.

In other words, we aren't just speculating about the possible benefits of high taxes. We can see them on full display.

Finnish journalist Anu Partanen points to a less obvious advantage that generous social programs create: more freedom. She notes that having a strong safety net is liberating; it frees Nordic citizens from the daily torment of worrying about financial security and allows them to get on with improving their lives and building their careers. This turns upside down the familiar notion that a strong social welfare system amounts to a nanny state that encourages dependence. On the contrary, Partanen argues, the *lack* of a social welfare system creates dependence in many Americans.

She elaborates on this in her book, *The Nordic Theory of Everything*, which she wrote after living in the United States for almost a decade. Partanen gradually noticed "how much people in America depended on their employers for all sorts of things that were unimaginable to me: medical care, health savings accounts, and pension contributions, to name the most obvious. The result was that employers ended up having far more power in the relationship than the employee." By contrast, she insists, the Nordic nations create "in individual citizens not a culture of dependency, but rather a new culture of personal self-sufficiency ... that many Americans could only fantasize about achieving in their personal lives: real freedom, real independence, and real opportunity."[4]

⟞⟝

Even if we confine our observations to North America, we can see a major difference between social supports in the United States and Canada, most obviously in health care, where Canada's public system is clearly superior to the largely private U.S. system. The statistics are familiar: the United States spends an astonishing 16 percent of its GDP on health care, while leaving millions without coverage; Canada spends 10 percent of its GDP and covers all Canadians.

These stats don't really convey the extent of the problems that private health care creates for Americans, millions of whom literally can't afford needed medical treatments and who live in fear of enormous medical bills, the leading cause of personal bankruptcy. Roughly two million Americans declare bankruptcy each year due to medical bills.

Perhaps a personal story better captures the superiority of the Canadian health care system. A friend of mine who suffered a massive heart attack was rushed to a Toronto hospital, where he underwent major surgery, followed by multiple days in intensive care and a lengthy stay while he recovered. When he checked out of the hospital a healthy man six weeks later, having received hundreds of thousands of dollars' worth of top-notch medical care, it occurred to him that "no one even mentioned money!"

This is why Canadians revere our public health care system, and why politicians who seek to privatize parts of it never admit to doing so. In 2004, CBC-TV conducted a cross-country series, asking Canadians to select the greatest Canadian of all time. Tens of thousands voted over several weeks. The winner wasn't a prime minister or a military leader, but Tommy Douglas, considered the father of medicare.

Medicare enshrines the principle of equality. Everyone matters; everyone is included. No matter how rich or poor you are, as a Canadian, you have access to the best medical care available.

This commitment to equality is all the more notable because it has been diminishing, even in Canada, in recent years. Increasingly, we live in a society riddled with elitism and special privilege. At our airports, passengers are separated by the degree of their elite status, with more privileges available for Air Canada passengers who are "Super Elite" than for those who are just plain "Elite." If you're anything less, you're made to feel like you shouldn't really be flying. At amusement parks, you can now buy your child a "fast pass" so she can push to the front, leaving in her dust the other children waiting patiently in line to go on a fun-filled ride.

At universities, where the principle of equality should be enshrined, it is apparently readily traded away for cash from wealthy donors. When the University of Toronto accepted thirty-five million dollars from the late mining magnate Peter Munk to set up a school of global affairs, the administration accepted his terms. Among those terms was a requirement that the front door of the mansion housing the school be reserved for senior faculty and guests (presumably including Munk's corporate guests). All others — junior faculty, students, and the public (who pay most of the school's costs through their taxes) — were required to enter through the back door.

So it seems that at airports, at amusement parks, at our universities, and just about everywhere else, the rich can buy their way to the front of the line. But when it comes to health care — where it really matters — they can't. We are all equal. What a triumph!

Right-wing critics counter, "Yes, but in Canada, a dog can get a hip replacement faster than a human!" And this may be true, because veterinary medicine operates under the rules of the private marketplace: with enough money, you can get whatever you want, as fast as you want. So, yes, you can get your dog a speedy hip replacement. With sufficient cash, you could probably get your dog a facelift or liposuction. But the flipside is this: if the owner can't pay, the dog is put down. That's the difference between a public system, based on equality and inclusiveness, and a private system, based on profit.

When it comes to the vital area of health care, Canadians have indicated a clear preference for a system that provides for everyone — a system where everyone enters through the front door.

～❧～

Hostility toward the public sector, encouraged by business, has led to a widespread ignorance about the crucial role governments actually play, even in a dogmatically free-enterprise country like the United States. In her provocative book *The Entrepreneurial State*, economist Mariana Mazzucato argues that the state has consistently played the critical role of financing the basic research that has resulted in innovation and economic growth in the United States. "From the development of aviation, nuclear energy, computers, the Internet, biotechnology, and today's developments in green technology, it is, and has been the State — not the private sector — that has kick-started and developed the engine of growth, because of its willingness to take risks in areas where the private sector has been too risk averse."[5]

Her point is amply illustrated by Apple. The phenomenal success of the technology giant is typically attributed to the creative brilliance of its founder, Steve Jobs. A mythology has grown up around how Apple innovations began with Jobs, a high-school dropout, tinkering around in the family garage. In a 2005 address at Stanford University, Jobs famously advised graduating students to be innovative by "pursuing what you love" and "staying foolish."

Mazzucato recognizes that Jobs had a genius for conceiving visionary products. But she maintains that "without the massive amount of public investment behind the computer and Internet revolutions, such attributes might have led only to the invention of a new toy — not to cutting-edge revolutionary products like the iPad and iPhone which have changed the way people work and communicate." She points out that Apple mastered and marketed "technologies that were first developed and funded by the U.S. government and military.... In fact, there is not a single key technology behind the iPhone that has not been State-funded." She points to the pivotal role of the State in "making the early, large and high-risk investments, and then sustaining them until such time that the later-stage private actors can appear to 'play around and have fun.'"

Acknowledging the state's vital role would have some important implications. Apple, like many leading U.S. corporations, has gone to great lengths to avoid paying taxes. It would be harder for it and other companies to shirk their tax bills and to press for ever-lower corporate taxes if the public appreciated just how much of their success had been funded by the state. As Mazzucato puts it, "Keeping that story untold has allowed Apple to avoid 'paying back' a share of its profits to the same State that funded much of its success." This corporate tax avoidance is not only unfair to the public, but has left the U.S. government with diminished resources to fund future path-breaking research. (It's also led to growing corporate pressure in other countries, including Canada, to match America's low corporate tax burden.)

One key area that is badly in need of major government funding today is green technology. Although the United States was an initial leader in pushing into wind and solar power in the 1980s, it has fallen behind, with Europe, Japan, and now China taking the lead. Washington's failure to invest significantly on the green front in recent years has been mostly due to the enormous clout of the fossil fuel industry, which feels threatened by the prospect of a green energy revolution. "Energy markets are dominated by some of the largest and most powerful companies on the planet, which are generally not driven to innovate," writes Mazzucato. "Leaving direction setting to 'the market' only ensures that the energy transition will be put off until fossil fuel prices reach economy-wrecking highs."

<hr>

In November 2018, Detroit-based General Motors dealt a staggering blow to 2,700 Canadian workers when it announced plans leading to the closure of a key automotive assembly plant in Oshawa, Ontario. In its heyday decades earlier, GM Oshawa had been the largest auto complex in North America and had employed twenty-three thousand workers. But those numbers had been steadily reduced over the years, and now it was to be shut down — along with several GM plants in the United States — as part of the ongoing move by the automaker to relocate ever more of its production to low-wage Mexico.

Unifor, the union representing Canadian auto workers, protested vehemently and focused on trying to negotiate a less draconian deal with GM in order to save at least some of the jobs. Meanwhile, the Trudeau government in Ottawa and the Ford government in Toronto signalled their willingness to accept the closure of the plant without a fight.

One veteran of the auto industry calling for a more robust response from government has been Sam Gindin, who served from 1974 to 2000 as research director of the Canadian Auto Workers (Unifor's predecessor). Now an adjunct professor at York University, Gindin argues that giving up on Oshawa amounts to a "disheartening failure of the imagination." Instead, he suggests serious consideration be given to expropriating the GM Oshawa plant and turning it into a publicly owned facility that would produce some of the vast array of products that will be needed in the transition to green energy: wind turbines, solar panels, energy-saving lighting, motors, appliances, and electric vehicles.[6]

A fleet of electric utility vehicles seems the most obvious alternative for the Oshawa assembly plant, he notes. "Public vehicles will inevitably have to be electrified or run on renewable energy resources, and this means a growing market for electric post office vans for mail and package delivery (as suggested by the Canadian Union of Postal Workers), hydro vehicles doing maintenance and repair work, mini-buses to supplement public transit … electrified vehicles in agriculture, mining and construction." Gindin points out that much of the needed equipment and skills for such an ambitious "green production" project already exist in the Oshawa complex; additional high-tech expertise could be pulled in from the Waterloo computer corridor, as well as Canada's experienced engineering, aerospace, and construction firms.

Of course, Gindin's idea for producing public utility vehicles would require co-operation from the federal and provincial governments, and it is hard to imagine such co-operation from our current political leaders. And business leaders would no doubt dismiss the notion that the public sector could handle something as complicated as vehicle manufacturing.

In fact, as we've seen, Canadian public enterprise has an impressive history and has made its mark in fields that are at least as complicated as vehicle manufacturing. The creation of a public hydroelectric power system in Ontario — and later in other provinces — was a stunning achievement that served as a model for U.S. president Franklin D. Roosevelt when he created highly successful public power systems, including the New York Power Authority, the Tennessee Valley Authority, the Rural Electrification Administration, and the Bonneville Power Administration. There was also Connaught Labs, the publicly owned Canadian drug company, which made remarkable contributions to the development of breakthrough vaccines and treatments for a wide range of deadly diseases. And the publicly owned CNR exhibited innovative business skills in creating a viable national rail network out of five bankrupt railway lines and in establishing, during the pioneering days of radio, a cross-country string of radio stations, which became the basis of the nationwide CBC broadcasting network.

And, as we've seen, some of Canada's most impressive public enterprises were created during the Second World War, when twenty-eight Crown corporations contributed enormously to Canada's war effort, manufacturing airplanes, weapons, and communications equipment. Crown corporation Victory Aircraft provided the foundation for the postwar Canadian subsidiary that developed the Avro Arrow, a state-of-the-art military fighter plane (discontinued by the Diefenbaker government for political, not technological, reasons). And Crown corporation Research Enterprises, teaming up during the war with Ottawa's National Research Council, produced highly innovative optical and communications equipment, including radar devices, binoculars, and radio sets — equipment with countless applications that could have been successfully developed for the postwar market if our political leaders hadn't succumbed to the notion that government shouldn't be involved in producing such things.

The rationale that the wartime emergency made government owner-ship acceptable could be resurrected today — with the substitution of the climate emergency. The possibility of producing electric utility vehi-cles at a nationalized GM Canada plant, or at another location for that matter, would open up truly exciting possibilities if we can get beyond our knee-jerk rejection of government entering the marketplace.

As *Toronto Star* business columnist David Olive observed, Canadians know a lot about building cars; we've been manufacturing them in southern Ontario for more than a hundred years.[7] It started in Oshawa in the 1890s when Sam McLaughlin, along with his father and brother, established McLaughlin Carriage Works, which produced horse-drawn sleighs and carriages. By 1908, the McLaughlins were producing car bodies for Buick Motor Company in Flint, Michigan. In 1918, their company was purchased by General Motors and incorporated as General Motors of Canada, with Sam McLaughlin serving as president of GM Canada and vice-president of the U.S. parent company.

GM, along with Ford and Chrysler, built a substantial auto industry in Ontario, particularly after Canada and the United States signed the 1965 Auto Pact, which provided automakers access to the Canadian market on the condition that they locate a specified amount of their production here. Effectively, the pact required that, for every vehicle sold in Canada, one had to be produced here. This "domestic content requirement" worked extremely well for Canada, leading to the creation of hundreds of thousands of well-paying jobs in Canadian auto production and spinoff industries.

In 1988, Brian Mulroney signed the Canada-U.S. Free Trade Agreement (later adding Mexico in NAFTA), which eliminated most of the force of these domestic content requirements. The Auto Pact continued to formally exist until 2001 (when it was overruled by the World Trade Organization). But as soon as the ink was dry on NAFTA, the auto companies began planning their migration to Mexico. In 2019, GM is expected to produce one million vehicles in Mexico, while GM's Canadian production, with the closing of the Oshawa plant, is expected to fall to just two hundred thousand vehicles — about half of what it was producing here a decade ago.

Yet, even as GM has drastically cut its Canadian operations, Canadian taxpayers have contributed generously to keeping the company alive. When the 2008 financial crisis pushed the U.S. automaker into bankruptcy, the Canadian and Ontario governments provided financial assistance worth more than ten billion dollars (including a 10 percent ownership stake in the company) as part of the joint U.S.-Canada financial rescue of GM.

Jim Stanford, former economist for Unifor, argues that the ownership stake gave Ottawa some real clout in dealing with GM. He points out that Ottawa could have held on to that stake and used it as leverage to pressure the company in the future to maintain production and jobs in Canada. This has worked elsewhere. France's 15 percent interest in Renault and a German public ownership stake in Volkswagen have helped ensure that Renault and Volkswagen maintain high employment levels in France and Germany, Stanford says.[8]

But the Harper government, with its strong ideological resistance to public ownership, made clear that it intended to be a purely passive investor in GM and that it would sell its stake as soon as possible. By 2015, the Harper government had sold off the last of Canada's shares, over the strenuous objections of Unifor.

This was a tremendous missed opportunity. Stanford recalls how much clout Canada had had when the rescue package was negotiated. He was in meetings where "the CEO of GM was basically on his knees begging for help from an assistant deputy minister of industry in Ottawa. That's not what normally happens." As part of the rescue package, Canada insisted that GM agree to maintain its Canadian production at the existing level of 16 percent of the company's overall production. That production requirement — reminiscent of the Auto Pact — was good, Stanford says, except that the Canadian negotiators allowed it to expire by 2017.

So, in 2018, after the expiry of the production requirement and with no remaining Canadian government ownership stake in the company, GM felt free to shut down its major Canadian plant in Oshawa and move those jobs to Mexico, which is exactly what it did. Given the Harper government's failure to take advantage of the clout we had with GM, we have been left with a dwindling, uncertain presence in a once-booming Canadian industry.

It's striking to think that we were veterans of the auto manufacturing industry by the 1960s, when Honda was just beginning its transition in Japan from making motorcycles to making cars. While Honda has gone on to produce some of the world's most popular cars, Canada is facing the end of auto making in Oshawa, amid fears about which of our remaining auto plants will be closed next.

Is it feasible to save the once-vibrant Oshawa complex and transform it into a publicly owned plant producing environmentally essential products, as part of a Green New Deal? Gindin notes that, during the Second World War, GM facilities were converted to produce military vehicles. And he suggests that the Oshawa plant be expropriated today without compensation, since Canadian taxpayers have already provided generous subsidies to GM. While he acknowledges that his plan is a long shot, he adds, "It seems criminal not to at least try."

What is needed is some bold, out-of-the-box thinking — a willingness to consider innovation that is not just Wall-Street-designed, self-enriching financial innovation, but untapped made-in-Canada innovation aimed at building something the world needs. Given the fact that Canada's historic auto-making centre is about to be shut down, we should at least give serious consideration to the possibility of creating a publicly owned company that could potentially start a transformative industry here. If that idea is ultimately rejected, the rejection should be based on something more than the notion that such a project is too ambitious for public enterprise and is best left to the private sector.

In truth, the very ambitiousness of the project seems to call out for public enterprise. For most of our history we've been mere "hewers of wood and drawers of water" and operators of branch plants. When we've risen above that, it's usually been because we've created public enterprises that served a broader public purpose than what private interests were offering. We became the country we are today in part because, at key moments in our past, some visionary figures had bold, ambitious ideas of what was possible and weren't deterred by the admonitions of the business elite.

Would Adam Beck have backed off from creating a public power system for Ontario, thinking that he couldn't possibly match the skill set of those in business? Would Henry Thornton have decided not to transform bankrupt railway lines into the profitable, publicly owned Canadian National Railways on the grounds that railways belong exclusively in the hands of private, profiteering monopolists? Would Dr. John G. FitzGerald have decided not to take great personal risks experimenting in a makeshift lab in a horse barn, considering it better to leave the production of affordable, life-saving medical treatments to the business world?

There may be a good reason not to turn the Oshawa plant into a green production facility, but let's not succumb to the ill-informed notion that Canadians aren't up to the task or that we don't know how to do public enterprise in this country.

❧

Advocates for business, including those in think tanks, the media, and academia, insist that private entrepreneurs are the very source of innovation and wealth. Yet, as Mazzucato demonstrates so well, even some of the best inventor-entrepreneurs, such as Steve Jobs, were able to accomplish what they did only because of massive, publicly funded investments in basic research. "Such radical investments — which embedded extreme uncertainty — did not come about due to the presence of venture capitalists, nor of 'garage-tinkerers,'" she writes. "It was the visible hand of the State which made these innovations happen. Innovation that would not have come about had we waited for the 'market' and business to do it alone."[9]

Downplaying the public contribution and exaggerating the contribution of entrepreneurs has encouraged a deferential attitude toward business, even as business has delivered fewer and fewer benefits in recent years. In the early decades following the Second World War, major corporations typically provided their workforces with significant benefits, including lifetime employment and job security, pensions, and, in many cases, acceptance of their right to unionize. To be sure, there was significant inequality, but unions were managing to improve the economic well-being of their members, with the ripple effects helping the broader workforce.

With the rise of a more aggressive stance on the part of corporations and their wealthy owners in the last few decades, progress for labour has not only been largely halted, it has frequently been reversed. It is now common for major corporations to offer mostly part-time or temporary employment, with little or no job security. Company pensions, where they still exist, have increasingly been transformed from "defined benefit" to "defined contribution," making them far less generous and reliable. The corporate world has also adopted a more hostile attitude toward unions, taking steps that have made it more difficult for workers to organize and to defend themselves.

These substantial changes are part of what's been dubbed "the neo-liberal agenda" — a set of policies based on flimsy pseudo-theories that boil down to the simplistic notion that the private sector is inherently good and the public sector is inherently bad. The result has been a massive transfer of society's resources from ordinary people to a small set of wealthy individuals and corporations. Workers have lost ground badly as the economy has become increasingly dominated by hedge funds and private equity firms, which typically take over a company, strip out its assets, slash its workforce, pay little or no severance to its terminated workers, and leave the company pension plan unfunded.

This sort of stunning corporate indifference to the welfare of workers was amply illustrated in the 2017 shutdown of Sears Canada, once the leading department store in the country with more than 130 stores. In 2004, its parent company was taken over by U.S. billionaire hedge fund manager Eddie Lampert, who had no interest in reinvesting Sears Canada revenue to keep the company's stores updated in the highly competitive Canadian retail market. Instead, starting in 2005, Sears Canada paid out more than $2.9 billion in dividends, with the lion's share going to its largest shareholder, Sears Holding, controlled by Lampert. "Sears Canada had been a bountiful piggy bank for Lampert," notes *Globe and Mail* business reporter Marina Strauss.[10] When the company closed its doors, it left sixteen thousand Canadian workers without severance pay, and a shortfall of $270 million in its pension fund, leaving eighteen thousand retirees uncertain about collecting future benefits.

The difficult situation faced by workers today has led some to turn to so-called populist solutions — usually advocated by rich right wingers — even though these solutions boil down to tax cuts, which mostly benefit the rich and lead to social spending cuts that hurt ordinary people.

Another alternative would involve tightening regulations over the corporate world by, for instance, amending laws so that those controlling corporations can be held personally liable for money owed to their employees. If Eddie Lampert had been personally liable for the severance and pensions of terminated employees at Sears Canada, he would have certainly covered these costs from corporate funds before paying out massive dividends, notes Harry Glasbeek, professor emeritus at Osgoode Hall Law School.[11] Similarly, we need to toughen laws governing corporate behaviour affecting health and safety. Governments remain committed to deregulation, despite the lessons that should have been learned from the deadly Lac-Mégantic train disaster. Little has changed in the wake of that catastrophe, and the Trudeau government remains committed to weakening, removing, or blocking regulations which annoy business, author Bruce Campbell has concluded after a thorough investigation into the tragedy and its aftermath.[12]

In addition to tougher regulations, we should also strengthen our public programs and enterprises. Most of our economy is in private hands, and that's probably in line with the desires of most Canadians, since it ensures opportunities for entrepreneurs and a range of choices on consumer items. But in cases where a strong public interest is at stake or where business has abandoned or failed to provide something of vital public importance, we should feel free to explore the public option, undeterred by corporate threats of departure or accusations of "socialism."

The rigid pro-business mindset of recent years has blocked us from properly understanding and acting in our own interests. It has prevented us, for instance, from seeing the obvious benefits in Norway's highly effective public ownership and management of its oil resources. The people of Alberta are about a trillion dollars poorer today because the province's political leaders refused to be as tough and demanding with the multinational oil companies as the Norwegians managed to be. This missed opportunity for Alberta is all the more striking in light of the fact that Peter Lougheed had already started the province down a more assertive path.

In the early years, Canada got off to a strong start by pooling our efforts and resources in creating promising public ventures and key public programs. In recent decades, however, a pugnacious corporate sector has attacked the public sector and undermined Canadians' confidence in the public domain. Under pressure from the corporate world, we have foolishly sold off impressive and innovative parts of our public heritage, including, among others, Ontario Hydro, Connaught Labs, and Canadian National Railways, not to mention the wartime Crown corporations that manufactured visionary products well ahead of their time. We have also recklessly allowed the privatization of Highway 407, costing commuters billions of dollars in extra fees over the rest of this century. Furthermore, we've dramatically overspent on privatized infrastructure — by more than eight billion dollars in Ontario alone, according to the provincial auditor general. And we've established a national infrastructure bank that, in the words of former parliamentary budget officer Kevin Page, will allow private investors to "rob us blind."

Yet it seems that no lessons have been learned. The push to privatize has only intensified with the passing years, and we can certainly expect more of it, for instance, from the zealously pro-business Conservative governments in Ontario and Alberta.

Rather than continuing to passively accept the corporate world's vision for our country, we should free ourselves to think boldly about what is really in our interests and not be intimidated if our conclusions don't fit with those coming from the business commentators who dominate public debate. Bold thinking would include a willingness to consider not just resisting further privatization, but actually expanding the public domain.

There is certainly a strong case, for instance, for establishing public banking through the post office's vast national network so that vulnerable Canadians don't have to rely on payday loan sharks and those in remote communities can have access to a bank. We might also consider establishing a publicly owned pharmaceutical company that could produce needed generic drugs and other drugs rejected as insufficiently profitable by private industry. And, as discussed above, we should consider creating a facility for manufacturing electric public utility vehicles, as part of a broader effort to contribute productively to the global campaign to avert climate disaster. An expansion of the public domain should also include a national child care program, and a universal pharmacare program, as well as an expanded national infrastructure, which would be owned and operated by the people of Canada.

All these innovations are possible, worthwhile, and within our reach. Above all, they involve a change in our mindset — a determination to stop being cowed by business and to start embracing our inner Viking.

Acknowledgements

Alarge number of people have helped me in the writing of this book. Bill Reno first suggested the idea of a book about privatization and inspired me with his own history of Ontario Hydro. Herschel Hardin, author of *A Nation Unaware*, led me to think about privatization as a betrayal of Canada's strong tradition of public enterprise.

I am indebted to many people who generously gave their time and whose expertise greatly assisted me, notably Heather Whiteside, Christopher Rutty, Joel Lexchin, Gordon Laxer, Bruce Campbell, Mel Watkins, Paul Kahnert, John Anderson, Sandford Borins, John Orrett, Toby Sanger, Karin Jordan, and Mark Anielski.

The crew at Dundurn has been extremely competent and creative, as well as a real pleasure to work with. I am particularly grateful to Scott Fraser, who first approached me to do a book, and to Dominic Farrell, whose smart and thoughtful editing was a big help. I'd also like to thank all the others at Dundurn who aided the project: Kirk Howard, Kathryn Lane, Jenny McWha, Laura Boyle, Elham Ali, Elena Radic, and freelance copy editor Susan Fitzgerald.

And I am grateful to the terrific cast of family members and friends in my life. Special thanks for years of encouragement go to Barbara Nichol and Daniel Wright, along with a great new addition, Juan Lopez.

Notes

Introduction

1. Quoted in David Biello, "How Much Will Tar Sands Oil Add to Global Warming?" *Scientific American*, January 23, 2013.
2. James Hansen, "Game Over for the Climate," *New York Times*, May 9, 2012.
3. H.V. Nelles, *The Politics of Development: Forests, Mines and Hydro-Electric Power in Ontario 1849–1941* (Toronto: Macmillan of Canada, 1974), pp. 1–2.
4. *Ibid.,* p. 39.
5. *Ibid.,* pp. 8, 11, 15.
6. *Ibid.,* p. 31.
7. Herschel Hardin, *A Nation Unaware: The Canadian Economic Culture* (North Vancouver: J.J. Douglas Ltd., 1974), pp. 54, 92.
8. *Ibid.,* p. 61.
9. Hugh Grant, David Wolfe (eds.), *Staples and Beyond: Selected Writings of Mel Watkins* (Montreal: McGill-Queen's University Press, 2006), p. 110.

10. Quoted in Hardin, *A Nation Unaware*, p. 94.
11. *Ibid.*, p. 140.
12. Sandford F. Borins, "World War II Crown Corporations: Their Functions and Their Fate," in J. Robert Prichard (ed.), *Crown Corporations in Canada: The Calculus of Instrument Choice* (Toronto: Butterworths, 1983), pp. 447–75.
13. Quoted in *ibid.*, p. 466.
14. Quoted in *ibid.*, p. 471.
15. Jeff Rubin, *Evaluating the Need for Pipelines: A False Narrative for the Canadian Economy* (Waterloo, ON: Centre for International Governance Innovation, Policy Brief No. 115, September 2017), p. 2.
16. Quoted in Geoff Dembicki, "Here's How Canada's Oil Sands Could Collapse by 2030," *Vice*, August 14, 2017.
17. Quoted in Audrea Lim, "How a Scandal-Plagued Company Gave Birth to Kinder Morgan," *National Observer*, November 14, 2016.
18. Rubin, *Evaluating the Need for Pipelines*, p. 5.

Chapter One: Justin Trudeau Meets the Smartest Guy on Wall Street

1. Sally Blount, "How Leaders Use Power to Drive Change," *Forbes*, November 16, 2017.
2. J.P. Morgan Asset Management, *Infrastructure Investing: Key Benefits and Risks*, 4Q2015 (New York: JPMorgan Chase, 2015), p. 7.
3. Suzanna Andrews, "Larry Fink's $12 Trillion Shadow," *Vanity Fair*, April 2010.
4. Bill Curry, "Private-Sector Role in Canada Infrastructure Bank Raises Conflict-of-Interest Questions," *Globe and Mail*, May 5, 2017.
5. Sean Craig, "After He Leaves the CCIB, Where Will Mark Wiseman Fit in at BlackRock?" *Financial Post*, May 19, 2016.
6. Advisory Council on Economic Growth, *Unleashing Productivity through Infrastructure* (Ottawa: Department of Finance, 2016), p. 10

7. *Ibid.*, p. 4.
8. This question was originally posed by economists Brian MacLean and Mark Setterfield.
9. McKinsey Global Institute, *Bridging Global Infrastructure Gaps* (New York: McKinsey & Company, 2016).
10. Bill Curry, "MPs Grill Morneau's Growth Adviser on Ambitious Infrastructure Plans," *Globe and Mail*, October 27, 2016.
11. Advisory Council on Economic Growth, *Unleashing Productivity*, p. 5.
12. *Ibid.*, p. 5.
13. *Ibid.*, p. 13.
14. *Ibid.*, p. 15.
15. *Ibid.*, p. 12.
16. *Ibid.*, pp. 12–13.
17. Author interview with Kevin Page, Randall Bartlett, Azfar Ali Khan, Ottawa, January 22, 2018. Bartlett is now economic research director at OMERS Capital Markets.
18. Toby Sanger, *Creating a Canadian Infrastructure Bank in the Public Interest* (Ottawa: Canadian Centre for Policy Alternatives, Alternative Federal Budget Technical Paper, March 2017), p. 3. Also, author interview with Toby Sanger, Karin Jordan, Ottawa, January 22, 2018. Sanger is now executive director of Canadians for Tax Fairness.
19. Jordan Press, Andy Blatchford, "Documents Suggest Taxpayers Poised for Bigger Risk in Infrastructure Bank," *Globe and Mail,* May 31, 2017.
20. Advisory Council on Economic Growth, *Unleashing Productivity*, p. 15.
21. Quoted in Tara Deschamps, "Sidewalk Toronto Faces Growing Opposition, Calls to Cancel Project," *Financial Post,* February 18, 2019.
22. BlackRock, *Infrastructure Rising: An Asset Class Takes Shape*, April 2015, pp. 2–4.
23. Heather Whiteside, "Austerity Infrastructure: Financializing, Offshoring, and Tax Sheltering Public-Private Partnership Funds," paper prepared for Austerity and Its Alternatives,

SSHRC Partnership Development Grant Workshop, McMaster University, Hamilton, ON, December 14–15, 2016. See also Heather Whiteside, *Public-Private Partnerships* (Halifax: Fernwood Publishing, 2016).

24. Author interview with Heather Whiteside, University of Waterloo, February 2, 2018.

25. Paul Wells, "Justin Trudeau's Trillion-Dollar Question," *Toronto Star*, October 16, 2016.

26. Barrie McKenna, "Many Things Will Have to Click for Canada Infrastructure Bank to Work," *Globe and Mail*, June 9, 2017.

Chapter Two: The Worst Deal of the Century

1. Nancy MacLean, *Democracy in Chains: The Deep History of the Radical Right's Stealth Plan for America* (New York: Penguin Random House, 2017).

2. Quoted in *ibid.*, p. 9.

3. *Ibid.*, p. 1.

4. Quoted in Hugh Stretton, Lionel Orchard, *Public Goods, Public Enterprise, Public Choice: Theoretical Foundations of the Contemporary Attack on Government* (New York: St. Martin's Press, 1994), p. 51.

5. Lars Udehn, *The Limits of Public Choice* (London: Routledge, 1996), p. 193.

6. MacLean, *Democracy in Chains*, p. 105.

7. Jane Mayer, *Dark Money: The Hidden History of the Billionaires Behind the Rise of the Radical Right* (New York: Penguin Random House, 2016).

8. MacLean, *Democracy in Chains*, p. 135.

9. Chandran Mylvaganam, Sandford Borins, *"If You Build It ... ": Business, Government and Ontario's Electronic Toll Highway* (Toronto: University of Toronto Press, 2004).

10. Martin Regg Cohn, "PC Blunder Over Highway 407 Looms Over Liberals on Hydro," *Toronto Star*, March 30, 2015.

11. Mark McNeil, "Bill for Driving on 407: $43,000," *Toronto Star*, February 1, 2014.

12. Quoted in Geoff Zochodne, "Highway 407 Could Be Worth up

to $45 Billion in a Decade, and That's Good News for SNC-Lavalin," *Financial Post*, September 27, 2017.

13. Quoted in *ibid.*

14. Author interview with Sandford Borins, Toronto, April 11, 2018.

15. Adrian Morrow, Karen Howlett, "Ontario Liberals' Gas-Plant Cancellations Cost $1 Billion: Auditor," *Globe and Mail*, October 8, 2013.

16. Karen Howlett, Paul Waldie, "Hedge Funds Reaped $149-Million from Cancelled Ontario Power Plant," *Globe and Mail*, November 7, 2012.

17. Martin Regg Cohn, "Privatization Mania and NIMBY Myopia behind Ontario Gas Plant Scandal," *Toronto Star*, April 16, 2013.

18. Adrian Morrow, "Government-Managed Projects Could Save Ontario Money: Auditor-General," *Globe and Mail*, December 9, 2014.

19. Yasha Levine, Mark Ames, "Charles Koch to Friedrich Hayek: Use Social Security!" *The Nation*, September 27, 2011.

Chapter Three: The Thrill of Hearing Organ Music on a Train Crossing the Prairies

1. Quoted in J.C. Herbert Emery, Kenneth J. McKenzie, "Damned If You Do, Damned If You Don't: An Option Value Approach to Evaluating the Subsidy of the CPR Mainline," *Canadian Journal of Economics*, Vol. XXIX, No. 2, May 1996, p. 256.

2. D'Arcy Marsh, *The Tragedy of Henry Thornton* (Toronto: Macmillan Co. of Canada Ltd., 1935), p. 52. This journalistic account from the time describes in detail the story of Thornton and the CNR.

3. John Walker Barriger, *Sir Henry Thornton, K.B.E., 1871–1933, Pioneer* (New York: Newcomen Society of England, American Branch, 1948), p. 24.

4. Quoted in E. Austin Weir, *The Struggle for National Broadcasting in Canada* (Toronto: McClelland and Stewart, 1965), p. 5.

5. Quoted in Marsh, *The Tragedy of Henry Thornton*, p. 37.

6. *Ibid.*, p. 172.

7. *Ibid.*, p. 66.
8. *Ibid.*, p. 218.
9. Weir, *The Struggle for National Broadcasting in Canada*, p. 10.
10. *Ibid.*, pp. 11–12.
11. *Ibid.*, p. 62.
12. Marsh, *The Tragedy of Henry Thornton*, p. 106.
13. Bruce Campbell, *The Lac-Mégantic Rail Disaster: Public Betrayal, Justice Denied* (Toronto: James Lorimer & Co., 2018).
14. *Ibid.*, pp. 26–27.
15. *Ibid.*, pp. 67–72.
16. "CEO of the Year," Report on Business, *Globe and Mail*, November 29, 2007.
17. Scott Deveau, "CP Rail May Cut as Many as 6,000 Jobs: Harrison," *Financial Post*, March 6, 2013.
18. Campbell, *The Lac-Mégantic Rail Disaster*, p. 79.

Chapter Four: Niagara Falls, Berlin Rises

1. There have been numerous detailed accounts of the battle between Henry Pellatt and Adam Beck leading to the creation of Ontario Hydro. I have relied particularly on Nelles, *The Politics of Development*; W.R. Plewman, *Adam Beck and the Ontario Hydro* (Toronto: Ryerson Press, 1947); Merrill Denison, *The People's Power: The History of Ontario Hydro* (Toronto: McClelland and Stewart, 1960); Howard Hampton, Bill Reno, *Public Power: The Fight for Publicly-Owned Electricity* (Toronto: Insomniac Press, 2003).
2. Nelles, *The Politics of Development*, p. 304.
3. Quoted in Denison, *The People's Power*, p. 41.
4. Quoted in Hampton, Reno, *Public Power*, p. 37.
5. Quoted in *ibid.*, p. 37.
6. Denison, *The People's Power*, p. 51.
7. Quoted in *ibid.*, p. 56.
8. Quoted in *ibid.*, p. 57.
9. Nelles, *The Politics of Development*, p. 288.
10. Both quoted in Denison, *The People's Power*, pp. 81–82.

11. Nelles, *The Politics of Development*, p. 301.
12. Quoted in *ibid.*, p. 302.
13. Quoted in *ibid.*, p. 302.
14. Quoted in Plewman, *Adam Beck and the Ontario Hydro*, p. 67.
15. *Ibid.*, p. 71.
16. Denison, *The People's Power*, p. 1.
17. Quoted in Plewman, *Adam Beck and the Ontario Hydro*, p. 440, and Denison, *The People's Power*, p. 160.
18. Denison, *The People's Power*, pp. 1, 4, 5.
19. Author interview with Bill Reno, Toronto, October 10, 2018. See also Hampton, Reno, *Public Power*.
20. Quoted in "Hampton Predicted Perils of Privatization," Editorial, *Toronto Sun*, April 21, 2018.

Chapter Five: From Horse Barn to World Stage: The Connaught Story

1. The story of Dr. John G. FitzGerald and the development of Connaught Laboratories has been well documented. I have relied particularly on Robert D. Defries, *The First Forty Years 1914–1955: Connaught Medical Research Laboratories* (Toronto: University of Toronto Press, 1968); Paul Adolphus Bator, Andrew James Rhodes, *Within Reach of Everyone: A History of the University of Toronto School of Hygiene and the Connaught Laboratories* (Ottawa: Canadian Public Health Association, 1990); James FitzGerald, *What Disturbs Our Blood: A Son's Quest to Redeem the Past* (Toronto: Random House Canada, 2010); and Christopher J. Rutty, *A History of Connaught Laboratories*, www.connaught.research.utoronto.ca/history.
2. Quoted in FitzGerald, *What Disturbs Our Blood*, p. 238.
3. *Ibid.*, p. 230.
4. Christopher J. Rutty, Luis Barreto, "The Speckled Monster: Canada, Smallpox and Its Eradication," *Canadian Journal of Public Health*, Vol. 93, July/August 2002, pp. I-1–I-20. See also Christopher J. Rutty, "Canadian Vaccine Research, Production and International Regulation: Connaught Laboratories and Smallpox

Vaccines, 1962–1980," in K. Kroker, J. Keelan, P. Mazumdar (eds.), *Crafting Immunity: Working Histories of Clinical Immunology* (Burlington, VT: Ashgate Publishing, 2008), pp. 273–300.

5. Quoted in Rutty, "Canadian Vaccine Research," p. 293.

6. Lorne Brown, Doug Taylor, "The Birth of Medicare: From Saskatchewan's Breakthrough to Canada-Wide Coverage," *Canadian Dimension,* Vol. 46, No. 4, July 3, 2012.

7. Author interview with Joel Lexchin, Toronto, July 25, 2018.

8. Kelly Crowe, "The Million-Dollar Drug," *CBC News,* November 17, 2018, newsinteractives.cbc.ca/longform/glybera.

9. Mariana Mazzucato, *The Entrepreneurial State: Debunking Public vs. Private Sector Myths* (New York: Anthem Press, 2013), p. 64.

10. Crowe, "The Million-Dollar Drug."

11. Bator, Rhodes, *Within Reach of Everyone*, p. 106.

12. Author interview with Christopher Rutty, Toronto, September 6, 2018.

Chapter Six: Driving Out the Loan Sharks: The Case for Public Banking

1. Tom Korski, "Canada Postal Banks 'Win-Win,' Secret Records Show," *Blacklock's Reporter,* February 10, 2014, www.blacklocks.ca /Canada-postal-banks-win-win-secret-records-show.

2. R.T. Naylor, *The History of Canadian Business, 1867–1914,* Vol. 1: *The Banks and Finance Capital* (Toronto: J. Lorimer, 1975), p. 74.

3. Gustavus Myers, *History of the Great American Fortunes* (Chicago: C. N. Kerr, 1910), p. 123.

4. Quoted in Naylor, *The History of Canadian Business, 1867–1914,* pp. 74–75.

5. *Ibid.,* p. 86.

6. Dan Bunbury, "The Public Purse and State Finance: Government Savings Banks in the Era of Nation Building, 1867–1900," *Canadian Historical Review,* Vol. 78, No. 4, December 4, 1997, pp. 566–98.

7. Quoted in *ibid.,* p. 566.

8. *Ibid.,* p. 567.

9. Quoted in *ibid.*, p. 580.

10. Naylor, *The History of Canadian Business, 1867–1914*, pp. 74–76.

11. Quoted in *ibid.*, pp. 75–76.

12. *Ibid.*, p. 76.

13. Bunbury, "The Public Purse and State Finance," p. 581.

14. Duncan McDowall, *Quick to the Frontier: Canada's Royal Bank* (Toronto: McClelland and Stewart, 1993), p. 245.

15. Bob Ascah, Mark Anielski, *Alberta's Public Bank: How ATB Can Help Shape the New Economy* (Edmonton: Parkland Institute, August 2018), p. 2.

16. *Ibid.*, p. 3.

17. *Ibid.*, p. 5.

18. Duff Conacher, "Stop Bank Gouging and Abuse," Release, Democracy Watch, December 20, 2018.

19. John Anderson, *It's Time for a Postal Bank for Everyone: How a Bank in the Post Office Could Help You*, research paper prepared for CUPW, 2018, p. 3, www.cupw.ca/en/campaign/resources/its-time-postal-bank-everyone-how-bank-post-office-could-help-you.

20. Quoted in Sophia Harris, "Canada's Major Banks Hiking Fees While Pulling in Big Profits," *CBC News*, June 13, 2016, www.cbc.ca/news/business/banking-fees-profits-1.3629701.

21. *Supporting a Strong and Growing Economy: Positioning Canada's Financial Sector of the Future* (Ottawa: Department of Finance, August 26, 2016), p. 10.

22. David Macdonald, *The Big Banks' Big Secret: Estimating Government Support for Canadian Banks during the Financial Crisis* (Ottawa: Canadian Centre for Policy Alternatives, April 2012).

23. Quoted in Daniel Tencer, "Canada Bank Bailout: Yes, There Was One, and Here's Why It's Important to Remember That," *Huffington Post*, May 1, 2012.

24. *Ibid.*

25. *Ibid.*

26. Anderson, *It's Time for a Postal Bank for Everyone*. See also John Anderson, "Why We Need Postal Banking," *Monitor*, November 1, 2018.

27. Financial Consumer Agency of Canada, *Payday Loans: Market Trends*. www.canada.ca/en/financial-consumer-agncy /programs/research/payday-loans.

28. Mehrsa Baradaran, "It's Time for Postal Banking," *Harvard Law Review Forum*, April 16, 2019.

29. Barrie McKenna, "Q & A: CEO Deepak Chopra on Canada Post's Future," Report on Business, *Globe and Mail*, December 17, 2013.

30. Task Force for the Canada Post Corporation Review, *Canada Post in the Digital Age*, Discussion Paper, 2016, p. 81, www.tpsgc-pwgsc .gc.ca/examendepostescanada-canadapostreview/rapport-report /consult-eng.html.

31. *Ibid.*, pp. 84, 81.

32. Mike Palecek, Brenda McAuley, Avi Lewis, "Canadian Postal Network Can Be National Green Machine," *Toronto Star*, October 11, 2018.

Chapter Seven: Oil and the Search for Our Inner Viking

1. Gary Lamphier, "Norway Offers Few Lessons for Alberta," *Edmonton Journal*, June 6, 2015.

2. For a comparison of the different approaches taken by Norway and Alberta, see Bruce Campbell, *The Petro-Path Not Taken: Comparing Norway with Canada and Alberta's Management of Petroleum Wealth* (Ottawa: Canadian Centre for Policy Alternatives, January 2013); Susan Ormiston, "Norway's Sovereign Wealth Holds Lessons for Canada," *CBC News*, March 20, 2015; Greg Poelzer, *What Crisis? Global Lessons from Norway for Managing Energy-Based Economics* (Ottawa: Macdonald-Laurier Institute, February 2015).

3. Quoted in Gillian Steward, *Betting on Bitumen: Alberta's Energy Policies from Lougheed to Klein* (Edmonton: Parkland Institute, June 2017), p. 13.

4. Ed Shaffer, "The Political Economy of Oil in Alberta," in David Leadbeater (ed.), *Essays on the Political Economy of Alberta* (Toronto: New Hogtown Press, 1984), p. 175.

5. Peter Lougheed, "Sounding an Alarm for Alberta (Interview)," *Policy Options*, September 1, 2006.

6. Kevin Taft, *Oil's Deep State* (Toronto: James Lorimer & Co., 2017). See particularly pp. 154–68.

7. Andrew Nikiforuk, "Peter Lougheed's Radical Legacy," *The Tyee*, September 17, 2012.

8. Quoted in Jim MacDonald, "Stelmach Plays Down Royalty Furor," *Globe and Mail*, November 12, 2007.

9. Tracy Johnson, "Oilpatch Wins the Day in Royalty Review," *CBC News*, January 29, 2016.

10. David Campanella, *Misplaced Generosity: Update 2012: Extraordinary Profits in Alberta's Oil and Gas Industry* (Edmonton: Parkland Institute, March 2012).

11. Quoted in *ibid.*, p. 11.

12. Mitchell Anderson, "Against Big Oil, Norway Channels Its Inner Viking," *The Tyee*, August 1, 2012.

13. See Campbell, *The Petro-Path Not Taken*, pp. 16–21.

14. Quoted in *ibid.*, p. 18.

15. Quoted in Mitchell Anderson, "Canada Doesn't Obey Oil-Rich Norway's 'Ten Commandments,'" *The Tyee*, August 8, 2012.

16. Rolf Wiborg, "Alberta Can Be Like Norway," Address to the Alberta Federation of Labour convention, April 15–19, 2015, www.youtube.com/watch?v=N01QUYBZQho. Description of meeting between Norwegian oil minister and multinational oil executives begins at 29:20.

17. Taft, *Oil's Deep State*, pp. 146–48.

18. Author interview with Gordon Laxer, Toronto, November 5, 2018.

19. Nerijus Adomaitis, Ron Bousso, "Statoil Plants Flag in Big Oil's Race for 'Cleaner' Crude," *Reuters*, November 21, 2017.

20. Bruce Campbell, "How Have Canada and Norway Managed Climate Change?," *Behind the Numbers* (blog), Ottawa, October 2, 2015.

21. Fatima Syed, "Canada's 'Insufficient' Climate Policies Would Help Increase Global Warming by 5 C, Study Finds," *National Observer*, November 29, 2018.

22. Barry Saxifrage, "Oilsands Pollution on Collision Course with Canada's Climate Plan," *National Observer*, February 20, 2018. See also Gary Mason, "A War Jason Kenney Neither Wants Nor Needs," *Globe and Mail*, April 18, 2019.

23. Ian Hussey, Eric Pineault, Emma Jackson, Susan Cake, *Boom, Bust, and Consolidation: Corporate Restructuring in the Alberta Oil Sands* (Edmonton: Parkland Institute, November 2018).

24. Emma McIntosh, David Bruser, Mike De Souza, Carolyn Jarvis, "What Would It Cost to Clean Up Alberta's Oilpatch? $260 Billion, a Top Official Warns," *Toronto Star*, November 1, 2018.

25. Quoted in Mitchell Anderson, "Alberta's Oil Wealth and the Big Question for Harper," *The Tyee*, April 13, 2011.

26. Nikiforuk, "Peter Lougheed's Radical Legacy."

27. Andrew Nikiforuk, "A Bold Clean-Up Plan for Alberta's Giant Oil Industry Pollution Liabilities," *The Tyee*, November 4, 2016.

Chapter Eight: The Triumph of the Commons

1. Karl Polanyi, *The Great Transformation* (Boston: Beacon Press, 1957), p. 141.

2. Jason Kirby, "Business Investment Hasn't Been This Crummy in 40 Years," *Maclean's*, July 4, 2016; Paul Krugman, "Why Was Trump's Tax Cut a Fizzle?," *New York Times*, November 15, 2018.

3. Linda McQuaig, Neil Brooks, *The Trouble with Billionaires: How the Super-Rich Hijacked the World and How We Can Take It Back* (London: Oneworld Publications, 2013), pp. 56–85.

4. Anu Partanen, *The Nordic Theory of Everything: In Search of a Better Life* (New York: HarperCollins Publishers, 2016), pp. 41, 44.

5. Mazzucato, *The Entrepreneurial State*, pp. 1–13.

6. Sam Gindin, "GM Oshawa: Lowered Expectations, Unexplored Opportunities," *The Bullet*, March 29, 2019. See also Sam Gindin, "GM Oshawa: Making Hope Possible," *The Bullet*, December 13, 2018.

7. David Olive, "It's Time for a Truly Canadian Automaker," *Toronto Star*, November 26, 2018.

8. Author interview with Jim Stanford, Toronto, March 21, 2019.

9. Mazzucato, *The Entrepreneurial State,* p. 3.

10. Marina Strauss, "Who Killed Sears Canada?," Report on Business, *Globe and Mail,* October 20, 2017.

11. Quoted in Linda McQuaig, "Demise of Sears Canada Should Be Catalyst for Change," *Toronto Star,* October 26, 2017.

12. Campbell, *The Lac-Mégantic Rail Disaster*, pp. 166–78.

Index

Hoskins, Dr. Eric, 138
Howe, C.D., 8–11
Howlett, Karen, 64
Hubbard, William, 97
Hughes, Howard, 9
Hughes Aircraft, 59
Hunter, Bill, 182
Hydro One, 117

Illinois Central Railroad, 90
Institute of Fiscal Studies and
    Democracy, 30
Intercolonial Railway, 73

J.P. Morgan Asset Management,
    21
James M. Buchanan Center for
    Political Economy, 47
Jasper Park Lodge, 75
Jetliner, 9
Jobs, Steve, 207, 214
John Birch Society, 46

Keynes, John Maynard, 43
Kinder Morgan, 1, 13, 15, 16
Kinder, Richard, 15, 16
King, Brian, 141, 142
King, William Lyon Mackenzie,
    9, 72, 82, 84, 108
Kiwibank (New Zealand), 168
Klein, Ralph, 179, 180, 192
Knudsen, Gunnar, 184
Koch, Charles, 41, 46, 47, 66, 67
Koch, David, 46, 47
Koch, Fred, 46

Krugman, Paul, 201
Kuwait Petroleum, 190

Lac-Mégantic rail disaster,
    88–92, 216
Lampert, Eddie, 215, 216
Lamphier, Gary, 174, 175
Lash, Zebulon A., 154
Laurier, Wilfrid, 156
Laxer, Gordon, 189, 190
Leap, The, 172
Lee, Ian, 162
Levine, Yasha, 66
Lewis, Avi, 172
Lexchin, Dr. Joel, 138, 140, 141
Lie, Einar, 186
Liquor Control Board of Ontario,
    49
Lougheed, Peter, 176–81,
    186–88, 198, 199, 217
Lysyk, Bonnie, 63, 65

Macdonald, David, 164
Macdonald, John A., 152, 153,
    156
Mackenzie, William, 94, 98,
    110
MacLean, Nancy, 40, 41, 47
Madison, James, 42
Manitoba Telephone System, 65
Manning, Ernest, 175
Marsh, D'Arcy, 75, 77, 84
Martin, Paul, 89
Massey, Walter, 99
Mayer, Jane, 47

Book Credits
Acquiring Editor: Scott Fraser
Developmental Editor: Dominic Farrell
Project Editor: Elena Radic
Editorial Assistant: Melissa Kawaguchi
Copy Editor: Susan Fitzgerald

Designer: Sophie Paas-Lang

Publicist: Saba Eitizaz

dundurn.com   dundurnpress
@dundurnpress   dundurnpress
dundurnpress   info@dundurn.com

FIND US ON NETGALLEY & GOODREADS TOO!

DUNDURN